WHAT'S LEFT?

A NEW DEMOCRATIC VISION FOR AMERICA

Robert McElvaine

Adams Media Corporation
HOLBROOK, MASSACHUSETTS

For
Kerri
Always Our First

Published by Adams Media Corporation
260 Center Street, Holbrook, MA 02343

ISBN: 1-55850-629-2

Printed in the United States of America.

J I H G F E D C B A

Library of Congress Cataloging-in-Publication Data
McElvaine, Robert S., 1947–
What's left? : a new Democratic vision for America / Robert McElvaine.
p. cm.
Includes bibliographical references and index.
ISBN 1-55850-629-2
1. Liberalism—United States. 2. Democratic Party (U.S.) 3. United States—Politics and government—1945–1989. 4. United States—Politics and government—1989– I. Title.
JC574.2.U6M34 1996
342.2736—dc20 96–14636
CIP

Contents

ACKNOWLEDGMENTS

I would like to give special thanks to the following public figures who talked with me in 1995 and early 1996 about the state of the nation, the Democratic party, and progressive thought: Paul Begala, Rep. David Bonior, Sen. Dale Bumpers, James Carville, Gov. Mario Cuomo, Sen. Tom Daschle, Rep. Rosa DeLauro, Rep. Chaka Fattah, Rep. Barney Frank, Bill Galston, Rep. Marcy Kaptur, Rep. Joe Kennedy, Madeline Kunin, David Kusnet, Rep. Jim McDermott, Rep. Patsy Mink, Del. Eleanor Holmes Norton, Bruce Reed, Rep. Bill Richardson, Secretary Richard Riley, Rep. Bernie Sanders, Sen. Paul Simon, Doug Sosnik, George Stephanopoulos, Rep. Nydia Velazquez, Sen. Paul Wellstone, and Carter Willkie.

In addition to these people who talked with me specifically for this book, I also want to thank a number of others whom I have interviewed at earlier times, and whose thoughts and insights have proved useful to me in this project: Les Aspin, Bruce Babbitt, Lloyd Bentsen, Joe Biden, Patrick Caddell, Lawton Chiles, Bill Clinton, Tony Coelho, Christopher Dodd, Wayne Dowdy, Michael Dukakis, Alvin From, Richard Gephardt, Richard Goodwin, Gary Hart, Jesse Jackson, Edward Kennedy, William Proxmire, Joe Rauh, Chuck Robb, Arthur Schlesinger, Jr., Pat Schroeder, Morris Udall, William Winter, and Jim Wright.

Louise Hetrick has provided enormous assistance in transcribing interview tapes and handling numerous other chores in the production of the manuscript. Kathy and Hugh Boyle and their children, Lisa, Hugh, and Charles, opened their home to me on my trips to the Washington area, providing good times as well as shelter and food.

My colleagues in the Millsaps College history department—Charles Sallis, David Davis, Laura Mayhall, and Sanford Zale—have been very supportive of my work. I also thank my agent, Fifi Oscard, and my editors, Ed Walters and Dan Weaver. Ned Chase deserves special thanks for much help with this and other projects.

All that I do is an extension of what I learned from my late parents, Edward and Ruth McElvaine. My children, Kerri, Lauren, Allison, and Brett, have been, as always, my inspiration. Brett has also been my companion and helper through much of the writing of the book.

Anne is my everything.

ROBERT S. MCELVAINE
Clinton, Mississippi
March 1996

PREFACE

In the early 1960s, more than half of Americans believed that other people can usually be trusted. Today, nearly two-thirds of Americans think that other people *cannot* usually be trusted.* No statistic better captures one part of the three-pronged crisis the United States faces as the twentieth century draws to its close: We have become a nation of cynics. We no longer even trust our neighbors. We believe that everyone is out for him- or herself and will say anything, without regard to the truth, that will advance his or her individual interests. Such an attitude on a widespread scale is poisonous to a society.

But cynicism is only one of a trio of intertwined problems that together constitute a major challenge to the future of our nation. One source of the ubiquitous cynicism is a collapse of values. A major reason why we tend to think people are "looking out for Number One" is that so many of us are doing just that. For far too many Americans, other people have come to be seen as objects to be used, ignored, or abused in a relentless pursuit of self-interest. We constantly hear talk of "rights," but rarely of responsibilities. The consequences, in terms of crime and violence, unwed pregnancies, family breakup, and many other social ills, are evident all around us.

The third part of the three-fold predicament that threatens to alter our nation beyond recognition is the rise of a two-tier, "winner-take-all" economy of increasing inequality. The combination of rapid technological change and the emergence of a largely free international market has created an economy that is constantly enriching a small segment of our society while the income of the vast majority stagnates or declines. If left unchecked, this phenomenon could make the twen-

* *Washington Post* / Harvard University / Kaiser Family Foundation survey, published in January, 1996.

ty-first-century United States resemble a Third World country, with an elite consisting of a relatively few fabulously wealthy people and a vast number of people struggling desperately to make ends meet.

The response to this crisis from one of our major political parties, the Republicans, is clear: The decline of values is the real problem, they insist, and it has been caused by liberal social programs, a government that has gotten much too big, and a cultural elite that sneers at traditional morality. Cynicism is just realism, many conservatives claim, because human nature is based on the maximization of self-interest (especially as measured in money) and any successful economy must be based on encouraging the very every-man-and-woman-for-him-or-herself attitude that breeds cynicism. The two-tier economy? To Republicans, this is not a problem, but the inevitable result of a free market that distributes rewards as it will, and we should not attempt to do anything to counteract the tendency towards ever-greater concentration of wealth and income at the top. In fact, they propose—through various schemes to shift the tax burden away from richer people and unearned income—to enlarge the gulf between the rich and the rest.

The Republicans' blueprint is one for disaster. They want to try to treat one symptom (the loss of values) of the underlying problem by addressing its supposed causes (which are actually only minor contributors to the problem), while ignoring another (cynicism) and intensifying the third (the two-tier economy).

The Democratic Party has, meanwhile, according to popular impressions, been placed on life-support systems and is classified—at least by Republicans—as "brain dead." One purpose of this book is to try to help reverse this situation by offering a friendly and committed, but also frank and critical, examination of the policies, practices, and ideals of American liberal/left politics and thinking, combined with an assessment of Gingrichism and its vulnerabilities and a vision for Democrats for the remainder of the 1990s and beyond.

But the book is much more than a prescription to cure the ailments of the American Left. It is also a diagnosis of what has gone wrong with America in recent decades, a prognosis for the nation's future, and an examination of what might be done to restore us to health. The book employs history and what used to be termed political economy to explore the causes of the three-pronged crisis we face today, and to suggest what might be done to begin to reverse our social, moral, and economic decline.

My basic argument is that the three major problems we now confront are interrelated and must be addressed in a comprehensive manner. I contend that the three afflictions are a result of deep economic forces that have been intensifying through the entire twentieth century, principally the development of a "supply-side economy" (using that term in a different way from that in which it has been used by one brand of conservatives since the late 1970s) which is so dependent on increasing consumption that it has been obliged to tear down traditional values in order to replace the work ethic with a "consumption ethic."

We must realize that the market, which has been almost deified by many self-styled conservatives, is an essential tool that provides us with fabulous productivity, but that it is not the omnipotent force in the universe. It can, and sometimes does, produce undesirable results. In those cases it is essential to take corrective measures.

A new progressive, Democratic vision for America must begin with an understanding of the source of our current malaise and the proper place for both the market and the government in our economy and our lives. The contours of such a vision will emerge in the pages that follow.

1

WHERE HAVE ALL THE DEMOCRATS GONE?

A PROPOSITION PARTY, NOT AN OPPOSITION PARTY

When I began writing this book in the spring of 1995, numerous political obituaries were being written for both Bill Clinton and the Democratic Party. The incumbent president was desperately trying to make the case that he had not become irrelevant, and he was considered to be a sure loser in a bid for reelection. As I finish the manuscript a year later, President Clinton enjoys a double-digit lead in opinion polls over each of his potential Republican challengers. Where the extremely volatile public opinion of Americans in the nineties will have gone when the book reaches readers is difficult to predict.

But one thing is certain: While a growing majority of voters have become alarmed at the extremist nature of the policies pushed by the Republican majority in the 104th Congress, this has not translated into much of an increase in committed support for the Democrats. The main reason is that the American people are looking for something more than an opposition party. They want a *"proposition party"*—one that presents a clear set of ideas with which they can identify.

"It is," as Deputy Secretary of Education and former Vermont Governor Madeline Kunin said to me, "easier to define what you are against than what you are for."[1] Or, as Senator Paul Wellstone puts it: "Part of the answer as to where Democrats need to go is in denunciation, but denunciation is not enough. There has to be *annunciation.*" "If you just look like you're for the status quo—you're just saying 'no' to everything," the Minnesota Democrat says. "I don't think that's very stirring to people."[2]

"We can't just be criticizing what they are doing," Congresswoman Nydia Velazquez agrees. "People don't like that. You have to come out with concrete solutions and new ideas as to how we can reform and why things are not working."[3]

The Democrats have not seemed to be much of a proposition party in recent years. "The country has no idea of what an affirmative Democratic program would look like and less confidence that Democrats could agree to pass such a program if they ever decided what it was," E. J. Dionne, Jr., correctly wrote in a fall of 1995 *Washington Post* column.[4] This is a succinct statement of the basic problem confronting Democrats and progressives in the nineties.

Republicans—and others—keep using such terms as "bankrupt of ideas," "brain dead," "stuck in the past," "uncertain," "indecisive," "despairing," "incoherent," "visionless," "leaderless," and "irrelevant" to characterize Democrats and liberalism.

Some of these charges are too harsh, but it is undeniable that the Left in the United States today is, to put the best "spin" on its situation, in disarray. Those who identify themselves with progressive politics and thought are drifting, rudderless and dispirited. Lacking a vision for the future, the Left is largely living in the past, nostalgic for the halcyon days of the thirties and sixties. If this corpse is to be resurrected—if Democrats are to get out of their Chapter Eleven of ideas—they have to develop new ideas, new visions, and new approaches to our national problems.

THE NATIONAL CRISIS

Today the nation finds itself at a critical juncture—a point at which dramatic social and economic changes are undermining our familiar ways of life, leaving large numbers of Americans apprehensive about their futures, both personal and national. The American social-economic-political system does not seem to be working for a substantial portion of the population. A mid-1995 *Newsweek* poll found that nearly two-thirds of white Americans think that the American national character has changed for the worse in the last twenty years. The grievances so many people feel are real, although unfocused (or, in some cases, focused on the wrong targets).

As the twentieth century draws to a close, the American people face a three-fold predicament that threatens to alter our nation beyond recognition. The three principal problems facing American society today are the rise of a two-tier, "winner-take-all" economy[5] of increasing inequality, the collapse of values, and a rampant cynicism (including, but not confined to, a collapse of faith in government and leaders).

The rapidly changing economy in which we find ourselves is constantly enriching a small segment of our society, while the income of the vast majority stagnates or declines. If left unchecked, this phenomenon could make the twenty-first-century United States resemble a Third World country, with an elite consisting of a relatively few fabulously wealthy people and a vast number of people struggling desperately to make ends meet. No statistics better capture what has been happening than these astounding facts: Between 1977 and the end of the Reagan administration in 1989, *70 percent* of all of the income growth in the United States went to the top *1 percent* of income recipients.[6] And, *100 percent* of the increased wealth in the United States went to the wealthiest *20 percent* of Americans.[7] This is to say, of course, that four-fifths of Americans saw absolutely no increase in their wealth during the "prosperous" eighties. The result of these trends is that the United States, which prides itself on being a largely egalitarian society, has come to have the largest disparity of wealth and income in any Western nation.[8]

Despite all of the talk about traditional values, the major force undermining these values in recent years is the extreme individualism advocated by Republicans. The "Look Out for Number One"/"Who Says You Can't Have It All" attitude that became the hallmark of the eighties is the principal corrosive agent that is eating away at traditional values. That hyperindividualism, in turn, has been promoted by an economic system that, driven by the vast increase in the supply side of the economic equation, has become dependent on ever-increasing consumption. The resulting "consumption ethic" fosters present-mindedness, self-indulgence, and immediate gratification; it increases competitive urges to dangerous levels, widens the gap between the rich and everyone else, and encourages—particularly through the advertising that is its lifeblood—the sort of deceitful communication that results in a cynicism as pernicious as it is pervasive, and promotes the breakdown of community and family.

The full scope of the crisis is best captured in the finding of a study done in 1996 by the *Washington Post*, the Kaiser Family Foundation, and Harvard University, that nearly two out of three Americans now believe that most people cannot be trusted. In 1964, more than half of Americans believed that most people could be trusted. An eighteen-year-old woman from Madison, Wisconsin, bluntly told those conducting the study why she doesn't trust government: "It's made up of people, isn't it?" We have not just lost faith in government and institutions; we have lost faith in each other—in humanity itself. The survey found that each "generation that has come of age since the 1950s has been more mistrusting of human nature, a transformation in the national outlook that has deeply corroded the nation's social and political life."[9]

In September of 1995, President Bill Clinton quickly retreated after saying that the American people are in a "funk." If that word indicates that there is something phony or inappropriate about the apprehension being felt by many Americans, the president was right to retract the statement. It was unfortunate that the flap over his using a term that seemed reminiscent of President Jimmy Carter's infamous 1979 "malaise speech" (a speech in which he never uttered the word *malaise*) overshadowed the effective description of what the American people are experiencing that Clinton gave in the same interview: "What makes people insecure is when they feel like they're lost in the funhouse; they're lost in a room where something can hit them from any direction at any time."[10]

It is these deep-seated problems that have produced the extraordinary volatility in the American electorate in the nineties. One consequence of voters' desperate search for answers to questions that previously did not have to be asked was the election of Republican majorities in both houses of Congress in 1994. That election could prove to be either a blessing or a disaster for the American people. It will prove to be a positive development if it obliges Democrats to develop a new approach that will bring the nation together to deal with the underlying causes of our current crisis; it will be a calamity if the Republican extremists get away with what they want to do.

WALKING AWAY FROM THE WORKING CLASS

What has caused the recent decline in support for Democrats and progressive policies? Many Republicans and self-styled conservatives contend that the Democrats abandoned ordinary working- and middle-class Americans. Obviously this is a self-serving analysis, but that does not mean that there might not be a kernel of truth in it. "I would like to call it the biggest heist in American political history," Ben Wattenberg says of the Republican seizure of popular Democratic issues, "but in truth the Democrats weren't robbed; they gave away those issues, gratis."[11]

There is a simple proposition that goes a long way toward explaining the success or failure of political parties in the American two-party system: Neither the very poor nor the very rich by themselves constitute anything approaching a majority of the electorate. At least since the New Deal, Democrats have been able to count on the support of an overwhelming majority of the former (if they vote at all); Republicans have enjoyed a similar degree of backing from the latter. What determines which party will win an election, more than any other factor, is whether a majority of the middle class identifies its interests more with those at the bottom or those at the top of the economic scale. Since most people would rather aspire to something higher than associate themselves with people in worse circumstances, the Republicans have something of a built-in advantage in this competition for the allegiance of the middle class.

The best way for Democrats to counter this, of course, is by demonstrating that Republican policies help the rich *at the expense of* middle-class people and that Democratic policies are aimed at giving *everyone*, including the middle class and the poor, an opportunity to better themselves.

The Great Depression brought together the working and middle classes because it threatened both. They shared a common experience, and the New Deal provided them with a common response. But the very success of Democratic programs began to drive a wedge between the party's principal constituencies.

The combination of Social Security, economic recovery (heavily stimulated by wartime—hot and cold—military spending), the GI Bill, and the unions Democrats had unabashedly promoted, gradually allowed the middle class to regain a feeling of security—and workers to become members of the middle class. Former House Speaker Tip O'Neill was right when he said that Democratic programs were so successful that they enabled many working-class people to rise economically to a point where they could become Republicans.

In the decades following the end of the Depression, many members of the increasingly comfortable middle stratum proved to be foul-weather friends of the poor and of an activist government. As the economic skies cleared, old divisions reemerged. Those who were left behind began to appear to many in the middle class to be shiftless ne'er-do-wells, looking for handouts. Many middle-class people began to identify more with those above them, rather than those below them, on the economic scale.

The great expansion of the middle class in the two decades after the end of World War II and the exponential growth in higher education furthered the potential fault line between an increasingly affluent, educated, liberal elite and the workers who had formed the base of the Roosevelt coalition.

This is the standard liberal interpretation of the breakup of the Democratic majority: liberal Democratic policies helped middle-class people so much that they came to identify with the rich rather than the poor and so deserted the political and economic philosophy that had helped them to achieve a degree of affluence.

But liberalism abandoned the middle class at least as much as the middle class abandoned liberalism.

WILL THE REAL POPULISTS PLEASE STAND UP?

"Conservative" Republicans now claim that they represent the interests of ordinary Americans. Many of them go so far as to label themselves "populists." It must have the Populists of a century ago rolling over in their graves when people using their name call for the elimination of the progressive income tax, an end to the taxation of all unearned income, the end of government regulation of corporations, undermining of labor unions, or restoration of the gold standard (an attack on which—using the immortal words, "You shall not crucify mankind upon a cross of gold!"—won the 1896 Democratic presidential nomination for populist William Jennings Bryan). Today's Republican "polo populists," as political commentator Mark Shields has cleverly dubbed them, are a far cry from their nineteenth-century namesakes.

But Democrats need to understand that they have not been true populists, either. Each of the major parties now has elites associated with it. Each also takes, with varying degrees of sincerity, "populist" stances.

Pat Buchanan made an attempt during the 1996 Republican primaries to claim that he fits this bill, but his is in fact a false populism across the board. While claiming to lead "peasants with pitchforks," all Buchanan offered hard-pressed workers was scapegoats. Far from being a genuine economic populist, he opposes unions, the minimum wage, health care, progressive taxation, and almost every other proposal that might actually benefit working people. His cultural populism falls at least as short of the genuine article as does his economics. It consists of a blend of protectionism, racism, anti-Semitism, xenophobia, gay-bashing, and religious intolerance. Pat Buchanan is a skilled demagogue, but he is not a populist of any sort.

Shedding the elitist image makes for strange mixtures on both sides. The Republican brew consists of economic elitism mixed with cultural populism; the Democratic blend is economic populism combined with cultural elitism. If either party could separate itself from its elitist allies and embrace populism across the board, in both economics and culture, it would be very likely to win lasting majority support.

This is not a simple task. As Vermont Congressman Bernie Sanders, a socialist and the only member of Congress in the mid-nineties not affiliated with either party, points out, "there are many Barbra Streisand Democrats, who are liberal on women's issues, good on the environment; but, you know, it's easier to relate to Barbra Streisand than to a truck driver."[12]

Progressives have usually identified with the most downtrodden elements in society. During the Depression, that identification clearly included white working men (and those who *wished* they were working). During the glory days of the New Deal and into the mid-sixties, Democrats were clearly the champions of both the poor and the middle class. They never hesitated to identify themselves with workers.

In the affluent postwar decades, especially from the sixties onward, however, liberals began to see their former allies in the white working class as no longer in need of their support. They rallied to the cause of the more clearly oppressed: first blacks and, subsequently, other minorities and women. In so doing, they resurveyed the boundary between "us" and "them" and placed white working men on the "wrong side" of the line. "By narrowing the definition of 'common people' to the most disadvantaged," Democratic pollster Stan Greenberg says, Lyndon Johnson "distorted the Democratic bottom-up vision . . . as a political formula, it could not embrace the middle class."[13]

It should not be forgotten that a party, program, and administration far more liberal than those of Franklin Roosevelt still enjoyed the support of an overwhelming majority of Americans, including union members and most of the middle class, as late as the mid-sixties.

What really eroded the New Deal coalition and launched the tensions and divisions that still plague the Democrats were the three defining events of that decade: the Civil Rights movement, the Vietnam War, and the rise of a "counterculture." All three divided liberals and intellectuals from the middle- and working-class people who had been their political allies since the New Deal. As liberals, students, and intellectuals identified—entirely properly—with the aspirations of African-Americans, they began to look down upon white workers, whom they saw (sometimes accurately, sometimes not) as racists.

The Vietnam War served as the second blow in the quick one-two punch of the early- and mid-sixties that left the New Deal coalition with wobbly legs. The war itself was unquestionably the work of the political and ideological heirs of Franklin Roosevelt. Ironically, this war that was the offspring of "the best and the brightest" embittered a large portion of a generation of the college-educated, turning them against New Deal liberalism, the government, unions, and white workers, whom young liberals now dismissed or castigated as warmongers as well as racists.

In fact, many working-class people were neither. They saw themselves as patriots; they had no particular liking for a war that was beyond understanding, but they could not abide people who attacked the American flag and called those who answered their nation's call to duty "murderers" and "baby-killers."

Rather quickly in the mid-sixties, white workers moved in the eyes of many liberals from being part of "us" (the New Deal coalition) to being part of "them" (the opponents of racial justice and peace). Simultaneously, liberals, especially intellectuals and other elites, moved in the eyes of workers from being a segment of the "us" of the Democratic coalition to being an element of "them" (those who ridicule patriotism, hard work, and traditional values). This metamorphosis was part of a larger transformation of liberalism from a movement primarily concerned with economic issues to one at least perceived as mainly interested in social and cultural matters. Since the sixties, liberals have paid little attention to the growing economic concerns of the stagnating or declining middle and working class, concerning themselves more with such subjects as environmentalism, women's rights, gay rights, sexual liberation, and freedom of artistic expression.

Jesse Jackson summarized the changed perceptions of liberalism in a conversation I had with him in 1986. By the early 1970s, liberalism "got labeled with 'free, but not responsible,' 'free without values,' and became the dumping ground for every fringe protest formation," Reverend Jackson said. "It became free speech turned into license for obscenity, pornography, abortion, smoking pot. The liberal movement got trapped with all the decadent fallout and no values."[14]

"We have too often given the impression that we sought to 'understand' rather than condemn antisocial and criminal behavior," Mario Cuomo notes.[15]

As liberals began to place white working men on "the other side" in the sixties, they also began to become increasingly elitist in a cultural sense, even while they remained steadfastly antielitist in terms of economic policy. But, particularly since they were dividing themselves from workers on the issues of civil rights and the war, their growing cultural elitism gradually came to define liberals more clearly than did their continuing, but rather de-emphasized, economic populism. As President Clinton's domestic policy advisor Bruce Reed said to me, there is a "longstanding minority complex whereby Democrats are afraid that if something is popular, then there must be something morally tainted about it."[16]

It now seems to many male, white working- and middle-class Americans that their problems and interests rank lower on the agenda of the Left than those, not only of minorities and women in the United States, but of illegal immigrants, flag desecrators, pornography peddlers, homosexuals, Somalians, Rwandan Tutsis, Bosnian Muslims, Canadian baby seals, Alaskan caribou, snail darters, spotted owls, and tropical rain forests. Many of these are worthy causes; many of them, particularly environmental issues, are in fact of great importance to working-class people.

But when liberals talk more, often *much* more, about these matters than they do about the very real problems confronting the shrinking middle class and industrial and service workers, they play into the hands of right-wingers. Workers might well accept the need to protect these "others," if they thought liberals really cared about *them*, too—that *their* needs and interests were not at the bottom of the list of liberal priorities. Oklahoma Senator Fred Harris put his finger on this problem for Democrats in the early 1970s when he remarked: "The blue-collar worker will continue to be progressive so long as it is not progress for everyone but himself."[17]

But today, Democrats find themselves identified in middle-class minds as not only the champions of the poor, but also as linked with an elite, and they face an almost insurmountable task in their attempts to construct a majority coalition.

The problem of holding working people at arm's length is at the heart of the Democrats' difficulties in the last quarter century. When liberals fail to show genuine concern for the plight of what once was the heart of their constituency, they make it possible for conservatives—most of whom quite demonstrably care no more for white male American workers than they do for minorities, seals, or any of the rest, especially if they get in the way of profits—to pretend to be on the workers' side while they are in fact working full-time against their economic interests.

"If the Democratic Party can't talk about stagnating wages in a time of rising prosperity," political consultant James Carville pointedly asks, "Why have one?"[18]

THE CURSE OF ELITISM

Of course Newt Gingrich, Rush Limbaugh, and other right-wing Republicans are selling white working men a bill of goods (or, more accurately, a bill of "bads") when they woo them by mocking the cultural elitism of liberals. "Intellectual elites" has also become one of their favorite terms of disdain.[19]

Earlier in the century, it was clear enough that the symbols of elitism were identified with Republicans. Figuratively, at least, members of the GOP were known by their taste for champagne. Democrats were folks who drank beer—and it was domestic lager, without a slice of lime floating in it. When brie and Chablis—not to mention BMW's—came to be associated with liberals, their days of allegiance from working people were numbered. (Some of this was self-inflicted; some was the work of skillful conservative propagandists who gleefully tarred liberals with the elitist stain that had so justifiably been used against them in the past.)

Bill Clinton certainly seemed to prefer relations with celebrities to those with workers during the first two years of his administration. "I was floored by Bill Clinton defining the party and his presidency by identifying with Hollywood," Congresswoman Marcy Kaptur told me. "The vacation residences, the haircut, and so forth—it was unbelievable."[20]

And I saw a clear reflection of what has happened to Democrats at a 1995 election-night party for Dick Molpus, the Democratic candidate for Governor of Mississippi. By any objective standard, Molpus's program was much more in the interests of working people than was that of his Republican opponent, incumbent Governor Kirk Fordice. But Fordice masterfully employed cultural populism to cloak his economic elitism and tarnish his rival with the brush of cultural elitism. He won the election by a wide margin.

The reason why Fordice, like so many other Republicans, was able to get away with this was apparent at the Molpus party, which was well attended, despite the outcome of the election. But what stood out was the almost complete absence of anyone who, as they say, "works for a living." Attorneys, professors, and other assorted yuppies—all very good people (many of them friends of mine)—were there in abundance but, aside from a few union leaders, the working class was virtually unrepresented.

There is, to be sure, nothing new about charges of elitism in American politics. Andrew Jackson got much mileage out of portraying his opponent, John Quincy Adams, as a "professor" and contrasting him with the commoner role of the "ploughman," which Jackson assigned himself.[21] And, more recently (to cite but a few other examples from what is an American cornucopia of anti-intellectualism[22]), Richard Nixon and Joseph McCarthy blasted political enemies as "eggheads," George Wallace expressed contempt for "pointy heads," and Spiro Agnew derided "effete intellectual snobs."

The current Republican resort to this tactic is, however, more than a little ironic. While Jackson, McCarthy, Wallace, and Agnew were hardly intellectuals themselves (the case of Nixon, a man who is difficult to categorize, is less clear), several of the leaders of the "Republican Revolution," including Newt Gingrich himself, House Republican Leader Dick Armey, and Senator Phil Gramm, hold Ph.D. degrees.

In this regard, the current Republicans are more like the Whigs of 1840, a party whose principal constituency was an economic elite but who concluded that the way to defeat the Jacksonian Democrats was cynically to adopt the trappings of the common man. With a military "hero" of their own, William Henry "Tippecanoe" Harrison, as a candidate and a log cabin and hard cider as their symbols—and the help of the Panic of 1837—the Whigs were able to unseat Jackson's chosen successor, Martin Van Buren.

Feigned or not, the castigation of their opponents as cultural or intellectual elites performs the invaluable function of concealing the Republicans' own unswerving loyalty to the interests of economic elites.

But we must recognize that liberals have, over the past three decades, provided the right-wingers with the ammunition needed to conduct their offensive. Limbaugh's ridicule of liberals would not resonate with the people Republicans actually seek to leave high and dry were there not some validity to the charges he makes. The economic elitists of the Right could not have gotten away with turning working- and middle-class white men against liberals had there not been enough truth in the accusations of cultural elitism to make the charges stick.

Liberals said that white male working- and middle-class people were on the other side—that of the "oppressors"—so often that people in those categories finally came to believe it. The answer to the classic question "Which side are you on?" depends upon how the "sides" are defined. In the sixties, Democrats and liberals began to alter the definition of their side in such a way that white working men no longer felt fully welcome on that side. "Which side is the other side is a very key ingredient to these folks, and we can't pooh-pooh that," House Democratic Whip David Bonior rightly says.[23]

Progressive Democrats will never get back on track until they can convince middle- and working-class Americans that they are on their side—and they will never convince those constituencies that they are on their side until they start really believing it themselves. This means that they need to adopt cultural populism to go along with their economic populism. That way lies a lasting Democratic majority.

For example, liberals may feel the need to defend the "liberty" to burn the American flag; but they need to make plain that such an action is abhorrent and that their defense of this outrage is a necessary evil if we are to maintain a free society, certainly not a positive good—and that such matters are not at the top of the Democratic agenda, above the needs of working people with diminishing incomes and futures. It would be easier for patriotic, hardworking Americans to accept the unpalatable necessity of allowing flag desecration as a cost of liberty if they thought that liberals cared more about their economic problems than they do about the "rights" of flag burners.

The demise of the Democratic majority and the transformation of liberalism was perfectly, albeit unintentionally, captured in Rob Reiner's 1995 film, *The American President*. The movie's transparent purpose was to send a message to Bill Clinton: "Get some backbone." (At the film's Washington premiere, Reiner eagerly asked political pundits, "Do you think this movie is really going to have an effect on American politics?"[24]) But when the Clinton clone in the cinematic White House finally does find his courage, his purpose is not to do anything to help workers; it is to stand up for environmental protection, gun control, and the ACLU. These are, for the most part, commendable objectives. But they do not begin to address the principal causes of the problems that frighten a majority of Americans in the nineties. Workers are wholly absent from the sets of *The American President*, as they have increasingly become in the councils of American liberalism and the Democratic Party. Reiner's president has gone to Washington, but he's no Mr. Smith.

TODAY'S REPUBLICAN AGENDA

The reaction of the putatively new thinkers of the GOP to the three-pronged menace to the American way of life has been a shrug of the shoulders coupled with a host of proposals designed to exacerbate the problems. Basically they suggest the trickle-down economics and unfettering of free enterprise that characterized conservative dogma from Alexander Hamilton through Calvin Coolidge and was discredited by the Great Depression. The Republican ideas are so old that they seem new to people whose knowledge of history is not what it should be.

The Republicans' "new ideas" to deal with an economy in which the rich are getting richer and everyone else is losing ground include the following: tax cuts weighted in favor of the highest-income groups; replacing the progressive income tax with a "flat tax"; excluding unearned income—interest, dividends, capital gains, and inheritances—from all taxes (which is to say: *If you had to work for your income, we'll tax it; if you got it without work, you can keep it all*); the substitution of a regressive national sales tax for the income tax; allowing corporations to raid workers' pension funds; sharp cutbacks in the Earned Income Tax Credit, which helps poor working families keep their heads above the waters of welfare; and slashing college loans, thus pulling the major ladder into a middle-class life out of the reach of more Americans who lack affluence.

The Gingrich Republicans say they want to complete the Reagan Revolution. In one sense, this is true enough. The unrelenting attack on the welfare state launched by the Republican majority elected in 1994 amounts to the falling of the second shoe of a scheme that was devised by Reaganites at the beginning of his presidency. The attempts of Gingrich Republicans to dismantle social programs as part of balancing the budget are the fulfillment of a long-term plan set in motion by the Reagan administration when it passed its tax cut in 1981.

Most of the Reagan insiders never believed in what Budget Director David Stockman bluntly referred to as "these tooth-fairy tales" that they fed to the public: that cutting the taxes of the rich would so stimulate the economy that the lower rates would produce more revenue and balance the budget. Rather, the goal from the start was to increase the deficit so much that it would appear that the country could no longer afford to maintain social programs. "The plan," Stockman said, "was to have a strategic deficit that would give you an argument for cutting back programs that weren't desired."[25] Then the case would be pushed that it was a matter of fiscal necessity to disassemble the welfare state in order to balance the budget. The "then" foreseen by the Reaganites in 1981 arrived when Newt Gingrich became Speaker of the House a decade and a half later.

Populist Republican Kevin Phillips argues persuasively that the GOP talk about balancing the budget has been "flim-flam" and an "economic con game" all along. "Since the Republicans started producing deficit elimination charts in the early 1980s, their three goals have been very different," Phillips contends. The real objectives have been to cut taxes for the rich, shrink the role of government and the safety net," and "help the stock and bond markets." And, while the budget has never come close to balance under all the Republican fiscal proposals, the genuine purpose has been admirably met: "the tax rates have come down, the rich have gotten richer, and the Dow Jones Average has jumped from under a thousand to over five thousand."[26] No objections to any of these results are likely to be raised by the principal beneficiaries of the new American economy.

Although the Republicans of the nineties are in some respects completing the unfinished business of the Reagan years, it is undeniable that they seek to go far beyond what Reagan tried to do. The Reagan Republicans weakened the social safety net; the Gingrich Republicans want to eliminate it, as they let slip from time to time when a candid but indiscreet remark unintentionally passes their lips. "Now we don't get rid of it in Round One," Gingrich said of Medicare when speaking before a Republican gathering in October 1995, "because we don't think that's *politically* smart. We don't think that's the right way to go through a transition. But we believe it's going to wither on the vine."[27] The Grand New(t) Party's free-market extremism would put each person on the high wire, and those who fall off would be left to splatter on the floor of the social Darwinian arena into which Republican extremists hope to turn America.

In the name of not harming our children by leaving them with large debts, Republicans are slashing education, training, nutrition, research, college loans, conservation, and child immunization. (Now there's a program that is designed to secure the future of our children.[28])

Dress up their ideas as nattily as they may, the Republicans will have a tough time persuading the American people to embrace their raw survival-of-the-fittest doctrine. But it is, as the maxim has it, hard to beat something with nothing.

DEMOCRATIC ALTERNATIVES

As I worked on this book in 1995, optimism was a scarce commodity among Democrats. I sat in a West Wing office in the White House and listened as a top advisor to President Bill Clinton told me how conservative Republicans had taken thirty years from the time of Barry Goldwater to that of Newt Gingrich to develop a comprehensive set of ideas and win the public over to their program. He suggested that progressive Democrats were at the beginning of a similar process and could look forward to many years in the wilderness before the pendulum would swing back in their direction.[29] That attitude would appear to fall a bit short of optimism. Such defeatism in high places is needed neither by Democrats nor Americans at this point.

"I don't know what the next Democratic Party is going to look like or exactly when it will appear," former Democratic National Committee Executive Director Brian Lunde said in the summer of 1995. "But the old one, based on programmatic liberalism, is clearly dying. It's going the way of the Berlin Wall."[30] There is much truth to this assessment. The conditions for which the philosophy and programs of New Deal/Great Society liberalism were developed have changed in important ways, and we must have new responses to new circumstances. Republicans charge that Democrats have no new ideas, that all they can do is offer warmed-over versions of the no-longer-New Deal and never-so-Great Society. These criticisms do not miss their target by much, and I readily agree that some tried-and-false liberal ideas should be rejected.

Following a May 1995 retreat for House Democrats, a mainstream liberal compared the condition of his party with that of the Soviet Communist Party in its dying days. "On the surface, the Communist Party looked pretty much like it always had," this junior Democratic congressman told columnist Robert Novak. "The apparatus was there, the hierarchy, the organization. But all of a sudden, the party was gone—just like that. I get the same feelings about the Democratic Party today."[31]

The principal problems with Democrats and liberals are an apparent lack of ideas and a crisis of self-confidence. Indeed, holding a "retreat" seemed appropriate for a party that had enjoyed majority support for most of the half century that began with the Great Depression, but by 1995 looked like it was in full-scale withdrawal. Worse, perhaps, than its ostensible shortage of ideas was the American Left's confidence deficit in the beliefs that its adherents had long professed. Today, many progressives lack both the courage of their convictions and the convictions themselves.

Democrats and progressives seemed to be shell-shocked in the wake of the Republican congressional victory in 1994. The only strategy some could think of was the "give them enough rope" approach. This meant that Democrats would simply wait for the Republicans to "go too far." It is a fairly safe bet that the radical rightists now dominating the Republican Party *would* go too far—and quite rapidly. But following such a "strategy" would be foolish for three reasons: First, the Republicans might do a great deal of damage before the public recoils at their excesses; second, it will take a lot longer for the public to turn against the Republicans if the Democrats are not offering an attractive alternative; third, there is no guarantee that people who are repelled by what the GOP does will turn to the Democrats.

Here is a sobering thought for Democrats: During the eighties, conservative proposals were far less popular than their chief salesman, Ronald Reagan. To the extent that people went along with the "Reagan Revolution," it was because they liked the man, not the ideas. Today, however, conservatism's leading advocate, House Speaker Newt Gingrich, is personally unpopular. (*Very* unpopular. A *Time*/CNN survey in December 1995 found that only 24 percent of Americans had a favorable impression of the Speaker. When this cross section of Americans was asked whether they would "like to see Gingrich as president someday," the result could not have been comforting to the Speaker: 9% Yes; 80% No.[32]) Despite this, many of the Republican ideas are popular. We cannot, as we could in the Reagan years, dismiss that popularity as a result of a cult of personality.

Some befuddled Democrats are trying to compete with the right-wing Republicans by taking up their ideas but saying that they will not take them to the extremes that the Republicans will. This "me, too, but not as much" argument is the one Republicans employed during the New Deal. It didn't get Alf Landon very far in 1936. But sticking with old, discredited ideas and opposing apparently new and popular ones is hardly a ticket to success, either. See Hoover, Herbert; sub-heading: 1932 Election.

If the party hopes to regain majority status, it must find a way to address the genuine concerns and grievances of those people who once played such an important part in the New Deal coalition and who are now so prominently threatened by the new economic forces. Democrats badly need a coherent program that will make clear that, unlike the Republicans, they favor policies that will provide assistance to middle-class as well as poor Americans in coping with the new economy.

Bonior summed it up when he said to me: "We have to somehow convince them [middle- and working-class Americans] that we are on their side and we understand their problems with their incomes and their wages and the fact that they have an all-working family, a job, and they're not home with the kids as a result and the whole social fabric starts to shred at home because of that. We need to get that message across—that we understand that problem."[33]

While Republicans would leave each American to face the enormous forces of technological change and international competition on his or her own, the basic Democratic philosophy must be to use the government to cushion the impact of these powerful influences and assist people in making their way in this frightening new world. This can be done through such means as education and training programs and tax policy.

But the new Democratic program will have to be something more than a rehash of the New Deal and Great Society. As Democratic political consultant Paul Begala put it in a 1995 interview with me: "You can't just blindly accept every mistake in the last thirty-four years."[34] Bill Clinton said basically the same thing in a conversation I had with him six years before he was elected president. "I don't think that the Democratic Party can recapture the majority of the American people in a national election by any sort of reversion to its former policies," the highly ambitious Arkansas Governor said.[35]

While policies must change with the times, however, it is essential that Democrats not abandon the "roots of our being," as District of Columbia Delegate Eleanor Holmes Norton put it. "We have been the party of the working person. We put together the most unlikely coalition around economic issues. If the Democratic Party does not go back to those roots," she said, "it has no raison d'etre." The difficult task facing Democrats, Congresswoman Norton rightly said, "is changing our own change—taking our reforms and changing them to meet new circumstances before the other side overthrows them."[36]

CHANGE WITH THE CHANGING TIMES

This certainly does not mean that Democrats should simply attempt to resuscitate the New Deal. FDR's policies—and LBJ's—were geared to a time that is now past. The New Deal was designed for an America of self-sufficiency and industry. Today we find ourselves in an increasingly free international market and a technology- and service-based economy. We need new approaches to new problems, not solutions to old problems offered by a No-Longer-New Deal.

In a sense, the New Deal is rather like NATO: each was devised to meet the problems of another era. Each did an estimable job of coping with the monumental problems of its time; but that time is now gone. This does not mean that either should be scrapped, but both need to be modified and redefined to meet new missions under new circumstances.

We live in a new and perilous age, unlike what Americans have experienced in the past—and especially different from the quarter century after World War II in which Americans enjoyed a unique degree of prosperity and world dominance. Great Society liberalism was a product of that era of unprecedented abundance and growth. "During the 1960s," as sociologist Paul Starr has noted, "many observers thought America was entering a post-materialist era; we had allegedly solved the problems of basic living standards and could afford to worry about long-ignored injustices and experiment with new lifestyles and states of consciousness."[37] (Believing this is one of the reasons that so many liberals drifted away from economic issues and into cultural matters.) In the 1990s, virtually no one believes that we have solved the problems of basic living standards, which have been eroding for a majority of Americans for two decades, so it is clear that important parts of that liberal approach are unsuited for the age of limits in which we currently find ourselves. "We're in a different world today from the one I grew up in," Senate Democratic Leader Tom Daschle said to me, "and we, as the party of government, have to be ready to propose different approaches that will work in this new world."[38]

A prime example of an old liberal approach that is no longer viable is Keynesian economics. Based as it is on stimulating consumption as the essence of economic policy, Keynesianism's promises were always dubious. If an overemphasis on ever-increasing consumption is at the root of our social and values problems today (as I shall argue in Chapter Three), liberals who hitched their wagon to Lord Keynes were choosing a horse headed in the wrong social direction from the outset. Stimulating more and more consumption inevitably undermines community and the values that go with it.

But Keynesianism seemed to work as an economic policy. Deficit spending helped to keep up consumer demand from the thirties (and particularly from World War II) onward. But a critical fact about the efficacy of the Keynesian approach has been largely overlooked: It can work *only* under conditions of national isolation. One of the most important decisions of the New Deal came when Franklin Roosevelt sent his "bombshell message" to the London Economic Conference in July 1933, indicating that the United States would go it alone rather than agree to an international monetary exchange. (Keynes himself understood the need for nations to control their own economies for his ideas to work. He praised Roosevelt's stand in an article entitled "President Roosevelt Is Magnificently Right."[39]) By standing in the way of free trade, FDR may have made worldwide recovery more difficult, but he also ensured that his domestic programs would have a chance of success. Trade barriers provided the needed assurance that the economy Keynesian deficits stimulated would be our own.

The largely free international market in which we now find ourselves makes Keynesianism obsolete. The products we buy with borrowed money are now as likely to create jobs in Malaysia, South Korea, or France as they are in the United States. Bill Clinton understood this in the midst of the huge Keynesian increase in deficit spending during the Reagan administration. "We've created virtually all of the Japanese growth in the last couple of years," Clinton said to me without much exaggeration in 1986.[40]

Another major change in the world further undermines the old liberal economic approach: the end of the Cold War. Peace is hell, at least in an economic sense in a country that has placed all of its prosperity eggs in a Keynesian basket. Add to the decline in military spending that follows peace a largely free international market, and the Keynesian approach becomes almost wholly passé.

The fact that conditions today differ from those in which the policies of the New Deal and Great Society were devised does not mean, however, that we can return to the ways of an even earlier day, as the radical reactionaries who have taken over the Republican Party are trying to do. If we are, in fact, entering circumstances fundamentally different from any previously faced by Americans, we need neither the stale ideas of New Deal/Great Society liberalism nor the petrified thought of McKinley/Coolidge conservatism. A new age demands a genuinely new approach.

The pages that follow constitute an attempt to provide such a new strategy. Before going on to the details of how we got where we are and what we need to do to alter our course, let me state briefly what I see as the guidelines and destination for a new Democratic vision:

1. There *is* a public interest.
2. There are also private interests, and these must be respected and encouraged, as long as they do not substantially undermine the public interest.
3. Morality must once again become a central theme of progressives.
4. We are connected, not only with other people today, but with past and future generations.
5. Government is inherently neither good nor bad.
6. Moderating the extremes of wealth and poverty is a highly desirable goal, but *how* this is done is of critical importance.
7. Limits do exist in terms of personal behavior, business practices, natural resources, etc.
8. Responsibility is the price of freedom.
9. The free-market system is the best economic system ever devised by humans, but—like the best political system ever devised by humans, democracy—it is imperfect and can produce problems. The Market is not God. We need to apply the wisdom our Founding Fathers used with respect to the political system, to our economic system: make it fundamentally a free market, but with the sorts of checks and balances that the Founders placed on pure democracy.
10. Basing our whole society on "market values", as extreme "conservatives" desire, is a prescription for disaster. Self-interest is part of

human nature and so cannot be ignored; but we are also social creatures. Both sides of our natures need to be taken into account.

11. At least as important as getting the government out of the lives of the people is getting the people *into* the life of the government.
12. If the Great Society envisioned by Lyndon Johnson is beyond our reach, we ought to strive for what is more important: to become a *good* society.

2

The Psychic Crisis of the Nineties

Who Stole Our Future?

"We are a nation at peace. But being at peace with others and being at peace with ourselves are different things."[1] These uncharacteristically sagacious words from a pamphlet issued by the 1992 reelection campaign of President George Bush say much about the mood of Americans in the last decade of the second millennium.

"I am not optimistic about the future. The world has changed in ways that I find to be extremely frightening. My children are not going to have the opportunities I have had."[2] This early 1995 statement, which Denise Woods, a sales executive in Chicago, made as part of a survey taken for the bipartisan Council for Excellence in Government, encapsulates a widespread feeling among Americans in the 1990s. That poll found that less than half of the adults surveyed "believed that their children would have a higher standard of living than their own." It indicated a people not at peace with themselves. Journalists Michael Shanahan and Miles Benson summarized the findings of this poll and the sense of conversations on the national mood in the mid-nineties that they had with a number of historians (including myself) by saying: "The unbridled optimism that once characterized American society has been replaced by a sense of economic desperation and gloom about the future for middle-class Americans and their children, a fear undiminished by two years of steady economic growth."[3] Another 1995 poll found even less faith in the future. Asked how "the next generation of children will live," 23 percent of the Americans surveyed said they thought the lives of the next generation will be better; 60 percent said they will be worse.[4]

Why should such seemingly "un-American" feelings of apprehension about the future persist in the face of figures showing a healthy economy? In a May 1995 *Newsweek* article, Joe Klein enumerated some of the symptoms of what he called "The Nervous Nineties": "The economy is good, but a majority (60 percent) worry about losing their jobs. The crime rate is down, but everyone knows someone who has been mugged (and 89 percent think that crime is getting worse)."[5] A "free-floating gloom"[6] is abroad in the land—an "anxiety—a fear that something [has] gone deeply wrong with the soul of the country."[7] "People don't see a future in which they have control over their lives, or knowledge of what things will be like," says Columbia University historian Alan Brinkley. "That is a profound change in our culture."[8]

Apprehension was even more apparent by late 1995. The Dow Jones industrial average gained a remarkable 1,282.68 points during 1995, piercing both the 4,000 and 5,000 milestones in a single year and increasing its value by more than 33 percent in twelve months.[9] Yet nearly three-fourths (73 percent) of Americans surveyed for the Times Mirror Center for the People and the Press said that they were dissatisfied with the "way things are going." Their fears were spread over a wide range of concerns, including inability to afford health care, not being able to save enough to retire, not having enough money to pay for their children's college education, and losing their jobs or suffering a cut in pay.[10]

Certainly this fear of the future is diametrically opposed to what we have come to think of as the characteristic American outlook. Bill Clinton has often said that the ideas of one of his professors when he was at Georgetown, the idiosyncratic Carroll Quigley, have shaped his thinking. Quigley maintained, Clinton says, that "the one reason for America's greatness is that for ten generations we preferred the future to the present. Americans believed that what we sacrifice today, we will benefit from tomorrow. A basic value of our society was: 'I'm going to sacrifice now so that my children and grandchildren will be better off.'"[11] "One thing will kill our civilization and way of life," Quigley lectured to his students, "—when people no longer have the will to undergo the pain required to prefer the future to the present."[12] Clinton's 1992 campaign theme song, Fleetwood Mac's "Don't Stop" (Thinkin' About Tomorrow), served as an abridgement of Quigley's interpretation of the centrality of "future preference" to American history.

Now, however, it seems that we *have* stopped thinking about tomorrow—or at least we have stopped believing that it will be better than yesterday and today. This is a profound change in the American outlook, but it is not without precedent. There was a similar, troubled, transitional period in our history exactly a century ago. A comparison with that era can be instructive on the sources of the seemingly irrational Great Fear that appears to be endemic in parts of America today. Yet, even when this useful comparison is completed, the questions will still remain: What has happened to Americans' future orientation and our confidence that we will have control over our prospects? To put it more simply: Who stole our future? Why have we ceased to act in the way that Professor Quigley said Americans always had in the past? These are central questions facing the nation today, and any revival of progressivism must address them squarely. Doing so will be a major concern of this book.

THE NINETIES—AGAIN

In '92, the electorate's growing discontent with the social and economic changes that seemed to be destroying the America they knew produced a strong third party and helped the Democrats to win the presidency and both houses of Congress, marking the first time in a generation that the Democratic Party had simultaneously controlled the executive branch and both houses of the legislative branch of government. Democratic hopes were brighter than they had been at any time since the tumultuous events of the sixties had discredited their party in the eyes of a large portion of the American public.

But the Democratic euphoria soon proved to be misplaced. Being fully in charge of the government meant that there was no one else to blame for problems. It seemed clear to voters that the Democrats must be responsible for their difficulties. In the Congressional elections of '94, irritated voters almost everywhere turned to the Republicans, who won control of the Senate and the House. There was, as one senator said, "hardly an oasis left in the Democratic desert."[13]

A massive realignment was underway, and Republicans gleefully awaited the '96 election, when they would surely regain the presidency. The huge GOP victory over the Democrats in '94 signalled the beginning of a more than thirty-year reign of the Republicans as the majority party. The '96 election shaped up as presenting one of the few really clear and meaningful choices between competing philosophies in the history of American presidential contests. It would pit the traditional ideas that had held sway for decades against a radical program of change linked with the word "populist."

When the ballots were counted in that year, 1896, the representative of continuity, William McKinley, had defeated the radical "populist" who promised to shake things up, William Jennings Bryan. The Republicans then enjoyed majority status (two plurality victories by Woodrow Wilson notwithstanding) until they were discredited by the Great Depression.

On the surface, it may appear that history is repeating itself in an exactly 100-year cycle.[14] But this eerie phenomenon becomes more curious when one takes a closer look. Grover Cleveland and the Democrats were undermined a century ago by the worst economic collapse in American history up until that time, the Panic of 1893.

We do seem to be experiencing another Panic today, but the Panic of the 1990s is based on nothing as tangible as the economic depression of the 1890s. People today certainly feel imperiled by economic afflictions, but they also feel "threatened by something far bigger than mere economic adversity."[15] A substantial majority of Americans throughout the first half of the 1990s said they believed the country is headed in the wrong direction[16]—and in the falls of both 1992 and 1994 they voted accordingly. Yet at the time of the 1994 electoral upheaval, unemployment was low, the economy was growing at a healthy rate, inflation remained under control, and the deficit was declining.

In the 1890s, public perceptions and economic reality were in tandem; in the 1990s they appear to be widely divergent. What could account for the peculiar dissonance today?

AVERAGES CAN BE DECEIVING

Part of the problem is that while averages indicate that the economy has been doing well in much of the 1980s and 1990s, averages often obscure the important details. As the diminutive Secretary of Labor Robert B. Reich, who is under five feet tall, tellingly points out, "Shaquille O'Neal and I have an average height of six feet."[17] While Americans whose wealth corresponds to O'Neal's height (in Shaq's case, his place on the wealth scale is similar to his position on the height scale, although even he would appear to be a midget in terms of wealth if compared to, say, Bill Gates) are doing very well these days, those whose economic position parallels Reich's physical stature are facing conditions more like those of the depressed 1890s. The same discrepancy between aggregate economic statistics and the reality facing millions of Americans was captured in a 1995 Jeff MacNelly cartoon in which a politician speaking at a banquet brags: "The current economic recovery has created over 7.8 million jobs." The response in the waiter's mind is to the point: "And I have three of them."[18]

In fact, the United States experienced a net increase of 27 million jobs between 1979 and the end of 1995, enough to provide work for all the laid-off workers and all the new people entering the workforce. The problem, as the *New York Times* pointed out in its early 1996 series on "The Downsizing of America," is that, "whereas 25 years ago the vast majority of the people who were laid off found jobs that paid as well as their old ones, Labor Department numbers show that now only about 35 percent of laid-off full-time workers end up in equally remunerative or better-paid jobs."[19]

Secretary Reich's message about what averages obscure can be seen in a few statistics. Between 1990 and 1994, more than a million manufacturing jobs were lost in the United States. (This continued a trend. Between 1981 and 1991, 1.8 million American manufacturing jobs were lost.[20]) During the same five-year period, the after-tax profits of American corporations rose by 44.7 percent. Over an eleven-year period beginning in 1984, the stock market rose by 600 percent, while wages for non-college-educated workers were stagnant or declining.[21] "Something is very wrong with an economy where the stock market is going through the clouds and wages are going down," Eleanor Holmes Norton points out.[22] "There is a difference," as Ohio Congresswoman Marcy Kaptur tersely notes, between 'money for a few' and the 'wealth of a nation.'"[23] Even Pat Buchanan is worth quoting on this point: "What, after all, is an economy for, if not for its people?"[24]

In fact, there is a connection between how much money the few are making and the problems of the nation. "What companies do to make themselves secure," as the *New York Times* said in early 1996, "is precisely what makes their workers feel insecure."[25] The stock market's remarkable rise in 1994–95 was due in part to "downsizing," layoffs, and falling or stagnant wages. These fundamental problems and threats to most Americans translate—at least in the short- and middle-term—into increased corporate profits. (In the longer term, it is likely that the decline in buying power for the victims of this new economy will decrease profits as well.) The phenomenon upon which many people have remarked with amazement in recent years—that Wall Street usually reacts favorably to bad news—should not be surprising. The market's rise is in some important respects an indication not of health, but of weakness, in the American economy and society.[26]

The apparent inverse relationship between the health of Wall Street and that of Main Street (or Frontage Road) was demonstrated anew in March 1996 when the stock market reacted to the good news that the economy had created more than 700,000 new jobs in February—the best it had done in more than a decade—by registering the third largest one-day loss in the history of the Dow Jones average.[27]

We—or, rather, a majority of us—have been caught up in a largely unnoticed slow-motion crash since the 1970s. Between the 1870s and the early 1970s, despite the ups and downs (including the very big down of the 1930s), the American economy enjoyed an average annual growth rate in excess of 3 percent. But between 1973 and 1993, the American economy grew at an average annual, inflation-adjusted rate of only 2.3 percent.

Put simply, since the mid-seventies, we have lost about one-third of our normal economic growth. Had growth during those two decades been sustained at its historic norm, the average American family would have received an additional $50,000 over the period.[28]

But the problem is not just that the pie has been growing more slowly; it is also that the slice going to the richest Americans has been growing larger while the whole pie is expanding less rapidly. The *Wall Street Journal* summarized the disturbing trend when it pointed in 1995 to "a major shift . . . as the 'social contract' fades and is replaced by a more Darwinian system under which the most able get a greater share of the rewards."[29] Ownership—wealth—has become increasingly important in determining income. Between 1979 and the late eighties, income from property ownership—dividends, interest, rent—rose three times faster than income from work.[30] (One reason for this boon to the wealthy is the massive federal deficits created by the Reagan economic plan; the huge debt built up in the eighties has made interest on public obligations the government's largest transfer program. It transfers wealth from working people to lenders, who tend to be those with an excess of wealth available to lend. And the federal debt further added to the earning power of wealth by keeping up interest rates across the economy.)

Between 1970 and 1990, the percentage increase in income of each fifth of Americans, ranked in descending order, was much higher than that of the fifth below it (even though, of course, the base for the higher income segments was much larger than that of the lower ones). The incomes of the richest fifth of Americans went up by 31.3 percent, the middle fifth by 13.9 percent, and the poorest fifth by a scant 2.9 percent.[31] Among the results is growing maldistribution of income. Between 1967 and 1992, the share of total income going to the richest one-fifth of American families rose from 42.6 percent to 44.6 percent, while that going to the poorest one-fifth dropped from 5.2 percent to 3.9 percent.[32]

A large part of what has happened is that we have become a "winner-take-all society." In 1974, the compensation of the CEO of a typical large American corporation was approximately 35 times that of an average worker in manufacturing; twenty years later the representative American large corporation CEO was paid *120 times* what the average manufacturing worker earned and 150 times the average for manufacturing and service industries combined.[33] Had the difference in the worth to the organization of top and bottom people become so much greater over two decades? Can there be any justification for such gross imbalances? Competition for the very best in each field has become so intense that they can virtually name their price. The rest—even the "next-best"—often find themselves with vastly lower compensation. The idea of loyalty to a company virtually disappeared over these years. The United States has become a free-agent society in which leading figures in each field simply go with the highest bidder.[34]

The results of the two-decade bonanza for the winners and slow-motion crash for non-affluent Americans are apparent in real average hourly earnings, which rose every year between 1960 and 1973, when they peaked at $8.55 (in 1982 dollars), 26 percent higher than they had been in 1960. Since the decline began in 1973, the story has been very different. Hourly earnings have drifted downward, stagnating at about $7.40 in the years 1992–1994. This rate of pay is lower than at any time since 1964, and is 13.5 percent less than what the average working American was earning in 1973.[35] Put another way, two-thirds of the gains workers made between 1960 and 1973 were lost between 1973 and 1994.

Even as economic growth picked up a bit and the incomes of the very rich soared in the mid-nineties, moreover, the vast majority of Americans felt none of the benefits. "While permanent layoffs have been symptomatic of most recessions," the *New York Times* noted in early 1996, "now they are occurring in the same large numbers even during an economic recovery that has lasted five years and even at companies that are doing well."[36] As the adage says, where you stand depends on where you sit. The rosy economic mean hides an economy that is increasingly mean for a majority of Americans.

THE NEW GILDED AGE

There are more similarities between the 1890s and 1990s than the gross or average economic statistics indicate. In both periods, the nation was moving from one economic age to another. In an essay he wrote more than forty years ago, the late historian Richard Hofstadter outlined a "psychic crisis of the 1890s."[37] That crisis had to do with a related set of wrenching changes that together marked a watershed for the American people. The source of the national anxiety of a century ago was people's fear that the conditions that had made America great were ending and the nation was headed into uncharted and dangerous territory that could bring the end of the world—or at least America—as they knew it.

The ingredients in this fear-inducing mix included a fundamental change in the economy and society, from agriculture to industry and from rural and small town to urban; the perceived "closing" of the frontier, the experience of which was believed to have been responsible for shaping the unique American character; massive immigration of "different" people (from eastern and southern Europe) who were thought to be inassimilable; a growing gap between the rich and poor (Mark Twain called the late nineteenth century "the Gilded Age," because the top of society shone brightly, but that veneer hid a shameful, decaying society beneath it); the rapid concentration of business power through corporate mergers; the rise of social Darwinism to a position of intellectual dominance, seemingly justifying the growing maldistribution of wealth and income and an increased indifference to the problems of the poor; the perception of rising crime and political corruption; and the submerging of the separate "island communities" that had characterized America up until that time and had provided numerous small stages on which many people could play major roles, into a national society and culture with far fewer places of prominence.[38] All of this added up to a contraction of opportunity for most Americans—and so to a fundamentally different situation in which the future would be looked upon, not with the traditional American optimism, but with apprehension.

In most respects, this description of the psychic crisis of the 1890s sounds similar to what we are experiencing a century later. "It was," Hofstadter said of the changing circumstances of the 1890s, "especially poignant for young people, who would have to make their careers in the dark world that seemed to be emerging."[39] Those young people did not call themselves "Generation X," but surely they could readily identify with the anxieties of young people today.

Once again in the 1990s, we sense that we are at the end of one era and staring into a very cloudy future—one in which, many Americans seem to fear, the fog may hide an abyss toward which we are moving. "People sense something fundamental has ended," as Robert Samuelson put it in 1995, "and they're fearful of an unseen future."[40] Once again, we are in the midst of a fundamental transformation of our economy and society. This time it is from an industrial to a "postindustrial" economy based on electronics, information, and services. Large-scale immigration of "different" people, this time mostly from Latin America and Asia, again worries "native" Americans. The two previous mass migrations to America that did the most to create a multicultural society were based on demand for types of labor that are no longer needed. Blacks were brought in to do agricultural work, which they continued to do long after slavery ended. But since about 1940, mechanization has taken away most of this kind of work. Similarly, the mass of eastern and southern Europeans who entered the United States between 1881 and World War I were allowed in because of a huge and growing demand for industrial labor. Now manufacturing jobs are disappearing almost as rapidly as agricultural employment did in the past. In this sense, the new immigrants of the late twentieth century may face an especially hostile reception: they are arriving at a time when there is no clear need for their labor.

Today, however, the greater fear is from people in other countries who stay in their own lands, but who compete with Americans for jobs.

There is now a worldwide oversupply of workers, skilled as well as unskilled. "We're moving into a new economy and a new world where average Joe in the street is literally going to be competing with manufacturing workers in Europe and Japan—probably even in Malaysia and Singapore," Paul Begala notes, "and increasingly white-collar workers are the same."[41]

We are in a New Gilded Age. We have a two-tier economy in which those at the top are doing very well, but those in the middle and lower ranks are stagnating or declining, as the 1995 Twentieth Century Fund study showing that the United States leads the industrial world in inequality of incomes and wealth indicates. This analysis found that in 1989 the wealthiest 1 percent of American households held almost 40 percent of the wealth in the country, nearly twice the share they owned in 1973—and more than twice the percentage (18 percent) of British wealth owned by the top 1 percent in that country, which has the greatest inequality in wealth distribution in western Europe.[42] After reciting similar statistics to me, David Bonior stated the undeniable: "So that frustration is out there."[43]

The attitudes of businessmen today also echo those of their Gilded Age forebears. At the time of the 1996 announcement that his corporation was letting 40,000 employees go, AT&T Chairman Robert E. Allen declared: "More and more companies are taking the realistic view that shareholders come first and employees are there to serve the shareholders."[44] This "new" outlook is about as new as the trickle-down economic doctrines touted by the "revolutionary" Gingrich Republicans. If not quite antediluvian, it is certainly ante-labor movement, ante-New Deal, ante-Progressive Era, pre-twentieth century. It is, in short, straight out of the first Gilded Age.

Most people fully understand where corporate priorities lie—or at least that they do not lie with their employees. A national poll in late 1995 found that a mere 4 percent of Americans believed that large companies put the interests of their employees first, while 34 percent said they put top executives first and 46 percent said stockholders receive the top priority.[45] "The people who run our corporations do not care for workers these days," Congresswoman Rosa DeLauro of Connecticut maintains. "If they can downsize, if they can make another dollar, if their stock options for the CEO can go up—OK, so let 2,500 people go. It's OK. That's better business. There is a whole sea change in a whole variety of areas."[46] That sea change is drowning working people, as did the similar attitudes in the first Gilded Age.

And, although the term itself is not often used, social Darwinism is again dominating important segments of American thought in the late twentieth century, as it did in the late nineteenth. This creed that replaces a benevolent God with a ruthless competitive Market as the omnipotent force in the universe is the unacknowledged secular deity of many conservatives and Republicans. The "intellectual" darlings of the Right, Charles Murray and Dinesh D'Souza, are full-blown social Darwinists, arguing that certain races are inferior to others and deserve what they get. Indeed, the philosophy of the omnipotent marketplace that holds sway almost as much today as it did a century ago, *requires* its adherents to argue that everyone deserves what he or she receives, good or bad. Thus Murray argues that rewards in our society are distributed on the basis of intelligence and blacks have less intelligence than whites, so they should just content themselves with lesser positions, and D'Souza contends that slavery really wasn't so bad for blacks.[47]

Business concentration proceeds at at least as alarming a pace in the 1990s as it did in the 1890s, eliminating jobs in its wake. In 1995, the value of corporate mergers and acquisitions surged to $866 billion, 51 percent above the previous record in this category, set only a year before.[48] Fear of crime dominates public discourse, and stories of political corruption are ubiquitous. We also are experiencing a phenomenon very similar to the loss of island communities with their many stages for people of moderate talents. The late-nineteenth-century submergence of the island communities into metropolitan, regional, and even national arenas with far fewer places, and those only for people with higher talents or skills, is being replicated in the late twentieth century with the emergence of a worldwide stage. In their highly insightful 1995 book, *The Winner-Take-All Society*, economists Robert H. Frank and Philip J. Cook quote a character from Kurt Vonnegut's novel, *Bluebeard*, who makes this point: "A moderately gifted person who would have been a community treasure a thousand [or, we might add, 150] years ago has to go into some other line of work, since modern communications has put him or her into daily competition with nothing but the world's champions."[49] It is increasingly the case that people all over the world read the same books, go to the same movies, listen to the same recorded music, and buy clothing created by the same designers.[50] If island communities were submerged in the late nineteenth century, continents are being submerged today. If nationwide competition reduced opportunities and induced anxiety in the 1890s, worldwide competition is doing the same in the 1990s.

There is no longer a frontier to be lost, and we are not suffering from a general economic depression, but many people in the 1990s are as troubled about the contraction of opportunity and the emergence of a very different kind of America as were their forebears a century ago. The result today, as it was then, is to push large numbers of Americans into what Secretary Reich calls "the anxious class."[51]

Democratic Congressman Jim McDermott of Washington found members of this new class when he was persuaded to visit a grunge bar in

Seattle early in 1995. A young person he talked with there told him that "almost everyone in the place is a college graduate, but most of them are 'permanent temps,' working without benefits, unable to get a mortgage, and with no provision for a pension beyond Social Security."[52] Young Americans are finding themselves in "a country and a world where employers (increasingly so) are offering less than full-time jobs because they either don't want to or can't afford to provide health care," Senator Wellstone says. "So it's not only that the job doesn't pay a decent wage; you don't have the health care, either."[53] What is rarely stated in the debate over the future of the welfare state is that it is not only government-sponsored benefits that are imperiled; corporate benefits are also shrinking and vanishing. At the same time that the government-provided safety net may begin to unravel, employer-provided safety nets are being shredded.

"As companies hire more temporary help," the *Wall Street Journal* pointed out in 1995, "the contingent-worker population has swelled." "Earnings and wages have become considerably less stable," notes Boston College economist Peter Gottschalk.[54] Approximately half of the American workforce today is enrolled in no pension or retirement plan whatsoever. And well over half of all Americans expect Social Security to be either abolished or severely slashed by the time they retire.[55] How could someone in such a situation be other than anxious? Surely they have reason to want to stop thinking about tomorrow.

DOWNSIZING THE AMERICAN DREAM

"There has been a downsizing of the American Dream," says Democratic opinion analyst Peter Hart. "I see the American public as struggling. Instead of having dreams about what can be done, the public seems to be saying, 'don't let this (layoffs or other economic calamity) happen to me.' These are the dreams of people who are scared and uncertain."[56]

"It's important to recall that throughout American history, discontent has always had less to do with material well-being than with expectations and anxiety," Harvard historian David Donald points out. "You read that 40,000 people are laid off at AT&T and a shiver goes down your back that says, 'That could be me,' even if the fear is exaggerated. What we are reacting against is the end of a predictable kind of life, just as the people who left the predictable rhythms of the farm in the 1880s felt such a loss of control once they were in the cities."[57]

Another striking similarity between the present and the 1890s is that in both eras a significant political movement arose in reaction to the perceived erosion of traditional ways. In both periods, a substantial portion of the American populace had concluded that America was "no longer working," at least for them. In the late nineteenth century, this discontent was greatest among farmers, and it was the People's Party, better known as the Populists, that grew out of the Farmers' Alliance movement of the 1880s to become a major force in the 1890s. The Populists had many good ideas, particularly on economic matters, but many of the movement's rank and file were also given to a conspiratorial view of the world. Many of them were staunch nativists; more than a few were anti-Semitic, and they quickly pushed what had started as a bi-racial movement into virulent racism.

Today the discontented groups are more disparate, but at least as widespread—and as convinced, not only that America "ain't what it used to be," but also that the social-economic-political system is no longer working for them, whatever it might be doing for various elites. The disgruntled in the late twentieth century include those who supported Ross Perot in 1992, the growing radical rightist groups (armed and otherwise), those who voted for Pat Buchanan in 1996, and, most importantly, the Christian Right.

"I think the reason we're talking about angry white men is that it's really mainstream American workers who are now unhappy," Congressman Barney Frank of Massachusetts told me. "These are people who for thirty-five years after World War II assumed that if you were hard-working, even if you didn't have a lot of talent or skill, you had economic security. Now that's not true anymore, and it's because of technological change and the internationalization of the economy." As Frank pointed out, it used to be that when there was a recession, everybody got hurt a little. If a person was laid off, he would be reading in the papers about an economy in recession. "But we've got the problem now," Frank said, "where guys are getting laid off—*fired*—and they're reading in the paper about how wonderful things are. And they say, 'Well, what the *fuck* is wrong with me? I mean, if everything is so good, how come *I*'m gettin' shafted?'"[58]

"They are living with constant anxiety," agrees University of North Carolina historian William Leuchtenburg. "Anyone can be fired and the uncertainty reaches right into the ranks of middle management. There was a time when you went to work for firms like IBM and you were told you would never be laid off. Those days are over. There is no longer any sense of loyalty in either direction."[59] AT&T vice president James Meadows placed an exclamation point at the end of the era of job security when he proclaimed early in 1996: "People need to look at themselves as self-employed, as vendors who come to this company to sell their skills." Americans can, he declared, look forward to a future that is increasingly "jobless but not workless."[60]

It is understandable that many Americans do not seem eager for such a future. An *Atlanta Journal-Constitution* editorial writer put the situation facing Americans without a college degree in the 1990s starkly: "A generation ago, anybody with a strong back and work ethic could make an honest living. That's not true anymore."[61] "There is no place any longer where people with a rudimentary working-class education can earn a middle-class living," Paul Begala points out.[62]

"If anything says we're living in a different world," Eleanor Holmes Norton said to me, "it's the movement away from the idea that new technology means more jobs."[63] That simply does not follow anymore, although there are those, such as Newt Gingrich, who continue to worship at that altar. Instead, technology is bringing us face to face with the prospect of "the end of work."[64]

"Today a high school graduate with five years work experience makes 27 percent less in real wages than his counterpart did in 1979," Representative Kaptur notes. "In the 1950s, one working person could provide for a family of four. In the '90s, it takes two family members working full-time just to keep the family afloat. Isn't there something wrong when worker productivity in America has steadily risen, but workers' wages and benefits continue to decline?"[65]

"People are working harder," says Congresswoman DeLauro. "The people in the workplace are killing themselves and they are barely able to make it. The most tragic part of what is happening today is that notion of the American dream where you could work hard, pass on something better to your kids. Folks, for the first time in this country, are fearful that their kids are *not* going to be better off. They are right, at the moment. Their jobs are at risk; their pensions are at risk; their retirement is at risk; their health care is at risk; education is at risk—their whole way of living and the values that are tied up with it. All of those pieces are truly at loose ends for people today."[66]

And all of these difficulties are being faced at a time when the United States confronts two other major obstacles to unity. In the 1990s, as in the 1890s, the nation is about three decades removed from a terribly divisive war. The two wars of the sixties split the nation to a greater degree than at any other time in our history. Obviously the breach caused by the Civil War was far greater than that generated by the Vietnam War, but the American people were more divided in the late 1960s than they had been at any time since the 1860s. In both cases, the wounds and mistrust had not fully healed by the nineties. Now we have the additional problem that we have lost the glue that helped—the Vietnam divisions notwithstanding—to hold us together for a half century: a clearly dangerous foreign enemy, first in Nazism and then in Soviet Communism. People seeking someone to blame for their difficulties in the post-Cold War era no longer have a clear foreign candidate and so can more readily be turned to the internal forces that unscrupulous politicians demonize. As Secretary of Education Richard

Riley put it, "You have a very serious anxiety out there, and a common concern about the future—and no enemy. That's a problem."[67]

WHO CAN WE SHOOT?

Discontent caused by genuine grievances—particularly falling living standards in a nation whose basic promise has always been a better tomorrow—does not automatically push the unhappy toward either the Left or the Right. The populism of a century ago leaned much more to the Left than the Right. When people find themselves receptive to the advice of nineteenth-century Populist Mary Lease, to "raise less corn and more hell," they want to find someone to blame for their difficulties. The operative question is that articulated by an evicted tenant farmer in John Steinbeck's *Grapes of Wrath*: "Who can we shoot?"[68]

In the late nineteenth century, the federal government was quite weak, so the "angry white men" (although, as is the case today, many of the angry were in fact not white and/or not men) of that time turned their ire against big business, which they generally castigated as "Wall Street" or, more vaguely, "the Interests."

The size and power of the federal government today have made it an inviting target for the wrath of the disaffected. Since the 1960s, there has emerged an odd coalition of populist elements with the party of Wall Street. Over the last three decades, Republicans have to a large degree succeeded in redirecting the seething resentment of people who feel left out of the benefits of the American system. No longer do most of them see big business as the culprit; rather than aiming their venom-soaked arrows at lower Manhattan's Wall Street, they now launch them in the direction of Washington's Pennsylvania Avenue. (But in early 1996, Pat Buchanan created panic within GOP ranks by rhetorically attacking *both* Wall Street and Washington.)

Despite this difference, another correspondence between the situations of the 1890s and the 1990s is that in both eras the wealthy were able to prevent a unified opposition by exploiting racial and ethnic differences to turn those who were suffering against each other. Those in power in the 1890s met the challenge expressed in Populist Tom Watson's famous declaration to white and black farmers: "You are kept apart that you might be separately fleeced of your earnings," by playing the race card and redirecting the fury of exploited whites away from "the Interests" to the even more exploited blacks. Today's carefully arranged attacks on affirmative action and immigrants serve a similar purpose. Republicans, the president's senior policy advisor, George Stephanopoulos notes, "argue against the workers' economic interests, but create new social problems to divert them."[69]

Vermont Congressman Bernie Sanders describes the right-wing strategy in the following way: "You deflect attention from the *real* issue: the decline in the standard of living. You play with race; you play with homophobia; you play with flags; you play with immigrants. You raise all of these specters and give people the opportunity to vent their anger against those things, rather than against the people who really have the power and are causing the problems."[70]

That these Republican "issues" are diversions should be clear. "If you believe that affirmative action is the reason white guys are out of jobs," as Congressman Frank says, "you must believe that there are these vast underground factories somewhere, where women and blacks are making cars and steel and rubber and glass. Obviously, that's not true. It's that these jobs are not here anymore; they've been lost technologically and internationally."[71] In 1990, U.S. Steel used 20,000 workers to make about the same amount of steel it had employed 120,000 workers to manufacture ten years earlier.[72] Most of those 100,000 lost jobs had been held by white men, but they were not lost to affirmative action; they were lost to high technology. Very few of the jobs that white men once had are now held by minorities and women; most are held by machines and computers. The government has no affirmative action program for these job takers; it is profit-maximizing corporations that insist on hiring and promoting machines and computers that displace human workers. The problem is not affirmative action, it is what corporate chieftains call "downsizing." Wall Street investors love this: it means more profits and fewer people on payrolls. Its meaning for middle-class Americans may be seen in the fact that from 1993 through 1995, American corporations permanently laid off 1.5 million employees.[73] When AT&T cut its workforce by 13 percent at the beginning of 1996, its stock price soared. It was, *Newsweek* commented, "like Wall Street spitting on the victims' bodies."[74] The news was greeted with less enthusiasm by the 40,000 newly unemployed workers whose lives were thrown into disarray. Downsizing, market analysts tell us, makes corporations lean and mean. It certainly does.

The loss of job security is an even bigger source of anxiety in the Psychic Crisis of the Nineties than are decreasing wages.

The temptation for those already enjoying economic power or seeking political power to divide the discontented along racial lines only grew greater in the wake of the decision in the O. J. Simpson case and the rise of Louis Farrakhan to prominence. The Simpson case is a particularly telling example of how race so often obscures class in the United States. The fact that almost completely escaped the notice of irate whites is that the defendant belonged to *two* minorities, one much more of a minority in America than the other. Simpson was (at least before his legal bills came due) a member of the very rich minority, as well as of the African-American minority. He has long identified himself much more closely with the wealthy than with the black, and it was his membership in the former minority, not the latter, that put Simpson in a position to be acquitted. Anyone who doubts this should consider this undeniable fact: Rich people are hardly ever convicted of major crimes; black people usually are.

It is true, of course, that in the end attorney Johnnie Cochran did not play the "rich card"; he played the race card. Fortunately for his client, race is much higher than class in the consciousness of most Americans. The jury was composed of Simpson's peers in a racial sense, but certainly not in a class sense. The point, however, is that it was only Simpson's membership in the very rich minority that enabled him to hire the attorneys, jury selection experts, expert witnesses, and so forth that put his lawyers in a position to utilize race to win the verdict they sought. The elite of super criminal defense attorneys pride themselves on hardly ever losing a case. O. J. Simpson is a free man today not because he is black, but because he had the money to buy the attorneys who always win.

But did the Simpson verdict exacerbate class tensions in our country? No. As is usual in America, ire was directed at the wrong target: race.

Robert Reich sums up the current situation well: "Today in America, millions of men and women are struggling to stay afloat. And as they struggle, they become uneasy. Some become disillusioned, distrustful; some, angry. And as their disillusionment and anger crest, they become ever more willing to heed the cries of cynical opportunists who orchestrate the politics of rage."[75]

BEING A *MENSCH*

Where the new economy that is responsible for the Psychic Crisis of the Nineties and the politics of rage that accompanies it has taken us was made clear by a December 1995 story that captured the hearts of people across the United States. After his textile mill in Methuen, Massachusetts, burned down two weeks before Christmas, Aaron Feuerstein became major news and was virtually canonized when he announced that he would continue to pay his employees for at least a month, give them their Christmas bonuses, carry on their health insurance, and rebuild the plant in the community in which his workers live. Mr. Feuerstein deserves the accolades he received. But what does it say about our economic system that a man who simply "does the right thing" becomes national news and is labeled a "great American hero"?[76]

Surely it suggests that in the totally unfettered free market of the 1990s, doing the right thing has become a remarkable occurrence. The "normal" thing for someone in business to do is whatever will maximize his profits. That often means "downsizing" the workforce, replacing human workers with computers, or moving the plant to Indonesia, without regard to the effects of these actions on the employees or on the local community. Today, Secretary Reich says in commenting on Feuerstein's kindness, "most workers expect the worst. The irony is that there's such an outpouring of public affection to a man doing well by his workers at a time when many companies faced, not with adversity, but with larger and growing profits, are laying their workers off."[77]

That a business is both profitable and an integral part of the identity of a community apparently means nothing in the nineties if larger profits are to be made elsewhere. Art Modell, the owner of the Cleveland—or is it Baltimore, or perhaps (fill in the blank with dollar signs)—Browns (or whatever they will now be called), said that he did not want to take his team out of Cleveland, but he "had no choice."[78] What took away his choice? Perhaps it was the fact that he could make a lot more money under the deal Baltimore was offering him. Under the ethic—if that word is at all proper in this context—of the new social Darwinism that is now the rule in business and the philosophy of the Republican Party, the only values that matter are those that have a vertical line through the final "s": value$ have replaced values.

Aaron Feuerstein explained his now unusual action by quoting Rabbi Hillel from 2,000 years ago: "When all is moral chaos, this is the time for you to be a *mensch*."[79] Surely ours is a time of moral chaos (about which, more in the next chapter) and, under the dictates of a society that takes the Market as its god and the value$ of our current economy, the person in business who acts as a *mensch*—a caring, just, compassionate human being—is likely to emerge as a loser. Leo Durocher's aphorism, "nice guys finish last," has become the guiding philosophy of our society to the extent that when a businessman does something nice it is the equivalent of "man bites dog": news. *Big News*.

Humans require limits. With them, it is possible to be a mensch; without them, it's survival of the most ruthless. The latter is largely our condition today. The radical Republicans want to lift all limits on economic behavior and make our world even more one of a few huge winners and many, many losers.

THE GREATEST GOOD FOR A SMALL NUMBER?

It is plain that we have reached another major turning point in American history and that it has produced another "Psychic Crisis of the Nineties." Many people no longer believe that the American Dream is available to them or to their children. This dread leads them to seek scapegoats. That is the most fundamental cause of a host of interrelated phenomena, from the 1994 election results through the uncivil discourse on talk radio, the rise of the "angry white male," the popularity of immigration restriction, and the unpopularity of affirmative action, to the increasing membership in "militias," and—at the extreme—people who imagine themselves at war with their own government.

"We are again going from one economic age to another," Paul Wellstone said to me. "You have all of the economic squeeze and insecurity that is giving rise to the politics of anger. I think there is a sort of vision vacuum out there that Gingrich *et al.* are filling for the moment, but it's also the most turbulent period that I remember in my adult life."[80]

Some observers belittle the psychic crisis in which the nation finds itself. Callers to right-wing radio talk shows—and the hosts, such as Rush Limbaugh and G. Gordon Liddy—frequently cite current entrepreneurial success stories as proof that there is "just as much opportunity in the United States today as there ever was—even more!"[81] This assertion may well be correct. *Some* Americans are doing very well in the new economy. But what the Pollyannas of the Right miss (in addition to the fact, which they deny, that luck—not just determination and hard work—often plays an important role in determining who succeeds) is that while the prospect of hitting it big may be as great (or as small) as ever, the opportunities to be moderately successful have tangibly contracted. There may be even more big winners in the emerging American economy; but it appears that there will be many fewer small winners—and a lot more losers. We need not concern ourselves with the interests of the big winners; they are being ably looked after by conservative Republicans, whose philosophy might be summed up as: *The greatest good for a small number.* They are sparing no effort in their quest to comfort the comfortable. A major task for progressives is to devise ways to assist the rest of the American people in coping with the wrenching transformation we are presently undergoing.

Senator Bill Bradley puts "the economic facts of life" in 1990s America simply: "The problem in this country, as it affects race and a lot of other things, is inadequate economic growth, unfairly shared. Until we confront that, we're going to be dealing with issues around the edge." As the New Jersey senator sees it, "there's no way to separate somebody's earning power from their prospects for life."[82] Republicans have made clear that they have no problem with the "unfairly shared" part of our new economy. In fact, they would contend that it is impossible for the distribution to be "unfair," since "fairness" has no place in economic matters; the great God Market simply distributes rewards, and whatever way he distributes them is, as Limbaugh might put it, "the way things ought to be."

"They feel vulnerable, off balance and in need of assistance to help them redefine their place in a newly confusing world," Ellis Cose says of men in his 1995 book, *A Man's World.*[83] Indeed men—angry, white, or otherwise—and women, too, who are facing the brave new world of high technology and low compensation, of foreign competition and corporate indifference, *are* in need of assistance. What they really need is *affirmative action*.

If progressives can redefine "affirmative action" to mean the government providing support for *us—all* of us who are threatened by the new economy—rather than advantages to *them* (as affirmative action is now seen by so many white males who have been misled into believing that it is a major cause of their troubles), affirmative action can be transformed overnight from a political liability for Democrats into their most powerful, defining battle cry. "We've just got to talk about that in terms of principle, of opportunity for everybody," David Bonior says, "and that principle of opportunity applies to them [white males] as well and that ladder has to be left out for them to climb, as well."[84] Polls indicate that a majority of Americans understand the need for affirmative action, which provides fairness to members of groups that have been discriminated against. Most people have no problem with this positive side of the program. Objections arise when gains for people from previously excluded groups appear to come at the expense of white males. "They think that the ladder has been held up for them and let down for women, for African-Americans, and others," Bonior notes.[85] Affirmative action to correct past injustices is much easier to accept in an affirmative economy than in a negative economy plagued by "downsizing."

One way in which many people decide how they feel about particular government programs is whether they believe that the program might someday be helpful to them. This is a major reason for the widespread support for Social Security and Medicare. Everyone is either old or hopes to be someday, so they can envision themselves as beneficiaries. So long as affirmative action is something that applies *only* to minorities and women, white men know that it can never be of direct assistance to them. But a useful definition of affirmative action is: compensatory steps taken to help people compete in circumstances for which their backgrounds have not adequately prepared them. This definition includes minorities and women, but it can also include anyone who has not been prepared to compete in the new economy.

If affirmative action were to one day connote government helping people—through such means as education, retraining, job placement, health insurance, and pension protection—to meet the challenges of the changing economy, it would include anyone displaced by economic change, as well as those disadvantaged by discrimination against their race or sex. This would make it possible for the angry white male to envision affirmative action working in his behalf.

The question would then become: Would most people rather face the ominous new world of technology and worldwide competition alone, as the Republicans want us to, or with the assistance and cooperation of our fellow citizens, through the instrumentality of government, as progressive Democrats propose? When the issue is cast in these terms, it is hard to see how the progressive position can lose. Indeed, this position becomes the genuinely *conservative* one in the sense that it provides a means whereby people can hope to conserve their living standards and hopes for the future.

THE DECLINE OF COMMUNITY

"America is deep in mid-passage between two economic eras," the *New York Times* correctly stated in its 1996 "Downsizing of America" series, "the old era of making things and of job security, and the new one of service and technology, takeovers, layoffs, and job insecurity." But the most frightening aspect of the upheaval that is at the heart of the Psychic Crisis of the Nineties goes beyond economics. It is that "the entire cloth of society . . . feels as if it is out of style and could just wear out." Citizens are withdrawing from community and civic life. "Many people," the *Times* study found, "are too tired, frustrated or busy" to participate in the community activities they used to enjoy. "People's expectations of security, stability and a shared civic life" are vanishing. "The tie between individuals and the community is less certain, and more fragile," Brad Tillson, the publisher of the *Dayton Daily News* says of his once-cohesive community. "It's scary for everybody."[86]

What is happening, as Robert D. Putnam of Harvard has said in his widely cited 1995 article, "Bowling Alone," is that our "social capital"—"features of social organization such as networks, norms, and social trust that facilitate coordination and cooperation for mutual benefit"—are in alarming decline.[87] The loss of trust in other people—in human nature itself—that polls have found reflects what is surely one of the worst crises Americans have ever confronted.[88]

Understanding the connection of the current transformation of the worldwide economy to the Psychic Crisis of the Nineties is only the first step toward finding solutions to the nation's—and the world's—problems. The processes of "stealing the future" and declining community have been under way for much longer than has the latest metamorphosis in the economy. Changes in the modern economic system dating back to about the time of the last Psychic Crisis of the Nineties a century ago have gradually weaned us from the traditional American future preference, the willingness to sacrifice today for a better tomorrow, and feelings of connection with each other. This alteration is the basic cause of our loss of the future—and the disintegration of our society and values.

3

"It's the Amoral Economy, Stupid!": How Our Supply-Side Economy Undermines Values

Values and Economies

The most pressing issue facing the nation today is the multifaceted collapse of community and values. "Over the past three decades we have experienced substantial social regression," former Secretary of Education William Bennett wrote in 1994. "Today the forces of social decomposition are challenging—and in some instances, overtaking—the forces of social composition."[1] I am in complete agreement with Bennett's diagnosis, (although not with all of his prescriptions), but I think he misses the most important microbe that is producing the symptoms he so well enumerates.

Ben Wattenberg was also right when he wrote in his 1995 book, *Values Matter Most*, that the "values situation [is] by far the scariest and most urgent part of our politics, and our lives."[2] The collapse seems most advanced in the inner cities, but it is now becoming apparent that those sections are the vanguard for a society that has lost its way and is coming apart. Liberals and conservatives have been in sharp disagreement about the causes of these problems. The positions they have taken are ironic. Although conservatives have historically been—and still are—more apt to make judgments on a monetary basis, it is liberals who usually attribute the problems of the underclass, now spreading up the economic hierarchy, to economic causes: the lack of jobs and income. For their part, conservatives see the root of the problems in non-economic terms; they say our troubles are the result of a collapse of morality and that the poisonous effects of the national decline in values are spreading through various levels of American society. Former Vice President Dan Quayle delineated this position in his famous 1992 "Murphy Brown" speech: "The intergenerational poverty that troubles us so much today is predominantly a poverty of values."[3] William Bennett, of course, agrees. "Values aren't a *part* of the game," the Republican moralist says, "they are the *whole* game."[4] "I have come to the conclusion that values issues are no longer merely *co-equal* with economic concerns," Democratic social conservative Wattenberg declares. "*The values issues are now the most important*."[5]

Both sides in this debate are partly correct, but the fundamental source of our problems is unseen by either. Some, like Senator Bill Bradley, understand that "this debate is not economics *or* values; it is *both*."[6] But even those who realize that both areas are involved usually do not perceive the way in which values and economics are related. Conservatives are right that the proximate cause of our problems lies in the area of morals; what they fail to realize, however, is that the basis for the decline in values is ultimately economic—yet not at all in the simple sense of people not having enough money, as liberals are wont to contend.

Among the ascendant conservatives, a consensus has emerged that the fault in the breakdown of values lies with liberal social policies and a liberal culture that places virtually no limits on personal behavior. David Frum, in his highly influential 1994 tract, *Dead Right*, stated the first half of this analysis succinctly: "The force driving the social trends that offend conservatives, from family breakup to unassimilated immigration, is the welfare function of government."[7] A year later, Wattenberg (a much less strident opponent of government than Frum) made almost the same point: "I believe that what government has caused, government should cure, through politics. I believe that what liberalism has caused, conservatism can cure."[8] The assumption that government and a type of liberalism have caused our decline in values is partly correct, but the supposition that conservatism, as presently understood and constituted, can cure this problem is completely and tragically mistaken.

In 1993, *The Wall Street Journal* published a very influential article by Charles Murray on "The Coming White Underclass." The right-wing social analyst, who achieved infamy less than a year later with a chapter in his *The Bell Curve* in which he argued that black people are genetically inferior, made a contradictory contention in this article. Rather than blaming biology for social pathology, as he would in 1994, in 1993 Murray saw the causes as being entirely social and cultural. He contended that welfare is the origin of family breakup because it allows young women to get maintenance support payments, provided they have a child, leave home, and do not marry. The solution Murray proposed to our social deterioration is very simple: abolish welfare and force unwed mothers back to their families. He would reopen orphanages for those children who could not be provided for by families.[9]

This "solution" attracted many people. Newt Gingrich and many other leading Republicans seized upon this Murray thesis as a wonderful rationale to stop doing what they did not want to do anyway. (Many of them backed away when they realized how expensive such a program would be.) There is no question that our current welfare system contains disincentives to family formation and needs drastic overhaul; but the idea that simply abolishing it would solve our deep-seated social pathology is, at best, simpleminded wishful thinking.* At worst, it is disingenuous cruelty.

Let us stipulate that the provision of welfare tends to undermine the initiative, self-respect, self-reliance, and marketability of those who receive it, especially if they do so for extended periods of time. "No one wants the current system," Representative Bonior said to me, "—it's broke, it's corrupt, it just doesn't work. It's demeaning."[10] Work is better than handouts; "something for something," not "something for nothing," ought to be the basis on which our society and economy operate. Liberals understood this when they began the welfare state. "Give a man a dole," Franklin Roosevelt's relief administrator, Harry Hopkins, pronounced, "and you save his body and destroy his spirit. Give him a job and you save both body and spirit."[11] This is the simple truth, and those liberals who bought into the argument that "welfare ought to be regarded as highly as work"[12] made a foolish and serious mistake: they defied common sense. Requiring work of able-bodied welfare recipients has always been the proper—and the *liberal*—course (although moral and values questions arise when mothers of very young children are forced, whether by government policy or economic pressures, to work outside the home). The trouble is, it has also always been the *expensive* course, and one with the potential of placing low-paid government-employed workers in competition with private enterprise. For these reasons, it has usually been "conservatives" who have finally opposed work relief programs, thereby showing themselves to be more interested in conserving low taxes and private profits than in conserving the dignity, skills, and self-reliance of welfare recipients.

Let us further stipulate another matter of common sense: that the availability of stipends, meager though they are, to young women—teenage girls, to be more accurate—who have a baby, leave their parents' (or, more often these days, parent's) home, and do not marry, encourages

* This is not to say that group living arrangements for children have no place. Clearly this is far preferable to leaving a child in "the abusive, alcoholic, drug-addicted, violence-prone family, or non-family, that is the normal habitat of many children" (Gertrude Himmelfarb, "The Victorians Get a Bad Rap," *New York Times*, January 9, 1995). My point here is merely that ending welfare would end neither poverty nor moral decline.

teen pregnancy, unwed motherhood, family breakup, and "family nonformation." Let us further recognize that these are not simply alternative lifestyles; they are, in fact, when they become widespread, social pathologies. (This is certainly not to say that every case of single parenthood, divorce, or teen pregnancy is automatically a disaster; but when such practices become the norm, that is a clear sign of a society in trouble.)

Welfare plainly has contributed to our social and values problems, and progressives should not deny this. This said, however, we must quickly make two other points:

First, the solution to the welfare problem is fixing the system, not simply condemning and abolishing it. Fixing the system, furthermore, will not save money in the short run; it will cost more than the current system. But transforming a dispiriting, dead-end system that subverts values and rewards undesirable, self-destructive behavior into a structure that genuinely provides assistance directed toward making people self-sufficient contributors to society is one of the best ways we can spend our money.

Second, solving the welfare problem will not by itself be of much consequence in reversing our fundamental deterioration of values. Welfare contributes to that problem, but only in a marginal way. Democratic political consultant Paul Begala correctly calls the idea that the welfare system is the cause of all our social and moral decay "preposterous." He points out that welfare payments have been declining in real terms for the last twenty years, yet we have more social and moral breakdown now than when the payments were higher. "If I'm not mistaken," Begala continues, slipping for effect into a more populist grammar, "the Menendez brothers weren't on no welfare and they shot and killed their parents in cold blood. You know, O. J. ain't on no welfare. The divorce rate among the affluent has got to be as bad as it is among the welfare population. It's just completely nuts to suggest that welfare causes all these problems."[13]

Cases like those of the Menendezes and Simpson should serve as reminders—should reminders be necessary—of the absurdity of Newt Gingrich's assertion that every horrible crime, from a South Carolina mother's drowning of her children to a Chicago woman's having a friend cut a baby out of the womb of another woman, is the result of liberal policies such as welfare. The principal source of our social and moral decline must be sought elsewhere.

As social disintegration has worsened, David Frum points out, "an awful doubt began to spread" among some conservatives: "What if government were not the only—or even the worst—subversive force?"[14] Such doubts were, I believe, well founded, although most of the right wing still clings to the dogma that government is the major cause of our values crisis.

"SITUATION TRAGEDIES" AND THE LOSS OF VALUES

The most popular "elsewhere" on which the blame for our moral decay is placed is on the various "liberations" associated with the 1960s. This argument also has its merits. Anyone who contends that the media's relentless bombardment of our senses with gratuitous violence and casual sex has no effect on our behavior is deluding him- or herself as much as Murray, Gingrich, Frum, and others who assert that ending welfare would solve the problems of the poor are fooling themselves and/or others.

"There are some *idiots* out there who don't know whether it's a good idea or not to preach violence, knocking girls around, beating people up," Bill Bennett says. "They're *wondering* whether this has an effect on our culture and activity. Well, I think what happens on TV and in movies and on radio and on the street has *more* to do with the future of this country than public policies."[15]

It should be beyond dispute that the media can influence behavior. William Manchester has said that when his World War II Marine rifle company was polled on why they had joined the Marines, a majority said that it was because they had seen a John Wayne war movie, *To the Shores of Tripoli*. If, by defining "manhood" in a certain way, a movie can influence young men to join the Marines, surely movies, television, and songs can influence young males to play such other supposedly "masculine" roles as "love-'em-and-leave-'em stud" or violent criminal.

Of course words and images that come to us from television, movies, radio, and sound recordings have consequences. That there is a connection between words and actions should be beyond dispute. Companies are willing to pay tens of thousands—under some circumstances, hundreds of thousands—of dollars to send us thirty-second messages via electronic media because they *know* that they can affect our behavior in this way. If a thirty-second commercial can sway some people to buy a product, it stands to reason that countless hours of sex and violence on television or assaultive talk on radio can influence the behavior of some viewers or listeners in other ways.

Nor is it just a matter of movies that are filled with graphic violence or explicit sex. Can anyone seriously argue that the fact that television sitcoms suggest that there is something abnormal about people who do not engage in sexual intercourse by their second date has no effect on the behavior of young people who watch hundreds of hours of this programming as they are growing up? Such fare is a major part of their instruction in what the society expects them to do. In some respects, a show like *Seinfeld* is more pernicious than the more-criticized *N.Y.P.D. Blue*. *Seinfeld*, which has been among the top-rated programs throughout its tenure on the tube, is surely one of the funniest comedies on the air. I watch it regularly. But what message comes through from the lives of the characters on it? Until the fall of 1995, none of the characters had ever given the slightest hint that marriage might be an option for them, even at some point in the distant future. All the primary characters move from one one-night to, at most, two-week affair to another. In one episode, Elaine discusses how it is necessary for women to have their diaphragms with them at all times, since you never know when you're going to meet a man you want to have sex with on the spot. In another installment, she buys the remaining supply of a contraceptive sponge she favors and proceeds to interview men to see if they're worth using one of her now limited supply on.

Funny though it often is, *Seinfeld* actually is, like many other "sitcoms," actually a "sit-trag": a situation tragedy[16] that reflects (and fosters) the decomposition of our society. It constantly promotes the view that marriage is beyond the realm of consideration and that casual sex with countless different partners is not only what everyone is doing, but that it is what we all *should* be doing. When the program finally did bring up the possibility of marriage for one of its characters, George, it was only to ridicule the institution as a trap that must be avoided.

Some progressive Democrats have begun to recognize both the importance of cultural images in our moral decline and the links between our economy's attempts to stimulate consumption and our values. "People come home from work, they both work and they have kids and they spend about twenty minutes with the kids," David Bonior says. "The rest of the time, they're in front of the tube. So what we're sending out over that tube affects the way people feel, it affects their expectation levels which are very, very high because of commercialism that they see on TV. It affects the value structure because of violence, sexual content. And all of that is very important. I think that parents need to be in power to control that more."[17]

One of the sad results of such things as "rap lyrics in which women are for using and abusing, movies in which violence is administered with a smirk and smile," has been described by Charles Krauthammer: "Nothing could be better designed to rob youth of its most ephemeral gift: innocence. The ultimate effect of our mass culture is to make children older than their years, to turn them into the knowing, cynical, pseudo-adult that is by now the model kid of the TV sitcom. It is a crime against children to make them older than their years."[18]

There is, furthermore, another way in which the "anything goes" culture that has emerged in recent decades contributes to our moral decline. It seems that many young people have a "need" to rebel, to demonstrate their independence. If this is so, an increase in the acceptance of previously impermissible behavior, such as we have had in the last quarter century, will surely serve to escalate what it takes to demonstrate youthful rebellion.

So let us also stipulate that the culture has played and continues to play an important role in the collapse of American values.

THE REAL DANGER IN SUPPLY-SIDE ECONOMICS

But while both the current welfare system and the culture have played roles in the social decomposition we are experiencing, that distressing phenomenon has much deeper causes than any liberal drift beginning in the 1960s (or the 1930s). Irving Kristol raised an important question when he asked in 1972, "How can a bourgeois society survive in a cultural ambiance that derides every traditional bourgeois virtue . . . ?"[19] But the sources of that cultural ambiance must be sought. The entire thrust of the modern world, most notably including the economic system championed by self-professed "conservatives," is toward the undermining of traditional values and the disintegration of society, community, and family. Indeed, the "anything goes" culture, usually associated in the popular mind with liberalism, is much more closely related to the "anything goes" economic system promoted by "conservatives" than is widely apprehended.

Those who insist upon the practice of economic laissez faire place themselves in a weak position for complaining about cultural laissez faire—and vice versa. Conservatives complain of permissiveness in culture, but favor utter permissiveness in economics; liberals generally reverse this. Neither "side" seems to understand that permissiveness is difficult to contain in one realm of a society.

The most basic source of the collapse in our values is what might be termed "supply-side economics," if that expression is given a larger and deeper meaning than that which has adhered to it since the 1970s.

Perhaps the best place to start pointing out the role of the modern economy in our problems is to turn again to the sex and violence on television and ask ourselves: *Why* is it there? Who is it that determines what will be on television? The sponsors. And, to them, the only purpose of the programs themselves is to keep an audience tuned in between the commercials. Companies buy commercial time on programs that they believe will attract large audiences. Their motive is to make money, and if peddling sex and violence is a way to do so, they care not at all. Businesses have more direct control over what appears in their advertising than they do over program content, and sex is constantly used in commercials to sell everything from automobiles to razors. Who, if not the business executives that "conservatives" generally praise, is responsible for the sexual content of commercials? To what extent does this contribute to our moral decline? Is not the sex and violence used, directly or indirectly, by American business to sell its products, a greater contributor to teen pregnancy and associated social pathology than welfare is? ("It is lunacy to believe," columnist Carl Rowan sensibly contends, "that withdrawing a pittance of money to support teenagers and their babies will counteract all the sexual forces ["sex-based ads, TV shows, movies, and song lyrics"] that are at work in America, causing young women to stop having sex—and babies—before marriage."[20]) Do most leaders of corporations really care what the answer to the latter two questions are? Sex sells, and nowadays selling is what life is all about. The values dictated by our supply-side, social Darwinian economy are, as I pointed out in the first chapter, actually value$. The only measure of values to many people today—pointedly including most of those who style themselves "conservatives"—is the dollar sign.

Thomas Frank made the point well in a 1995 piece in the *Atlanta Journal-Constitution*, in which he argued that it is business executives and the advertisers they hire, not Snoop Doggy Dogg and Quentin Tarantino, who constitute "the most effective assault team" on traditional American values.[21] But even if this assertion is accepted, the question remains: *Why* have businesses and advertisers undermined traditional values?

Who Really Killed Traditional Values?

Our current problems began at least a century ago (around the time of the last Psychic Crisis of the Nineties), when the remarkable productive powers of our economic system had become so efficient in increasing supply that the essence of that system began to change. Put simply, after industrialism had first removed the limits on production, it would eventually be obliged to remove the limits on consumption: unlimited production requires unlimited consumption. The demand side would have to be artificially stimulated in order to keep the economic equation balanced as the supply side grew at phenomenal, wholly unprecedented rates. Paradoxically, this new situation, driven by the extraordinary expansion of the supply side of the economic equation, obliged business and the entire society to focus on the demand side: increasing consumption. Economics, which had always been concerned with the allocation of scarce resources, would now have to deal with the allocation of abundant resources. The economic system was entering a fundamentally different stage.

In 1940, economist Alvin Hansen captured the essence of the modern, supply-side economy in a sentence: "Consumption is the frontier of the future."[22] This new economic situation produced an essentially different view of people, which led its adherents to practice a very different set of values. Businessmen through the late nineteenth century looked upon most people as potential producers; in the twentieth century business has looked upon people more as potential consumers than potential workers.[23] This has resulted in a drastically altered outlook and the undermining of most of our traditional values. The "work ethic" that was appropriate for a society whose members were seen principally as producers was replaced by a "consumption ethic" when they came to be seen primarily as consumers. The old virtues that had been inculcated into a majority of the population had to be overturned. The belief that there is no such thing as "enough" began to be spread to the masses so that they could be persuaded to consume the products that the system was now able to produce in such unprecedented quantities. No other aspect of the twentieth century has had as large or as detrimental an impact on traditional values as has this economically dictated change in focus from work to consumption. Ultimately, it reversed the future orientation that had been central to the definition—and success—of America.

The features of the new economic system had been outlined by two economists during the 1890s. Simon Patten argued in *The Theory of Social Forces* (1896) that the modern economy is no longer based upon fear and pain, but has come to be a "pleasure economy" based more upon consumption than production.[24] Thorstein Veblen noted in his *The Theory of the Leisure Class* (1899) that the "economic man" who had emerged a few centuries before, "whose only interest is the self-regarding one and whose only human trait is prudence," had been ideal for early capitalism, but "is useless for the purposes of modern industry." People now were led to become "continually more narrowly self-seeking." What was taking place, Veblen rightly said, was that the whole society was assimilating the practices—such as "conspicuous consumption" and "conspicuous waste"—that had previously been confined to the leisure class.[25]

The new supply-side economics dictated that the work ethic be replaced by a "consumption ethic." That, in a sentence, is the explanation of the deterioration of values as the twentieth century has progressed.

Our modern economic system has proved to be the most radical force in the twentieth-century world. Though beneficial in many other ways, the radicalism of the consumption-ethic phase has been extremely harmful in its effects on values. Most of the system's practitioners were—and are—leading advocates of traditional values and consider themselves to be conservatives. Yet it was this highly efficient productive system's need for ever-expanding consumption that manufactured the most devastating assault that has ever occurred against the traditional values to which most of the business leaders themselves continue to pay lip service.[26]

The ultimate contradiction in the modern economic system is that its production depends upon the work ethic, of which sacrifice, saving, prudence, conservation, self-denial, and deferred gratification are essential parts; but the pace of consumption that this level of production needs to sustain itself requires that people's appetites be stimulated rather than repressed. Such maxims as "Save for a rainy day," "Waste not, want not," and "A penny saved is a penny earned" had suited the production-oriented needs of an earlier day; but they had to be weakened, if not entirely abolished, if demand was to be brought up to the extraordinary level of supply so that the new system could work. The hallmarks of the new consumption ethic of the twentieth century are the opposites of those of the work ethic: spending, borrowing, imprudence, waste, self-indulgence, and instant gratification. Self-indulgence had to displace self-denial if the products of modern industry were to be sold; but if this happened, the work ethic would be undermined and that, in turn, might ultimately weaken the productivity that had called forth the self-indulgence in the first place.

An "ethic" based on indulgence rather than restraint is a direct reversal not only of the work-ethic values that had become traditional in the early, production-oriented phase of capitalism, but of the whole purpose of values from their first inception, which was to rein in just those natural traits, such as acquisitiveness, that had become maladaptive. It would be more accurate to call the "consumption ethic" an antiethic.

(I CAN'T GET NO) SATISFACTION

"There are no limits," the advertising slogan for Swatch watches boldly proclaimed at the end of the 1980s. Ronald Reagan had been preaching the same message throughout the decade.

Certainly Americans have always had trouble accepting the idea of limits. From the start of the European penetration of America, the apparent boundlessness and abundance of the New World created what might be termed a geopsychology of limitlessness. But this modern American attitude that mobility, geography, and plenty had produced has been enormously extended by the consumption-ethic economy. By the last third of the twentieth century, there existed a widespread belief that *any* limits constitute an unacceptable imposition on personal freedom. Joan Didion nicely expressed this ultimate American and modern objective in a 1967 essay on Howard Hughes: "absolute personal freedom, mobility, privacy . . . to be a free agent, to live by one's own rules."[27] The consequences of this doctrine are apparent all around us.

The limitless expansion of individual rights necessarily means the contraction and eventual disappearance of any sense of responsibility toward others. If the self expands without bounds, there can be no place left for the community or society. The modern world's infinite expansion of the self causes the infinitesimal contraction of the society.

"Let us leave each other alone," "conservative" columnist Charley Reese of the *Orlando Sentinel* wrote in a remarkable 1990 statement. "Let each adult suffer the consequences of his or her own choices. That's my recipe for a good society."[28] This is the recipe of those now in control of the Republican Party. This utterly modern formula is in fact a recipe for no society at all, but for a chaotic conglomeration of "free," self-absorbed individuals. And no society at all is apparently just what some "conservatives" desire. In 1987, Margaret Thatcher put this conviction starkly in a radical, late-twentieth-century version of the seventeenth-century notion of natural independence (although one that echoes Jeremy Bentham): "There is no such thing as society. There are individual men and women, and there are families."[29] David Frum agrees, contending that there is no place in the conservative lexicon for the first person plural, at least not beyond the family. He vociferously objects to William Bennett's use of the construction "our children" in the subtitle of his 1992 book, *The De-valuing of America*. "What is the locution 'our children' doing in Bennett's mouth? The phrase contains the thought that one's obligations to all other children in the country are similar in nature to one's obligations to one's own," he complains.[30] The echoes of Emerson ("Are they *my* poor? I tell thee, thou foolish philanthropist, that I grudge the dollar, the dime, the cent that I give to such men as do not belong to me and to whom I do not belong."[31]) reverberate through such personal declarations of independence. In this hyper-individualistic worldview, there is *no* society, *no* community, *no "we."*

The consumption-ethic economy is based on telling us "that no discomfort can be tolerated and that every desire deserves to be satisfied."[32] But one of the consumption ethic's most important results is to make it almost impossible for *anyone* ever to find any lasting satisfaction. The main motivating force behind the modern economic system is for everyone's goal to be, as American Federation of Labor President Samuel Gompers put it late in the last century, "More, more, more." If consumption is to be kept rolling along, people must *never* feel that they have "enough"—they must never be satisfied. "The key to economic prosperity," General Motors executive Charles F. Kettering wrote in 1929, "is the organized creation of dissatisfaction."[33] The anthem of the modern consumption-oriented economy should be "(I Can't Get No) Satisfaction."

One reason for the feeling of dissatisfaction that characterizes the Psychic Crisis of the Nineties goes beyond the fact of economic stagnation or decline for a majority of Americans discussed in the second chapter. It is simply that, in our supply-side economy, businesses, through their advertisers, are constantly telling us that we are *not* satisfied.

Funhouse Values

An important part of traditional values was the recognition that there must be limits if individuals are to live together in society. "Civilization," it has rightly been said, "is a function of boundaries."[34] But under the forces of our consumption-oriented economic system, all remaining notions of limits are removed. The proverbs that embodied many of our traditional values, geared as they were to sacrifice, cooperation, and the acceptance of limits, no longer serve the interests of our economic system.

"People, especially young people, have embraced an ethos that values self-expression over self-control," political scientist James Q. Wilson notes with alarm. Our society now places higher value "on things like self-expression, individualism, self-realization, and personal choice" than on sacrifice, what we owe others, and "observing the rules," a Yankelovich poll confirms.[35] *Why?* What most "conservatives" fail to see is that the principal reason for this change in values is the promotion of consumption by the very businesses that they defend. "The expectations that TV creates are totally out of perspective," as David Bonior says. "People just sit there three or four hours a day and are just hit with commercial after commercial—expectation after expectation."[36]

It is the slogans of television commercials that tell us what our values—values *New York Times* columnist Bob Herbert has aptly called "funhouse values."[37]—are supposed to be. They constantly bombard us with messages of self-indulgence, self-realization, and personal choice, and preach against sacrifice, deferred gratification, caring about anyone but the self and other traditional values. The values that come from commercials are a far cry from those taught in *Poor Richard's Almanack*: "Who says you can't have it all?"; "Preference. . . because *I*'m worth it"; "The one thing you always wanted—*every*thing"; "You only go around once in life, so grab all the gusto you can"; "I believe in Crystal Light, because I believe in *me*"; "Too much of a good thing is—a good thing"; "On Planet Reebok, there are no rules"; and many similar messages. Planet Reebok seems, in fact, to be a metaphor for the disintegrated modern world; on it there are neither limits nor rules. Most companies and their advertisers try to make us believe that we live on such a planet, but we do not. We live on Planet Earth, where there are limits—and where there need to be rules.

Consumption-ethic "values" are also proclaimed on bumper stickers, such as: "Shop Until You Drop"; "Born to Shop"; "I'm Spending My Children's Inheritance"; and "He Who Dies with the Most Toys Wins."

When the implications of our consumption-maximizing advertising and bumper sticker slogans are considered, it becomes apparent, as the social-minded Christian evangelical Jim Wallis says, that the problem with young people who get into trouble, whether in the inner cities or the suburbs, is not that they haven't gotten our values, but that they *have*. It should be obvious that there is a connection between kids killing for a pair of sports shoes and a bumper sticker that announces: "I Shop; Therefore I Am."[38] Many of thc young pcoplc who turn to crimc say that it is the only way that they can get what they "need." This raises the question: How do they come to think that they *need* $150 athletic shoes? The answer, plainly, is from our supply-side, consumption-ethic economy and its advertising.

Let me cite another example of how culpability for our values problems is usually misplaced. "Conservatives" love to blame feminists (or, in Rush Limbaugh's endearing demonology, "femi-nazis") for family problems stemming from mothers working outside the home. (George Gilder has offered an alternate right-wing explanation. He attributes the decline of morality, which he believes can be traced to women working outside the home, to the Internal Revenue Service. Cut the tax rates, he maintained in 1981, and women will not be obliged to work. Then morality will revive.[39]) But, once again, the real culprit is our supply-side, consumption-ethic economy. It is clear that far more women with young children, especially those in the economic strata that cannot afford good, reliable care for those children, are working because of economic pressures—making ends meet and/or consuming ever more—than are doing so because of the urging of the women's movement. It is doubtful that working in a dead-end, low-paying, no-responsibility job is more "fulfilling" than staying home and caring for one's own children. But such a job *does* pay more—and makes it possible to buy more. Is it feminism that is constantly telling women (and their families) that they should buy more and more? Or is it the consumption-ethic economy and its advertisers?

THE CREATION OF LIMITLESS DEMAND

Although almost everyone would agree that greed is not among the traditional values to which we say we subscribe, the centrality of greed to our current economic practices has been acknowledged—even boasted about—by some. Prior to his legal difficulties resulting from insider trading, arbitrager Ivan Boesky lectured business students on his views of the modern, limitless economic system's sin of choice: "I think greed is healthy. You can be greedy and still feel good about yourself."

In his 1970 novel, *Mr. Sammler's Planet*, Saul Bellow outlined the effects of the consumption ethic on modern attitudes: ". . . in the name of perfect and instant freedom. For what it amounted to was limitless demand—insatiability, refusal of the doomed creature (death being sure and final) to go away from this world unsatisfied. A full bill of demand and complaint was therefore presented by each individual. Non-negotiable. Recognizing no scarcity in any human department."[40]

As the Berlin Wall was coming down in late 1989, a young woman wrote a piece for the *New York Times*' series, "Voices of a New Generation," which amounted to just the sort of "full bill of demand and complaint" that Bellow had described. She whined that, as a late-twentieth-century American, she faced her own "more subtle, elusive walls" that blocked her "independence." Although she griped about "walls" or limits of all kinds, her most revealing grievance was that "familial responsibility—another wall—exacts a high price on my personal freedom."[41]

The poor thing! Were it not for the danger of compassion overload, we would surely get all choked up about her plight. Her statement sums up much of what is wrong with the modern mentality, induced by the supply-side economy. She wants to "have it all," at no cost to herself. Her demands are limitless. In this, she is a perfect embodiment of the outlook of the eighties. While Nancy Reagan was urging people to "Just say no" to drugs, her husband, his administration, and the business interests they championed were pushing the consumption ethic to an extraordinary new level, in effect urging people to "just say yes" to every impulse, every desire.

The philosophy followed by the Republican administrations from 1981 through 1992—the same philosophy that the Republicans are currently trying to put back into practice, but to a much more extreme degree than it was ever followed in the Reagan-Bush years (as Paul Wellstone said to me, "this agenda today goes way beyond ketchup-as-a-vegetable"[42])—played an important part in producing the crises we now face in both our economy and our values. The problems in America today, once again, do not stem *either* from economic policy *or* the decline of values, but from both. The "Who Says You Can't Have It All" attitude that became the hallmark of the eighties is *the* chief corrosive agent eating away at traditional values.

In a 1995 speech before the National Governors' Association, Republican Senator Pete Dominici of New Mexico said that what has been forgotten in recent decades is "affordability." "We stopped asking the question: 'Can we afford it?' when a program was proposed," he pointed out.[43] Dominici was right, of course, but (like most others) he did not see the wider implications and application of his point. Our whole society has been induced to stop asking that question. The reason is our credit-based, consumption-ethic economy. Affordability is not an issue when "Who Says You Can't Have It All" is the motivator.

What most of us think of when we hear the phrase "traditional values" are such qualities as community, responsibility, sacrifice, frugality, conservation, sharing, and family. These are precisely the values that have been undermined by the every-man-for-himself, the-devil-take-the-hindmost approach that "conservatives" preach. That approach causes society to disintegrate, destroying any sense of community or family—eradicating the very basis of the traditional values longed for by so many Americans today.

THE TEMPTATION INDUSTRY

If the modern supply-side economy's need to stimulate mass consumption is the underlying cause of the decline of values and the atomization of society, the principal means through which this has been accomplished is advertising.

Although the trends had already been apparent to some for a quarter century, it was during the 1920s that the new industrial system's level of productivity reached the point at which it became clear that its practitioners would be obliged, if they were to maintain their own rapid expansion, to undermine the old values.

In the 1920s, advertising became an "industry." That word usually connotes a process that manufactures a product; its use for advertising is a striking indication of the change in purpose that the economy was undergoing. What advertising "manufactures" is demand; its "product" is consumption. This reverses the usual meaning of the words. As in so many other areas, in language the new consumption ethic was turning things upside down.

Advertising is the defining "industry" of the new, supply-side economy. Advertising produces nothing tangible, but focuses exclusively on consumption. One advertising executive summed up the new consumption ethic when he said: "Make the public want what you have to sell. Make 'em pant for it." This does not sound much like what most of us would think of as traditional values. And for good reason.

It can scarcely be doubted that advertising has been one of the most powerful forces eroding traditional values in the twentieth century. One of the most important functions of values since their inception has been to restrain impulsive actions. Impulses are undiluted, unfettered biological predispositions and, since we no longer live in the sort of environment for which some of them evolved, following them can be dangerous. Innate drives are likely to emerge whenever they are not restrained by community values.[44] Such values raise cautionary flags, telling us to stop and consider the consequences of yielding to our impulses. One of the principal purposes of advertising is to counteract these values by encouraging us to go along with our impulses. The fundamental, generic message of advertising is the exact opposite of that of traditional values. It is: "Aw, go ahead!"

Christians pray: "Lead us not into temptation." But the whole thrust of the modern, consumption-ethic economy is to lead us into temptation. That is the raison d'etre of advertising.

Advertising is a call to break out of limits. The most significant boundary that advertising shattered was that between needs and wants. As the rock group R.E.M. has lyrically commented, "what we want and what we need have been confused—been confused."[45] There can be no doubt that the source of that confusion is the consumption ethic or that the chief agency through which that confusion has been achieved is advertising. The confusion of wants and needs is essential if people are to be persuaded to buy all the modern economic system can produce. Creating such confusion has been the major function of advertising in the era of the consumption ethic.

(The connection between the Republican Right and the replacement of needs by wants was well illustrated by Texas senator and Republican presidential hopeful Phil Gramm when he proclaimed before a National Rifle Association gathering in 1995: "Ah own more shotguns than Ah need, but not as many as Ah *want*."[46])

The funhouse values promoted by our supply-side economy help to create large numbers of young Americans who can shout with Kurt Cobain, the late songwriter and lead vocalist of Nirvana: "Here we are now, entertain us!"[47] (That the cover of the album on which this classic statement of consumption-ethic values is made depicts a baby in water over his head pursuing a dollar bill on a fishhook, apparently being pulled away from him, suggests that this leading grunge band was well aware of the source of the maladies facing Generation X and the rest of America.)

Actually, the case that our economy's emphasis on consumption is destroying values is so strong that even someone as extreme as David Frum cannot bring himself wholly to deny it. "But if capitalism creates new opportunities to misbehave," he writes in a revealing comment, "it is welfarism that makes the exercise of those opportunities safe, or at least safer than ever before."[48] He apparently fails to notice that what he is really complaining about is that "welfarism" makes it possible for *the poor* to misbehave. If Frum and his fellow travelers think receiving a small stipend from the government makes misbehavior "safe" for the poor, how safe does having a million-dollar portfolio make such activities? Perhaps a decline in morality among the non-poor is of no concern to these guardians of tradition? Maybe they would say something like: *As long as people use their* own *money, let them do what they want; just don't ask us to subsidize vice in the poor.*

SPENDING THE FUTURE

"Here's how to get what you want, when you want it."[49]

I found this notice on the outside of an envelope I received a few years ago, offering me a "preapproved" credit card. It could stand as the motto of the modern consumption-ethic economy—and as the epitaph for traditional values.

Among the most important of learned human values has always been prudence—concern for the future. As we have seen, this future orientation has also been an essential feature of the American tradition. Avoidance of debt had—until quite recently—always been considered a major virtue. But not under the consumption ethic. "Prudence," Veblen noted, "is useless for the purposes of modern industry."[50] Patten summed up the change in values in 1907 when he proclaimed in a book grandiosely but not inaccurately entitled *The New Basis of Civilization*: "The non-saver is now a higher type than the saver. I tell my students to spend all they have and borrow more and spend that."[51]

But it was no easy task to persuade people who had been brought up on the aphorisms of Benjamin Franklin to abandon the values that had been inculcated in them and start borrowing in order to enjoy now what they would pay for only later. One of the more ingenious manipulations of language—a skill that has come to the fore in the business world under the supply-side economy—was to call borrowing for consumption "credit" rather than "debt."[52] Traditional values taught people that debt is bad; but *credit*—that seemed to be something else altogether. What could be wrong with *that*? Credit is something to be sought, not avoided.[53]

The most familiar use of the word "credit" in this sense today is the "credit card." The importance of using positive-sounding terminology becomes evident when we consider how less likely we might be to use these cards if they were called "debt cards."

"Credit" or "installment purchasing" is one of the most powerful of the modern solvents that have eaten away traditional values. One of its important effects was to destroy prudence and enhance the present-mindedness—the withdrawal from the flow of history—that characterizes the modern era.

While the "credit" system was "freeing" most people from the limits imposed upon them by old restrictions and values, it was simultaneously placing new fetters of debt upon them. The democratization of debt did not mean the democratization of freedom. On the contrary, credit—going into debt for current consumption—amounts to a disguised form of slavery—voluntary servitude. MasterCard uses as one of its catchy slogans, "Master the opportunities!" But for those who are caught by the catchy slogan, it is often the opportunities that master them.

MasterCard—like other credit cards—might more accurately be called "SlaveCard."

It is the economy's need for maximizing consumption that has subverted the essential American value of future orientation. Throughout most of the twentieth century, and particularly in recent decades, businesses have encouraged us to do the opposite of what Americans have traditionally done. Advertising urges us to indulge now and forget the future: "Buy now; pay later." Since almost anyone finds buying preferable to paying, this system necessarily leads people to focus on "now" and to think as little as possible about "later." *Sacrifice*, so central to the building of our nation, has all but disappeared from the American lexicon, having been replaced by *gratification*.

Saving is an essential feature of future orientation. To save is to "live for tomorrow." But our consumption-ethic economy leads us to do the opposite of saving today's earnings for tomorrow. Instead, businesses encourage us to spend tomorrow's income today. We use "credit" to *spend the future*.

In recent years, as incomes have stagnated or declined for most Americans— "when," as Chicago attorney Thomas Geoghegan has put it, "the Affluent Society is going in reverse, and diabolically so, giving us more and more 'wants' and less and less cash"[54]—the temptation to spend the future has grown larger. The tempters have become more persistent. In the nineties, it has become common for people to use credit cards even to buy groceries. In one of its brief statements as a corporate sponsor for National Public Radio's *Morning Edition*, MasterCard International says it "urges consumers to use credit responsibly." If they are serious about this, why do we find several preapproved credit card applications in our mail each day? Why do teenagers and college students who have never been gainfully employed at anything beyond baby-sitting or lawn-mowing receive such unsolicited applications? The unfortunate fact is that if people were to heed the advice to use credit responsibly, the supply-side economy would collapse.

Not to worry: We are *not* heeding the advice to use credit responsibly. Average family debt beyond mortgages in the United States rose from about $7900 in 1990 to more than $10,000 in 1994.[55] And ever more of that debt is on credit cards, with their extraordinarily high interest rates. (It is a reflection of what has happened to our economy and our values that *usury* is a concept that has fallen into unfortunate disuse; but charging 18 percent and more on credit-card borrowing when the prime rate is at 8.5 percent is a very effective way to transfer wealth from have-nots to haves.) Americans increased their credit-card balances (another interesting use of language; the amount owed might better be termed an "imbalance") by 28 percent in 1994 and 19 percent in 1995.[56] Incomes were increasing by less than 5 percent in those years.

The net national savings rate in the United States has dropped from its 1950s level of 7 percent (even that was low by international standards) to 1.8 percent in the 1990s.[57] The normal situation for Americans today is that what we owe on our credit cards exceeds our savings. We no longer have life savings, accumulated by sacrificing over a lifetime; today we have "life debts," amassed by buying beyond our means over a lifetime of "todays."

The most important underlying reason why Americans have lost faith in the future is that the needs of a highly productive economy led businesses to use advertising to persuade us—consumers—to "live for today." "Credit" then makes it possible to live fully for today by consuming future income now. People adhering to the traditional American concern for the future do not make good consumers. The modern economy's message to most of us is: *Do* stop thinkin' about tomorrow.

But we cannot succeed in completely forgetting about the future. When it does intrude upon our thoughts, many of us realize that, at the behest of advertisers working for business interests, we have, to paraphrase Kris Kristofferson, traded all of our tomorrows for a single today. This realization can make the future look dim, indeed.

The bumper sticker "We're spending our children's inheritance" explicates American practices today. This is, of course, the opposite of the traditional American ideal of "I'm going to sacrifice now so that my children and grandchildren will be better off." But many Americans are spending more than their children's inheritance; they are spending their own old ages as well. We are already seeing "retired" people working at Wal-Mart and McDonald's. If that's our future—spending our golden years working under the golden arches—no wonder most of us would rather "live for today." (Of course, it is a lifetime of living for today that produces that sort of future.)

JUST SAY YES

There is a further twist to the relationship between the consumption-ethic economy and values that has done so much to shape our current society. The need to increase sales to keep up with production has meant that large numbers of people had to be enticed into forsaking the old virtues, such as future orientation, thrift, and delayed gratification; but this in no sense means that these qualities have ceased to be virtues—or that they have ceased to be the route to success. In the free-market game, those who sacrifice in order to save and invest will be the winners; those who consume beyond their current means will lose. So the person (or corporation) that practices the old virtues while inducing others to abandon them will emerge as a winner in the free-market game. This is to say that advertising and credit are weapons whereby a small number of people try to persuade the rest to take up behaviors that will assure that the latter become losers in the quest to accumulate wealth.

On the same day in July 1995 that Secretary Reich and the Department of Labor were launching a new program to encourage workers to save, the juxtaposition of two messages on Rush Limbaugh's radio program served to highlight a major cause of the paucity of savings—and a basic contradiction in our economy. First, the jovial host appeared in his role as shill for whatever sponsor will pay him to promote consumption of their products. The gist of what he told his followers was that they all need to have a backyard spa. It is, he said, a place for the family to get together at the end of the day, relax, and enjoy each other's company. You *need* and *deserve* this, Limbaugh assured his gullible listeners.

Moments later (separated from the spa pitch only by a few more commercial messages), the host took a call from a woman in Arkansas. The two of them proceeded to discuss for a few minutes how anyone could achieve a comfortable living and financial independence if he or she would learn to just say "no" to themselves and their children, thereby saving rather than spending. The key to achieving personal prosperity, they agreed, is not how much you make, but how little you spend.[58]

First, Rush, the pitchman, says: "Just say 'yes' whenever I and other wealthy business people urge you to indulge yourself!" Then Rush, the "conservative," says: "If you expect to make anything of yourself, you had better just say 'no'!"

Is it any wonder that people do not save when they are constantly besieged by advertising that uses every method of persuasion to induce them to buy, buy, buy—often from the same people who reproach them for buying instead of saving?

Now, adding insult to injury (or, if they succeed, injury to injury), the political champions of the economic winners (that is, the Gingrich Republicans) propose to change the tax system in order to further reward the winners and penalize those they have talked into becoming losers. The same people who spend huge fortunes on advertising, trying to coax us into spending and borrowing, now say the tax system should be set up to reward saving and penalize consumption. This is a major part of the argument for both Rep. Bill Archer's proposal to replace the income tax with a national sales tax and the proposals of Rep. Dick Armey, Malcolm Forbes, Jr., and several others to eliminate taxes on capital gains, interest, and dividends (money that is saved rather than spent on consumption). The commercials on which corporations spend billions say: "Consume! Consume! Consume!" Then their political spokespeople say we need a tax system that discourages consumption. In other words: If you listen to our ads and follow our entreaties to consume more and more, we'll make you pay the price twice. (If discouraging consumption were really their objective, businesses could achieve it more directly by stopping advertising.)

THE ADDICTIVE ECONOMY

In the consumption-ethic economy, the consumer is to the corporation what the drug user is to the drug pusher.

For all of the "dropping out" that drug users once spoke of, they are in some respects the ultimate consumers, the ideal of the consumption-ethic economy. The product they consume is one intended purely for self-indulgence; it provides no benefit to anyone and it cuts its consumer off from others, putting him or her into a private world. Best of all for making money, consumption of the product increases demand for it. And the seller makes his profits (which are usually as high as the customer) with no regard for the consequences to the consumer. Here is the plainest case of the seller benefiting at the expense of the consumer, a general rule of a completely free market.

The connections between the drug problem and the consumption-ethic economy are abundant. The beliefs that nothing should ever be wrong, that we can buy something that will "fix" whatever we think is wrong, that all pain can be eliminated, and that every desire should be fulfilled, are constantly proclaimed by corporate advertisers. These notions pave the way for people to believe that they can purchase instant solutions to their problems. Drugs offer the same promise. And if television commercials tell us again and again that happiness is something that can be had for a price, why should we be surprised when people believe it and purchase chemicals they think will make them happy?

Those businesspeople, advertisers, economists, and politicians who preach the consumption ethic are in fact very similar to drug pushers. They push a different form of addiction, that to buying and having "things." In the process, these dealers have themselves become dependent on the continued addiction of those to whom they sell. The modern economy is suffering from the effects of long-term addiction. Our economy is hooked on the sale of all sorts of "stuff" that people are convinced they need. This is, certainly, a psychological, not a physical, dependence. Like addictive drugs, consumption of products is sold to people on the promise that it will bring them pleasure, and it often does—for a brief period. But when the effect wears off, the "fix" has to be increased.

In both the consumption-ethic economy and drug addiction, the dealer is dependent on the "user" for income, but has no other concern for his or her well-being. In both habits, "now" and "me" are all that matters to the consumer. What is sought is an immediate "high" for the self. As with drugs, so with buying products and services, there is no such thing as "enough." Ever-increasing doses of one sort of "junk" or another—drugs or material things—are needed to provide a fleeting sense of satisfaction. But no matter how much a person has, he or she will soon want more. The consumption ethic, like drug addiction, is by definition—or, rather, by *in*definition—insatiable. Both forms of addiction promise unlimited pleasure, but this is something that cannot be. Pleasure, like everything else, is meaningless without limits. Limits provide definition, so nothing can be defined without limits. In both types of addiction, the quest for unlimited pleasure results in unlimited consumption. We know where that leads with drug overdoses; there can be little doubt that a similar fate awaits a society that overdoses on material consumption.

All the addict can hope for is a series of brief "highs." Lasting satisfaction is never achieved by the junkie, whether the junk to which he or she is addicted is heroin, consumer "goods," or "junk bonds." (It is interesting that the official name for this last form of junk is "high-yield bonds." Some people use other kinds of junk to yield their highs; but, whatever the substance they abuse, their highs never last.) None of these different types of junkies attains lasting satisfaction; the modern, supply-side economy would collapse as quickly as would a drug dealer's business if his buyers achieved satiation. Satisfaction, were it possible, would be great for the addicts, but a disaster for the pushers (which in the case of the consumption addiction means businesses and, hence, the whole economy). The other alternative to continuing and increasing addiction, withdrawal, would be a wrenching experience for both.

Cultural and Economic Radicals

As the example of the drugs suggests, bitterly opposed though cultural radicals and modern business have usually appeared to be (and generally believed themselves to be), they are two sides of the same coin—the coin by which the values of the modern world are measured. Cultural radicalism and the modern, consumption-ethic economic system are, if not siblings, at least first cousins. They have usually been at war with each other, but it has actually been a civil war. Both have been attacking the same enemy: traditional values. The cultural radicals openly attacked traditional values, not realizing that those values were the main bulwark against the ravages of greed that they so despised; the businessmen generally pronounced their support for traditional values, not comprehending that their own supply-side economic system required the destruction of many of these values—or that their own actions were already destroying them.

The exponents of the new, supply-side, totally free-market economic system and the cultural radicals have been dipping from the same well: the well of complete individual freedom. Both are committed to self-centeredness. Both are "now" oriented, paying little heed to the future. Both encourage hedonism and instant gratification. Both seek to break down limits, though the limits they want to escape are in different areas.

Despite all the similarities, these two flanks of the rapidly advancing armies of the modern world have generally held each other in contempt. The reason for this is simply that neither group fully welcomes the social decomposition that the practices they advocate have helped to bring about, so each has attacked the changes in the area in which it was not radical. Businessmen are radicals in economics but seek security by being conservative in cultural matters; those who are radical in culture seek security by condemning the selfish materialism of the new consumption-ethic economy while most of them are deep in self-indulgence of other forms.[59]

THE SEXUAL FREE MARKET

The relationship between economics and values can be seen in another area. Let me put it directly: a completely free market is incompatible with family values and monogamy. Even David Frum recognizes this to some extent. "The spirit of the family is at odds with the individualism that prevails throughout American society," he admits.[60]

Most self-professed conservatives fervently believe that a man should be completely free to accumulate all the wealth he is able to lay his hands on. Certainly this is the view of George Gilder, whose 1981 book, *Wealth and Poverty*,[61] became an important part of the conservative canon. Yet while Gilder has no problem with powerful men getting most of the wealth, he does not want them to be free to accumulate all the women that they might be able to. "Under the regime of monogamy," he notes, "there are limits."[62] He does not seem to see the contradiction between his sexual economy and his political economy. Under a completely unfettered free-market system, there are no limits. Monogamy, Gilder says, is "designed to prevent a breakdown of society into a 'war of every man against every other man.'" "The removal of restrictions on sexual activity does not bring equality and community," he warns. "It brings ever more vicious sexual competition." Gilder is oblivious to the fact that the word *economic* can be substituted for *sexual* both times the latter appears in that quote without lessening the statement's accuracy. Apparently he sees no downside to vicious economic competition.[63]

Gilder is, in short, a sexual socialist, but a monetary capitalist. He favors equal distribution of the wealth in mates ("one to a customer," he proclaims), but not even a hint of limitation on inequality in the distribution of dollars. But, as I have been arguing throughout this chapter, the economy and the culture are not separate realms. If the former is based upon the doctrine of "to the strongest," that concept is likely to work its way into cultural attitudes toward accumulation of sexual partners. In an economic system the motto of which is "Who Says You Can't Have It All?" the men who emerge with "all" the money are likely to want to have all—or at least a lot—of the women, too. As Gilder correctly states, "the only undeniable winners in the sexual revolution [which is to say, the unshackling of the market in mates—the provision of "regulatory relief" in sexual relations] are powerful men."[64]

If we are going to defend a winner-take-all economy, why shouldn't the winner be able to take all the mates, too?

Conservatives like Gilder fail to see that grossly unequal distribution of wealth and income leads to the unequal distribution of sexual partners. What, after all, is it that makes the powerful men who emerge as winners in the sexual revolution so powerful? In the United States, power is mostly a function of wealth and income. A highly stratified society is conducive to polygyny (particularly in the sort of social system that men like Gilder favor, in which women are not self-supporting), because a few men have the resources to support many women, while many men have insufficient resources to support one wife in the style to which she would like to be accustomed. As Robert Wright, a champion of evolutionary psychology and the author of *The Moral Animal*, says: "conservatives may be surprised to hear that one of the best ways to strengthen monogamous marriages is to more equally distribute income."[65] One reason for the increase in unwed mothers is that the earnings of poorly-educated men have fallen so much that marriage to them does not seem advantageous. The welfare system discourages marriage, but so does the current economic system.

In an economy in which there are no limits, families will necessarily be on the endangered species list. This is a large part of the explanation of what has happened in America in recent decades.

When Value$ Replace Values

Throughout most of the twentieth century, and especially since the mid-1970s, the "values" (value$) of the marketplace have been replacing traditional values in one area after another. We have created a society that is literally a Super-Market: marketplace value$ have taken over almost all areas of our lives.

Marketplace values are those that attempt to measure numerically. This is done by assuming that values can be gauged in terms of money. (A traditional values proverb to the contrary notwithstanding, under the "value$" of the present system, money *is* everything—or at least the measure of everything.)

Bill Bradley summarizes the distinction between marketplace value$ and traditional values in the following way: "The governing ethos of the private sector is: 'Get as much as you can, as quickly as you can.'. . . But the ethos of the civil society is: 'giving something to someone without expectation of return.'"[66]

In his 1995 Hollywood speech attacking entertainment companies that purvey sex and violence, Bob Dole came—presumably quite unintentionally—close to the heart of the contradiction in the American system (and even more in the Republican philosophy). The Senate Majority Leader suggested that film, music, and television corporations should be motivated by considerations of decency and responsibility, not merely those of profit. "I'm just saying sometimes you have to have corporate responsibility and remember the impact on children," Dole pronounced.[67] Whether he realized it or not, the man widely expected to be the 1996 Republican presidential nominee was implying that value$ can undermine values and so values should sometimes take precedence over value$.

Speaking on the same subject about a month after Senator Dole did, Tipper Gore hinted at the wider implications of what the Republican leader had said. Ms. Gore declared: "We need the will of the people to say to the producers of this violence, all across the way, this is not in the public interest. This is not in the interest of the next generation. This is not in the interest of society."[68]

If we measure only by value$, marketing such noxious trash as songs encouraging the murder of police officers or sexual assault against women is "right": it turns a profit and, under value$, nothing else matters. But if we consider values, selling products that advocate such horrible actions is reprehensible.

It is the fact that companies generally consider only *what sells*, not *what they are selling* or the possible consequences of using any means that work to sell as much as possible, that is at the root of our social and moral disintegration. If corporations have responsibilities in the area mentioned by Dole, why can values not be placed above value$ in other areas as well? If some Republicans are willing to say that the marketplace should not be the final arbiter of the culture, of what appears on television or in movies or music, why should not the same standard be applied to other areas of life? Might corporations not also be urged to consider the impact on children and families of "downsizing" that puts parents out of work, of moving plants overseas, of keeping wages down while profits soar, of using tantalizing advertisements to induce people to buy all sorts of stuff they do not need, of polluting our air and water, and so forth? Does using "Joe Camel" to entice children into smoking cigarettes not have a negative impact on children?

Anywhere that we allow marketplace value$ to be the sole determinant of what is "right," many wrongs will ensue.

To propose that values should take precedence over value$ is not to say that there is anything wrong with making money. Profit-seeking is what makes our economy work. Problems arise when the pursuit of profit is allowed to become the *only* criterion, the *sole* measure of value. We must recognize that there are other consequences of corporate and individual actions besides profit or loss, that these results should always be taken into consideration, and that sometimes, at least, some of them should be given more weight than profit maximization.

If businesses were to start to consider the impact of their actions on the areas Tipper Gore mentioned, we would have a very different—and much better—society. It would amount to companies and individuals recognizing that there is such a thing as "the public interest." That would constitute a major change in the philosophy that has dominated American thought and action for much of the twentieth century, an outlook that has become increasingly dominant and deleterious in the last few decades.

The Republicans have reached the point where they must choose which side of their coalition they want to represent. The God of the Judeo-Christian-Islamic tradition often points us toward very different behaviors than does the god of the Market. To which deity will "conservatives" and Republicans give precedence? So far, all indications are that whenever that choice must be made, the religious God will be placed below the god of the Market and family values will be sacrificed to the sort of value that is determined by the dollar sign. Until the Republicans are prepared to change that measure of value, their protests about the loss of values cannot be taken as anything but political opportunism.

Like Mr. Dole and the Republicans, the American people have to choose which will take precedence: traditional values or marketplace value$. No question is more important for the future of our country.

4

The Two Sixties—And What They Mean to Us

The Evil Twin of the Sixties

Politics today are largely shaped by events, policies, and memories of "the sixties" (an era that goes beyond the calendar decade and ends in the mid-seventies, with the Nixon resignation and the final American pullout from Vietnam). The key events are readily recited: the Civil Rights movement, the Kennedy assassination, the Goldwater movement, the Civil Rights and Voting Rights Acts, the War on Poverty, the Black Power movement, urban uprisings, the Vietnam War, Medicare and Medicaid, the counterculture, the Johnson and Nixon presidencies.

The sixties defined liberalism and conservatism for the remainder of the century. By linking the former with antiwar protest, minority rights movements, violence, and licentiousness, the decade set the stage for the decline of liberalism, leaving a void that the brand of conservatism that emerged in the sixties was gradually able to fill over the following quarter century.

It has become fashionable to vilify the sixties. Many liberals have joined with conservative attacks on the decade as a time of extremism, drug addiction, "free love," and excess of all sorts. There is, to be sure, much truth in this assessment—or, more accurately, much *half*-truth. Those who like to put down the sixties with blanket denunciations are often those who delight in the failure of dreams. Studs Terkel speaks to the other half of the truth about the sixties when he comments that the decade was the one time in the second half of the twentieth century when young Americans were involved in causes beyond themselves—the Mississippi Freedom Summer, civil rights in general, and opposition to the Vietnam War.[1]

If we are to understand the decade and its continuing effects on our politics and culture, it is essential that we realize that there were two "sixties." Democrats were central to both; Republicans were peripheral to both. The sixties to which Terkel pays deserved homage is the early sixties, or "good sixties," which ran from the sit-ins that began in Greensboro, North Carolina, in February, 1960, through the middle years of the decade, and centered on the Civil Rights movement, attempts at rebuilding community, optimism, integration, sacrifice, and confidence in the capacity of government to play a role in making people's lives better. What is more often remembered today and what is properly denounced by conservatives is the late sixties, or "bad sixties," which ran from about 1967 through the early 1970s, and centered on hedonism, the self, individual freedom, pessimism, disintegration and separatism, and the conclusion that government was inept, corrupt, and evil. These two sixties have become almost inextricably intertwined in the public mind, but separating them is essential to the future well-being of both the Democratic Party and the nation.

Democrats won only two of the seven presidential elections between 1964 and 1996, the point at which this book was completed. A major reason for this is that Republicans have skillfully identified Democrats with the "bad sixties." In this effort, they have enjoyed great assistance from Democratic liberals, many of whom slid easily from their support for the "good sixties" into needlessly tying themselves to the excesses of the later sixties. Since the Republicans were not associated with either of the sixties (although they trace the origins of today's right wing to that decade), they have been able to market themselves as what amounts to the "anti-sixties" party. They have done a good job of convincing a large number of Americans that their country was nearly perfect prior to the sixties, when Democrats, liberals, hippies, and their fellow travelers (including, although this is usually not said explicitly, blacks and women) destroyed our society.

DEMOCRATS AND THE PURSUIT OF RACIAL JUSTICE

Although they came by the later sixties to be fused in the public mind, the "radical movements" that began in the fifteen years after World War II and came to the center of attention in that turbulent decade were two distinct streams based on very different ideas. The Civil Rights movement that spawned the politically conscious "New Left" and the hipster-beat movement that led to the counterculture did have certain points in common. Both, for instance, were characterized by young whites attempting to pattern their behavior after that of blacks. Both, too, were deeply influenced by the American and modern idea of "freedom" or "liberation," but in significantly different ways.

The real downfall of the Democratic Party and liberalism is that it came to be associated with the latter as well as the former. There can be no question that championing the quest for civil rights for African-Americans has been costly to Democrats; but that is a cost that is well worth bearing.

Paul Begala told me a story that illustrates this well. Early in 1995 he was sitting in on a television talk show "and a guy called in from Dayton, Ohio—Ray from Dayton. And he said, 'I was a union shop steward. I was a Democrat all my life, and Lyndon Johnson drove me out of the Democratic Party.'" Begala responded: "Well, Ray, what was it about Lyndon Johnson that drove you out of the Democratic Party? Hmm, you think maybe it was Medicare? Was that it? Was that what drove you out? Do you think maybe it was, oh, college loans, which he basically helped to create? Hmm, what could it have been? Was it all the environmental progress we made under Lyndon Johnson—is that what did it?" Begala said the man "just stammered around and finally he said, 'Well, you know, the Gulf of Tonkin Resolution.' I said, 'Oh, yeah, I'm sure that was it, right.'"

Begala's argument is that the largest factor in the decline of support for Democrats since the sixties has been race: "When two parties switch sides on the greatest issue in American history, that has massive consequences. It's hard for me to find a bigger issue that has defined the Democrats. And I think, proudly. I think we ought to stand four-square for it. But you have to be clear-eyed enough to say there are a lot of folks in this country who stand four-square against civil rights."[2]

One way to look at what has happened to liberalism since the sixties is that racial justice has become an essential ingredient in the liberal definition. From the New Deal until about 1965, the Democrats and liberalism were identified with the working and middle classes, and class was more significant than race, at least outside the South. During that period, it was possible for people to be economic liberals without at all embracing racial liberalism. Such notorious racists as Mississippi's Theodore Bilbo could enthusiastically support New Deal economic programs. So long as government intervention was seen primarily as something that was done to help people on the basis of their economic status, not their race, many whites who had no liking for minorities were prepared to support activist government.

With the Civil Rights movement and Lyndon Johnson's civil rights legislation, federal government intervention came once more to be associated, as it had been during Reconstruction a century before, with racial liberalism ("forced integration"). This began to discredit the idea of government intervention in the minds of those who were less than enthusiastic about integration, and so it began also to discredit economic liberalism.

In the 1890s, when Populists abandoned their attempts to build a biracial coalition and took up race baiting instead, economic populism had been uncoupled from racial liberalism. In the 1960s, they were fused again. It appears that the Left can succeed *only* when class is the issue. When race becomes the issue, the odds shift dramatically.

Allow me to oversimplify in order to make what I believe to be a very important point: Both liberals and conservatives tend to be on the side of one majority and one minority. Liberals are the champions of the working/middle-class majority and the black racial minority; conservatives are the proponents of the wealthy-class minority and the white racial majority. It follows that when the basic cleavage in the country is perceived to be class, Democrats and liberals have an advantage, but when the fundamental dividing line is seen as race, Republicans find themselves on the side of the majority.

There can be no question that the displacement of class politics by racial politics has played a major role in the declining fortunes of Democrats and liberals since the sixties. But that is far from the whole story. Lyndon Johnson, after all, won a landslide victory four months *after* he signed the Civil Rights Act of 1964. Their association with that the linking, in the late sixties, of Democrats with extreme cultural liberalism has been more harmful to the party's fortunes than has its association with racial liberalism.

Whatever the cost, the cause of racial justice was—and is—a noble one, and Democrats will just have to do without anyone who wants the party to abandon it. The same, however, cannot be said of what came to be known as the counterculture. Their association with that hedonistic movement was far more damaging to the party and liberalism than was their connection with civil rights. And in this case, the price is not at all worth paying. Democrats and progressives today need to reidentify themselves with the goals and ideals of the early sixties and the Civil Rights movement, while disassociating themselves from the counterculture and the late sixties.

CIVIL RIGHTS AND INDIVIDUAL RIGHTS

For all the talk about "the people" and all the emphasis on eliminating distinctions and limits, "liberation" in the late sixties almost always meant the lifting of limits on the self. Once removed from any personal context, unlimited individuals knew no one besides themselves. They could deal with nothing else, and the culture of the "power to the people" decade was pre-eminently self-centered. Its essence became "power to the person." Autobiographical works became ubiquitous. Particularly revealing was the tendency of some writers to place themselves at the center of history and then to refer to themselves in the third person (a habit they shared with Richard Nixon and Bob Dole). This was the technique, for example, of Norman Mailer in *The Armies of the Night* and *Miami and the Siege of Chicago*.[3]

The wide philosophical divide between the two sides of what was often spoken of in the singular, as "The Movement," is suggested by the early emphasis of the social-political side on *civil* rights and the persistent calls by the cultural radicals for *individual* rights or individual freedom. The implications of these two adjectives are strikingly different. "Civil rights" imply rights as citizens, and so carry with them obligations to the community; they are rights inextricably bound up with responsibilities, and they are the rights of people who are situated—members of a community—not free-floating "selves." Civil rights are entirely compatible with traditional values; indeed they are rooted in those values. But "individual rights" imply no necessary connection with anyone else, and so no connection with responsibilities. This idea matches the "every man for himself" doctrine of the modern, supply-side economy. Individual rights are fully compatible with the consumption ethic and, carried to an extreme, they become subversive of traditional values.

It may be instructive to put the difference between the movements of the sixties in another way: The Civil Rights movement sought integration; the counterculture sought *dis*integration.

Allen Ginsberg, the leading figure in the Beat movement that was the precursor of the counterculture, completely misunderstood the Civil Rights movement when he told writer Milton Viorst that its essence was "a rediscovery of their own private self."[4] That was certainly the essence of *his* movement and of the subsequent counterculture, but it was not at all that of the Civil Rights movement.

Although whites in both of the sixties movements patterned themselves after blacks, they were not the same blacks. There was a critical but often overlooked difference between the African-Americans that the political and cultural radicals attempted to emulate. The former took the black civil rights activists of the rural South as their model. The ways of the early Civil Rights movement were southern, rural, religious, "brotherly," and oriented toward family and community. It is highly significant that the anthem adopted by this early phase of the movement was the old union song, "*We* Shall Overcome." The southern Civil Rights movement was one that came from a premodern (or at least early modern) social environment in which it was still possible to think in terms of "we," rather than the modern "me." These traditional characteristics did not transplant well to the urban North and West. The country became aware of the change in 1965, with the massive uprising in the Los Angeles ghetto of Watts.

Outside the South, the modern social and economic environment with its disintegrative, nonreligious, atomistic anomie infected the black movement and civil rights began to give way to individual rights. It is telling that with the move to the urban environment the movement's goal began to shift from integration to black separatism and its means from nonviolence to violence. Separatism was in keeping with the disintegrative forces of the modern economy (although it might be argued that for some of its advocates this was an attempt to build a smaller, more cohesive community among African-Americans).

Well before the Civil Rights movement entered the North and became uncivil, white hipsters and Beats were setting the tone for the counterculture by patterning themselves after the mobile, rootless, live-for-today black city culture. Both churches and families were disintegrating in the urban environment. While the southern, church-based Civil Rights movement maintained community values, the life of the northern ghetto was increasingly self-indulgent and nihilistic. Many urban blacks had become disconnected "selves," withdrawing through music and drugs from the impersonal social environment into worlds of their own. The white cultural radicals who took these blacks as their models would do the same.

There was also a remarkable contrast between the sort of people who were central figures in the social-political movements, both black and white, of the early sixties and those who came to prominence in the individualistically oriented movements of the later sixties. The first half of the decade produced people who attempted to play a modern-day Cincinnatus role, such as Bob Moses of the Student Nonviolent Coordinating Committee (SNCC) and Mario Savio of Berkeley's Free Speech Movement. These were people who distrusted the very idea of leadership and withdrew from the limelight when they became uncomfortable with their own prominence. How different were the leading figures of the various "movements" of the later sixties, such as the megalomaniacal Stokely Carmichael of SNCC and such self-promoters as Eldridge Cleaver of the Black Panthers, Jerry Rubin of the Yippies, and Mark Rudd of Students for a Democratic Society (SDS). As the late historian Christopher Lasch once noted, most of the "radicals" of the late sixties and early seventies were less interested in practical results than in "self-dramatization."[5]

Music was central to both of the movements of the sixties. The music of the civil rights and subsequent political radicals was, like their values, much more traditional than that of the cultural radicals. The civil rights and later antiwar activists protested to the strains of folk music, while the cultural rebels gyrated to rock.

The symbolic turning point for the political movement came in July of 1965, when the man who was perhaps its greatest icon, Bob Dylan, made the move from political to cultural radicalism by employing an electric guitar and playing rock at the Newport Folk Festival. Pete Seeger, a traditionalist who was utterly committed to social and political causes, was so outraged that he considered cutting Dylan's cables.[6] The symbolism of Dylan's turn away from politics and tradition to the modern and personal was complete. That summer he hit the top of the pop charts with a song that perfectly captured the essence of the modern, excessively mobile, unconnected life that is a reflection of the supply-side, consumption-ethic economy, "Like a Rolling Stone": "How does it feel / To be on your own / With no direction home / Like a complete unknown / Like a rolling stone?"

DO YOUR OWN THING

The later sixties were replete with attempts to reconstitute community, but most were doomed because, while seeking to recreate community, people insisted on trying to maintain absolute personal freedom. This is oxymoronic. The absolutely free person is disconnected from others and so is necessarily in impersonal surroundings. There cannot be a totally free person, only a totally free "imperson." The hippies were people who had "dropped out," which meant that they had removed themselves from whatever vestiges of community they had previously experienced. They were desperate for both "somebody to love" and a personal group with which they could identify. The hippies failed because the biological need for "*some*body to love" could not be satisfied by trying to love *any*body or *every*body.

The hippies did show some understanding of what it was they were looking for when they spoke of their "tribe." "Everybody was part of your tribe," one said of the Summer of Love, "—your group; they all looked the same."[7] Clearly this was an attempt to answer a basic, biological motivation. The dress and lifestyle of the hippies provided some of the sorts of identification that genuine tribes and similar groups use to identify each other and distinguish themselves from "others." But these were not bands that could satisfy the demands of human nature, because they were not personal, because they were based on complete freedom for each "member" (which is to say that they were not members at all; a member must be a constituent part of something larger, not a totally free "individual"), and because they were not enduring.

One of the most insightful comments on the first of these principal deficiencies that prevented the hippies from forming genuine communities came from a Hopi spokesman when he was asked to allow a hippie "be-in" to be staged in the Grand Canyon. He refused the request because, as he told Ginsberg, "you mean well, but you are foolish. . . . You are *a tribe of strangers*."[8] A "tribe of strangers" is, of course, a contradiction in terms.

The hippie tribes (and rural communes) were not organized on any basis; rather, they were *dis*organized on the principle of "Do your own thing." This most famous of all sixties clichés is the ultimate antisocial statement, the extreme in self-centeredness and self-indulgence. It is perfectly compatible with the needs of a consumption-ethic economy, but utterly incompatible with genuine community. And, sad to say, it is the sixties advice that most clearly survived into the succeeding decades of selfish materialism.

The "do your own thing" maxim indicates what a short path it was from the self-indulgent hippie to the self-indulgent "yuppie." The former blazed the trail for (and in numerous cases *became*) the latter. Business likes nothing better than people doing their own things—so long as those things require them to spend money. The only trouble with the hippies from a marketing viewpoint was that their indulgences of choice were less expensive than those of their yuppie successors (or reincarnations): Brooks Brothers suits cost more than blue jeans; Rolex watches fetch more than love beads; BMW's command higher prices than VW buses; and cocaine goes for more than marijuana. But, as the last example shows best, these are differences of degree rather than kind; both types were extremely self-indulgent. There was nothing inappropriate about the late 1980s adoption by the manufacturer of superexpensive sports shoes of a variant of Jerry Rubin's motto: "Just Do It!"

Community without obligation is impossible. In calling for an utterly free community, the young people of the counterculture were seeking what never was and never can be.

Not only were relations among hippies impersonal and without responsibility; they were also transitory. People in the counterculture believed in "free love," which is the supreme oxymoron. Someone who is genuinely in love *cannot* be free; to be in love is to be connected, tied, bound to another. It necessitates the acceptance of responsibility and mutual obligation. Totally free people can have sex, but never love, because to have love is to give up freedom. Liberation breaks bonds; love creates bonds. "Liberated sex" is pure *self*-indulgence; what is liberated is the self, which then treats all other people as objects—things to be used for the pleasure of the self. "Sex in the counterculture," as historian Allen Matusow has said, "did not imply love between two people, but merely gratification of the self—ecstasy through orgasm."[9]

THE TRIUMPH OF THE INDIVIDUAL

By the time of the assassination of Martin Luther King, Jr., in 1968, the values and ideals of the early sixties had already been largely submerged. His death, followed as it was by symbolically meaningful major rioting by blacks in cities across the country, left the field to the self-promoters and charlatans of the counterculture and the pseudo "left."

The switch from the cooperative values of the early sixties to the resurgent individualism of the latter part of the decade can be seen in the differences between the sorts of people who were taken as heroes or revered as icons in the two halves of the decade. The reconciliation of Martin King gave way to the heavily armed defiance of such Black Panthers as Bobby Seale and Huey Newton; pacifist folksinger Joan Baez was succeeded by the vocal violence and hedonism of Janis Joplin[10]; the early, socially oriented Bob Dylan made way for the later, introspective Bob Dylan; Peter, Paul, and Mary were eclipsed by the Rolling Stones; Pete Seeger's music was supplanted by that of Jim Morrison.

Other shifts from the early to the late sixties make the same point. Rock bands, which became the norm with the British invasion that began with the Beatles in late 1963, broke up at the end of the decade, with individual members moving on to "solo" careers. The change was evident, too, in the moral distance from the March on Washington to the violence of the Altamont concert of 1969, from "The Times They Are A-Changin'" to "Let It Be," from "Ask not what your country can do for you" to "Look Out for Number One," from "I Have a Dream" to "Burn, Baby, Burn!"

In 1962, the SDS's Port Huron Statement echoed Martin Luther King's values when it proclaimed: "we find violence to be abhorrent because it requires generally the transformation of the target, be it a human being or a community of people, into a depersonalized object of hate."[11] This early New Left was hopeful and morally oriented.[12] By 1969, the SDS (dis)organization was enthusiastically condoning violence, and its attitude toward "others" was summarized by the shout, "Up against the wall, motherfucker!"

If Bob Dylan's 1962 line, "How many times must those cannon balls fly, before they're forever banned" had captured the mood of the beginning of the era, Rick Nelson's 1972 line, "You can't please everyone, so you'd better please yourself" encapsulated the sentiment of its end. King's "We must meet hate with love" was supplanted by H. Rap Brown's "violence is as American as cherry pie."[13] Antiwar activism gave way to rioting in the streets, integration to white backlash and black separatism, Mississippi's Freedom Summer to SDS's Days of Rage, the Peace Corps to the My Lai massacre, freedom marches to free-fire zones, *satyagraha* to violent confrontation, prophecy to profits, love to hate, inclusion to exclusion, "we" to "me." On one point after another, the more cooperative values of the early, "good sixties" were displaced by more individualistic thinking in the late, "bad sixties."

This scheme of early sixties=good sixties, late sixties=bad sixties is, of course, greatly oversimplified. Surely there were aspects of the early sixties that were not so good (although, in terms of those trying to bring about change, none comes readily to mind). More certainly, many of the developments of the late sixties, such as the women's movement, were clearly good. But the contrast, as the preceding paragraphs indicate, is sufficiently stark to justify this useful simplification.

It is the association of liberalism and Democrats (an affiliation that was confirmed in 1972, as I shall discuss in the next chapter) with the legacy of the late sixties, not that of the early sixties, that has been so detrimental to both the political philosophy and the party for the last quarter century.

The great irony that has generally escaped notice is that the "conservative" social and economic philosophy of the right-wing, libertarian Republicans is actually closer than that of liberal Democrats to the outlook of the late, "bad sixties." Conservatives, after all, have nothing against self-centeredness or against excess, at least when it comes to the accumulation of wealth.

A GREAT SOCIETY?

The "good sixties" were a time in which optimism and confidence in the capacity of government to ameliorate social problems were at a peak. We have come to associate these feelings with the memory of John F. Kennedy, and the nation has never entirely gotten over his assassination. It serves both as a metaphor for and a catalyst to our belief that everything would be right, except for . . . . We can't quite bring ourselves to believe that a single person—or even a relatively small conspiracy—could kill a president and alter the course of the world. Yet we have little trouble accepting the notion that a single person—JFK himself—could alter the course of the world. It was this schizophrenic view that Oliver Stone brought to the screen in his film *J.F.K.* The movie was successful because Stone's viewpoint mirrors that of many Americans: Everything was going great in the early sixties, but then it all fell apart and someone—no, a conspiracy of powerful, evil people—must be responsible for diverting the trajectory of American history from the paradise toward which we were headed before November 22, 1963.

This ignores the fact that the most significant and progressive accomplishments of the decade took place after that fateful date. Kennedy had the style that liberals love, but Johnson was the man who could get things done, and no president other than Franklin Roosevelt ever got more done than LBJ did in the two years after JFK's assassination. In 1965, with an undeniable mandate from the electorate and huge Democratic majorities in both Houses of Congress, liberals were in a stronger position than they had been since 1935. "We would sit around in the White House and ask each other, 'What needs to be done?' We should be able to pass anything we want to," Kennedy-Johnson speechwriter and aide Richard Goodwin once told me.[14]

Surely no American president has ever been a greater believer than Johnson was in the power of the government to be an instrument in the building of a better life for people. "Is our world gone?" LBJ asked rhetorically in his 1965 Inaugural Address. "We say farewell. Is a new world coming? We welcome it, and we will bend it to the hopes of man."[15]

The design of Johnsonian liberalism was an activist government helping people in need, but without asking for significant sacrifices from those who were already affluent. The achievement of this objective was predicated on sustained economic growth. "As long as everyone was getting richer—Johnson always felt that was the key—they wouldn't mind helping others," Dick Goodwin said. "When things get tight for them, they aren't willing to do that anymore."[16] Part of the tragedy of Johnson and the "good sixties" is that the economic growth upon which his true love, the Great Society, was dependent, was undermined by his application of the same principle to the War in Vietnam. Johnson believed that people would be as unwilling to support the war as they would the needy if things "got tight" for them financially, so he declined for the first two years of his full-scale ground war to ask the American people to pay for it. (Even when Johnson finally did ask for a tax increase in 1967, Congress took another year to approve it. By then the damage had been done.) Allen Matusow has explained why Johnson failed to seek to pay for the war when he should have: "To squeeze an unpopular tax increase from a reluctant Congress, he would have to wrap himself in the flag and frankly ask for a war tax. But, if he did so, conservatives would enforce austerity on his Great Society programs, and liberals would have additional evidence that the war was hurting America."[17] So LBJ fell back on what came naturally to him: he lied and hoped for the best.

Johnson's attempt simultaneously to fight wars against Vietnamese communism and American poverty without raising taxes to pay for either started the nation down the road of inflation and budget deficits—and so undermined the foundation upon which he was trying to construct his Great Society.

Most of the programs that Johnson initiated have come under attack from Republicans in recent years. It is beyond question that one of the fondest goals of the nineties Republicans is to dismantle what the sixties Democrats built. Yet many of those Johnsonian programs remain popular. This obliges the Republicans to cloak their real intentions; but sometimes they can't stop themselves from blurting out the truth. In October 1995, for example, Senator Bob Dole declared: "I was there, fighting the fight, voting against Medicare—one of twelve—because we knew it wouldn't work, in 1965."[18]

The reality is that the results of Great Society programs have been a mixed bag. Some of the programs have worked well; others have failed. Most have had some successes but need to be modified in light of experience. Advocating this common-sense approach is a far better position for Democrats to take than either blind endorsement of everything the government has attempted or blanket rejection of government as a tool for improving people's lives.

VIETNAM AND THE DEATH OF THE DEMOCRATIC COALITION

One of the main factors that made the second half of the sixties so different from the first was the War in Vietnam. It is now clear that this war constituted a spiritual defeat for America even more than it did a military defeat. Since things turned sour for the United States in Vietnam, we have never again been so sure of ourselves or the future. The optimism that has so long been a defining characteristic of America and of progressive thought—an outlook that survived even the Great Depression—nearly evaporated as the war escalated.

The instant renewal of quarter-century-old animosities over the Vietnam War when Robert McNamara's *In Retrospect* was published in 1995 served to remind us just how much that divisive event shaped a generation. The stance we took on the war defined us as perhaps nothing else did.

This is not the place to go into the causes of the war or the merits of the positions in support of or in opposition to it. Rather, we are here interested in its lasting effects on the political, social, economic, cultural, and ideological conditions in the United States.

The war jumbled the usual positions of various political and ideological groups in the country. Since the days of Woodrow Wilson and Franklin Roosevelt, Democratic liberals had been identified with patriotism, internationalism, and strong military action. The Vietnam War was principally the product of the worldview of liberal Cold War intellectuals, but as it unfolded it rapidly soured many of the best educated, most liberal young Americans on these traditional liberal principles. At the same time, this war conducted by the most liberal administration in American history turned the natural constituency of government—the Left—against the government.

Opposition to the war also subverted community feeling and promoted individualism. If one was an advocate of community-mindedness, the proper course would seem to be to go to war when the nation (community) called. In order to oppose a national policy, it was necessary to argue for individual, as opposed to civil, rights. So, as opposition to the war was impeding support for and confidence in the government, it was also having the more profound, if less noticed, effect of converting normally community-minded progressives into zealous champions of individual rights—sometimes transforming them into virtual anarchists.

Many Americans who answered the call of duty, even for a cause that they did not understand or support, could never abide those who condemned the war (and, all too often, those who fought in it) and found ways to avoid service themselves. Many of those who first saw the war as a mistake and an aberration in American history moved over a period of months or years to the conclusion that it was *not* a deviation from the American norm and so, in many cases, they started seeing the United States itself as evil. It has long been difficult for those who opposed the war and did not go to Vietnam to understand why veterans usually seem to dislike their behavior much more than that of the so-called "chickenhawks," such as Newt Gingrich, Phil Gramm, and Dan Quayle—men who found ways to avoid service themselves but insist that the war was a good thing, thereby saying, in effect: "This is a noble war, *you* go fight it while I stay safely at home." One reason is that at least the chickenhawks do not tell veterans that they were fighting for nothing worthwhile—or, worse, that they were acting as criminals.

But this war was no more popular among the working-class people whose family members had to fight it than it was among the college-educated who generally avoided service. It is a very important, but generally overlooked, fact that the Vietnam War weakened support for government as much among the working class that did most of the fighting as it did among the elite that led the protests against the war. "The whole goddamn country of South Vietnam is not worth the life of one American boy, no matter what the hell our politicians tell us," a construction worker proclaimed.[19] As much as they came to hate the war and the politicians who conducted it, though, few working-class Americans were willing to make common cause with the elite opponents of the war. There were two reasons for this. One was that so many of the college students and radicals attacked the United States, the military, and the American flag. Most working-class people were deeply patriotic; they would have no dealings with those who they thought were acting like traitors. Many workers came to hate the politicians who were conducting the war precisely because the workers saw it as something that was out of character for the United States, not as something that revealed the true character of the country they loved.

The other obstacle to an alliance between working-class and elite opponents of the war was summed up by a worker whose son was serving in Vietnam: "We can't understand how all those rich kids—the kids with beads from the fancy suburbs—how they get off when my son has to go over there and maybe get his head shot off."[20] The war deepened class antagonisms. But it also reshaped them by turning working-class resentment, which had previously been directed principally against the big business elite, against the liberal elite, which workers perceived as responsible for getting the country involved in a war it could not win and should not have been in, using its influence to keep its own sons out of danger, and then trashing America and waving the flags of the enemy. After this, it would be a hard road back to the New Deal alliance between workers and the liberal elite. The last political figure who seemed capable of bringing these two factions of the Democratic coalition back together was Robert Kennedy. His 1968 assassination, more than his brother's less than four years before, marked the end of hope for large numbers of Americans.

Just how hard—and long—the road back for an alliance on the Left would be, became apparent with the bitter controversy that erupted in 1992, when details of Bill Clinton's dealings with his draft board came to light. The fact that Clinton was "one of them," the elite who got out of service and protested the war, is one of the main reasons that a substantial portion of Americans will never be able to abide him, no matter what they think of his accomplishments as president.

The damage that the Vietnam War did to American liberalism in such areas as optimism, faith in government, community spirit, alliances between intellectuals and workers, patriotism, and the economic underpinnings for social reform is incalculable. It is plain that neither liberalism nor the Democratic Party has yet recovered from the blows struck to them by this tragic conflict three decades ago.

EXTREMISM IN DEFENSE OF LIBERTY *IS* A VICE

What happened to conservatism in the sixties was as dramatic as what happened to liberalism. After World War II, the consumption-ethic economy ran wild, eroding traditional values as it went. The irony of "conservatives" undermining conservative values was deepened with the emergence of the "new conservatism" (an appropriately oxymoronic concept) that gained control of the Republican Party in the early 1960s. Barry Goldwater's winning of the party's presidential nomination in 1964 created a coalition between the defenders of traditional values and those who were doing the most to destroy those values. Goldwater's achievement was to redirect the anger of populist traditionalists of the hinterlands, which had previously been aimed against New York, "Wall Street," and "the Interests," against Washington and the federal government. Thus those most alarmed at the erosion of traditional values were brought into alliance with the forces that were most responsible for that erosion, the proponents of the new economy based upon the consumption ethic.

The most famous lines of Goldwater's acceptance address are of great import in understanding the causes of the disintegration of society and the destruction of traditional values in modern America. "I would remind you that extremism in the defense of liberty is no vice," Goldwater told the delegates to the 1964 Republican National Convention. "And let me remind you also that moderation in pursuit of justice is no virtue."[21] Goldwater was generally assumed to be attempting to justify some of the extremist groups, such as the John Birch Society, that were backing his candidacy, and the reaction to his remark was, for the most part, hostile.[22]

But few observers perceived the larger meaning of what Goldwater was saying—and so they did not realize that the statement was even more disturbing than they thought it was. Goldwater was getting at—and embracing—what is most fundamental in the modern malady. Extremism in defense of liberty is not *a* vice; it is *the* vice of modern America. Liberty is, to be sure, among our most important values. But an extremist version of liberty amounts to the limitless expansion of self-interest. Extreme liberty necessarily implies the destruction of community. It means dismissing the social side of human nature and giving free rein to its selfish side.

Despite the stunning internal contradiction at its base, the "conservative" coalition that Goldwater launched, which is not really conservative at all, became the most powerful force in American politics during the quarter century after his lopsided defeat in 1964.

Since the 1960s, one wing of the "conservative" coalition—that advocating a return to "the good old days" of a completely unfettered free market (extreme liberty)—has moved ever more completely to subvert the traditional values advocated by the coalition's other wing. The fact is that the move toward a totally free market has done exactly the opposite of restoring the good old days, since the values that underlie what most people mean by "the good old days" are precisely the values that the every-man-for-himself, consumption-ethic economy advocated by "conservatives" has subverted.

INTO THE CREDIBILITY GAP

The sixties left us other legacies, most notably the extreme cynicism that permeates American society today. In the realm of politics, this is primarily a consequence of two men and two events associated with them: Lyndon Johnson and Richard Nixon, Vietnam and Watergate. In 1964, 76 percent of Americans said they trusted the federal government all or most of the time. By 1996 this figure had collapsed to only 25 percent.[23]

Even at the peak of the popularity of his Great Society domestic programs—and before the major escalation of the Vietnam War in 1965—President Johnson was distrusted by a substantial number of Americans.

The reason was what we today term "the character issue." He suffered from a self-inflicted "credibility gap," since he seemed incapable of speaking the truth, even when there was little or no advantage to be had by prevaricating. A trivial, but revealing, example: LBJ ordered his physician to report that the president drank only bourbon, when almost everyone acquainted with him knew that his only drink was Scotch.[24] By the last two years of his presidency, Johnson's words, especially those concerning the war, were routinely dismissed as fabrications. Reporters who covered him liked to say that much could be told about the president by observing his mannerisms. When he touched the side of his nose, they said, he was telling the truth; when he smoothed down the hair on the back of his head, he was telling the truth; when he raised his eyebrows, he was telling the truth; but when he moved his lips, he was lying.

Yet the sources of our current problems must be sought at a deeper level. Cynicism is not confined to politics; it pervades our entire society. The major force producing that cynicism is, once again, the supply-side, consumption-ethic economy. Advertising keeps this system going by stimulating consumption. This end is often achieved through misleading statements and images. We learn at an early age that we should not believe what we see and hear in television and radio commercials. This predisposes us toward cynicism; the various political prevaricators simply reinforce a tendency that the economic system points us toward from our childhoods.

But the Left also must accept a large share of the culpability for the growth of cynicism. We took delight in Watergate, Iran-Contra, and every other scandal and conspiracy, real or imagined, that came along from the sixties through the eighties. We jumped with glee on every example of corruption in government. We failed to realize that the delinquency of such government leaders as President Nixon was actually advancing the right-wing argument against government. Many of those on the Left who made careers in academe did more to promote cynicism. We found few, if any, heroes in our past or present, and too often gave students the impression that history is filled only with self-seeking villains. Some on the Left may have thought that this viewpoint would radicalize the next generation. In some respects, it did. But the result has frequently been the production of radical cynics who, having been taught that the only thing that motivates people is self-interest, believe it and pursue their own gain while ignoring the common good.

Positions first taken in the sixties continue to taint liberals in the eyes of many Americans, but now Republicans' association with the other (yet similar) extreme may become a larger problem. The "counterculture" that seeks extreme freedom and totally distrusts the government was on the Left in the late sixties; today it is on the Right. By the early seventies, most liberal Democrats were reluctant to criticize anyone on the Left, no matter how outrageous their positions. The operative axiom was "no enemies on the Left."[25] Today, however, it is the ascendant conservatives who decline to criticize the extreme counterculturalists on the Right, following a doctrine of "no enemies on the Right." They are forgetting, as liberals did a quarter century before, that those whose major objective is to have no enemies on one of the extremes thereby assure that they will have enemies in the center.

"One of the problems Democrats *had*, beginning in the mid to late sixties and continuing into the eighties," as Barney Frank said to me, "was that we were intimidated—politically, emotionally, and intellectually—by our own crazies." Democrats came to be seen as "the party of irresponsibility, violence, and anti-Americanism." Frank correctly contends that Democrats "finally got over that and now the Republicans have the same problem. They're the ones that have G. Gordon Liddy and the militias hangin' around their necks." The Republicans have benefitted from their association with the right wing. "They rode that tiger across the finish line" in 1994, Frank stated. "But the tiger won't go away."[26]

5

In the Shadow of the Sixties: American Society and Politics, 1972–1992

The long shadows cast by the sixties, good and bad, have continued to influence American society and culture and to shape our politics in the ensuing decades. The 1970s and '80s were liberalism's decades in the wilderness. (Most observers would say that exile is lingering in the nineties.) In the former decade, liberals continued to self-destruct, but the degree of the damage was somewhat obscured by the even greater self-destruction of Richard Nixon. Watergate gave Democrats a temporary stay of execution in the mid-seventies and allowed a Democrat to win the White House in 1976. But by 1978, the turn to the right was unmistakable and two years later Ronald Reagan's election would signal the apparent demise of the American Left.

The Laissez-Faire Society

If the theme of the late sixties was "All you need is love," that of the seventies and eighties was "All you need is to love yourself."[1] But for all the apparent difference, the two periods had much in common. The irony that has characterized the twentieth century, of cultural radicals and economic "conservatives" subscribing to the same basic worldview, became particularly pronounced in the years after the sixties.

Many radicals and liberals, while adamantly opposing laissez faire in the economic realm, have insisted upon cultural laissez faire; conservatives usually take the opposite position, demanding economic laissez faire while denouncing the doctrine of no limits in cultural expression. Neither "side" in this dualistic debate seems to realize that the complete lifting of limits in one area is highly likely to lead to an assault on limits in other areas. Those who want to be "let alone" to do as they please in making money, regardless of the common good or traditional values, encourage an atmosphere in which others will argue that they should be let alone and allowed to do as they please in matters of personal behavior and the arts. The same is true in the other direction. Those in the late sixties whose idea of social responsibility was expressed in the maxim "Whatever turns you on" were in no position to complain when others said, in effect, that making millions of dollars was what turned them on.

The Beatles' 1970 hit "Let It Be" was as clear a theme song of laissez faire as any ever written. Those who were advocating a return to the "natural" could not justify opposition to what was purported to be a natural economy (one with no restrictions). As had happened in the first half of the nineteenth century, a period of romanticism in the early part of the second half of the twentieth century led "naturally" into an era of no-holds-barred, social Darwinian capitalism in the 1970s and, especially, 1980s.

It was actually more in the seventies than in the sixties that American values and society collapsed. By the middle of the decade, almost all of the idealism that had characterized the good side of the sixties had dried up, replaced by a rampant cynicism. The romantic view that glorified nature had been based on the assumption that nature, including human nature, is essentially good. It had provided hope that society could be improved, and had made moral judgment between good and evil seem possible. With the disillusionments of the late sixties and early seventies, ranging from the assassinations of Martin Luther King and Robert Kennedy through the police riot at the 1968 Democratic National Convention, the revelation of the My Lai massacre, Altamont, the Manson murders, Kent State and Jackson State, through Watergate, however, the general view of human nature quickly evolved into a much more negative, Darwinian conception. "By the late seventies," as historian Peter Carroll has remarked, "middle-class Americans often doubted the clarity of those [moral] judgments, [and] perceived instead a world in which evil itself had become natural."[2] By this time, though, the idea that nature should be allowed to take its course had become well established.

The lifting of all limits is bound to lead to outrages. Cultural laissez faire produced the infamous 1980s "work of art," consisting of a photograph of a crucifix in a jar of urine.[3] Most self-styled conservatives were duly incensed by this example of boundlessness in taste, but few of them complained of its economic equivalent, Michael Milken's income in excess of $550 million in 1987.* The art that Senator Jesse Helms and his followers have deplored is the product of the same forces that created the economic system they praise.

* For those who have difficulty grasping such a figure, it means than in 1987 Milken made $1,046.43 each *minute*, day and night, awake and asleep, and just over $1.5

A NATION OF DEBTORS

From the 1930s through the late sixties, the position of the Democratic Party in American politics generally paralleled that of the United States in the world. The party did suffer a brief decline in the fifties, but for most of this period it enjoyed almost as much dominance of American politics as the nation did of the world economy. This experience served both the party and the nation poorly when it came to an end. Both had difficulty recognizing the change; neither reacted properly to it. Both Democrats and the nation as a whole suffered in the seventies and eighties from self-delusions based on their previous circumstances. Both failed to realize that they now lived in an altered environment that required new adaptations.

First, the nation:

Americans continued to act in the seventies and eighties like we were still in the position of economic dominance that we had enjoyed from World War II through the sixties. We lived beyond our means, both personally and as a nation, transforming ourselves by the early eighties from the world's largest creditor to its largest debtor. This shift has dramatic consequences for the American people. Being a net creditor nation meant that Americans could consume more than we produced; being a net debtor nation means that we must now produce more than we consume. Of course, we have not yet done this. Instead, we continue to live beyond our means, running up more debts and making certain that our living standards in the future will have to be reduced more substantially in order to pay for our past and present excesses.

While the largest factors in the decline of the American economy that ultimately produced the Psychic Crisis of the Nineties are technological change and international competition, important events in that decline can be seen in a series of developments from the late sixties through the early eighties: Johnson's refusal to ask the people to pay for the war until it was too late to stem the rise of inflation; the movement of American capital to countries with cheap labor, from which American corporations could then "export" finished goods to American consumers;[4] the rise of OPEC and the two oil crises of the seventies; and the Reagan plan to create a massive budget deficit in order to provide a rationale for dismantling the welfare state.

Mileposts in the American fall from world economic dominance occurred periodically through the seventies and eighties. Due principally to the movement of investment funds overseas, in 1971 the United States suffered a deficit in international trade for the first time since 1893.[5] Due

---

million each day, all year round. Such figures give a new meaning to the terms "excess" and "limitless."

primarily to the huge Reagan deficits, in 1984 the United States became a debtor nation for the first time since 1917.

The downward trajectory of the American economy was apparent early in the process. When the AFL-CIO charged in the mid-seventies that we were becoming "a nation of hamburger stands, a country stripped of industrial capacity and meaningful work . . . a service economy . . . a nation of citizens busily buying and selling cheeseburgers and root beer floats,"[6] it exaggerated the contemporary situation, but accurately forecast the future if the nation's course was not altered.

Surely "conservative" policies pursued by corporations and Republican administrations have played a major role in what has happened to the American economy in the last quarter century. But the traditional Democratic approaches are also of limited usefulness in dealing with the new problems. When President Nixon said to Howard K. Smith of ABC News in 1971, "I am now a Keynesian in economics," Smith's comment was to the point. It was, he said, "a little like a Christian crusader saying, 'All things considered, I think Mohammed was right.'"[7] But it would have been even more to the point to say that Nixon's embrace of Keynesianism should have been a sure sign to Democrats and progressives that, all things considered, Keynes was wrong.

As the high lord of the consumption ethic, Keynes had never been a natural ally of either progressives or those who advocated community values. His was an expedient approach for the restoration and maintenance of symptomatic economic health under the peculiar circumstances of the period from the beginning of the Great Depression into the 1960s. But Dr. Keynes's prescription was making the patient ever more dependent on increased doses of the drug of consumption, from which it could then scarcely hope to be weaned, despite this medication's very detrimental side effects. Keynes's lack of concern with long-run consequences was reflected in his oft-repeated pronouncement, "in the long run, we are all dead."

From One Extreme to Another

Democrats continued to consider themselves the natural majority party, largely ignoring such warning signs written in bold, capital letters as the fact that in the brief span of eight years, from 1964 to 1972, the party's fortunes in presidential elections went from the largest victory in American history to the largest defeat in Democratic Party history. Lyndon Johnson received 61.3 percent of the popular vote in 1964; in 1972, George McGovern obtained only 37.5 percent, the lowest share of the popular vote ever won by a major party nominee in a two-way race, and 23.5 points less than LBJ had won two elections before. To put this in another, perhaps more startling, way: over eight years, almost a quarter of the electorate deserted the Democrats.

The contrast between the outcomes of the elections of 1964 and 1972 is instructive for a number of reasons. In both years, the nominations of the opposition party were won by men who were out of step not only with the majority of Americans, but also with the majority within their own party. The Republican Party in 1964 and the Democratic Party in 1972 were seized by minority factions that represented distinctly minority viewpoints in the nation as a whole at the time. In both years, the soundly defeated challenger to an incumbent president was identified in the public mind with extremism. In both cases, the party controlling the presidency skillfully exploited the public's perception of extremism in the challenger. Democrats in 1964 used commercials that skewered Goldwater on his own words, depicting him as a man who, under the proper circumstances, was quite willing to incinerate the world with what he fondly termed "nukes," would like to see the East Coast "sliced off and cut adrift," and would destroy Social Security.[8] Republicans in 1972 portrayed McGovern as a man who, if not actually in league with the Vietnamese Communists, was at least their dupe. McGovern was also made out to be the champion of those who burned bras and flags, aborted babies, imbibed drugs other than alcohol, nicotine, and prescription medicines, and—well, the list went on and on until it created a picture of a man who, if not eager to incinerate the world himself, would allow the Soviets to blow up the United States with nuclear weapons or the hippies to destroy the nation from the inside, in effect slicing off middle-class America and cutting it adrift. Here, the Republicans intimated, was a man who would destroy not Social Security, but the security of society and perhaps society itself.

The out parties in each of these years held conventions that confirmed their extremist image in the public mind. At San Francisco's Cow Palace in 1964, the Goldwaterites jeered at members of the press, party security forces shoved reporter John Chancellor off the convention floor, and when Nelson Rockefeller tried to speak in favor of placing in the party platform language that would condemn the John Birch Society and the Ku Klux Klan, along with the Communist Party, Goldwater's supporters booed the "liberal" Republican Governor of New York so loudly and persistently that he could not make himself heard.[9]

At Miami in 1972, Democrats gathered in a national convention that looked very different from any other that a major American political party had ever before held. The percentage of women and blacks among the delegates approximately tripled from four years earlier, to 38 percent and 15 percent, respectively. Even more dramatic was the surge in the percentage of delegates under the age of thirty, which was nearly nine times what it had been in 1968. These youthful delegates constituted almost one-fourth of the convention. This convention marked the Democrats' first serious move toward multiculturalism and inclusion. This was admirable, to be sure. But the composition of the convention was not quite as diverse as it appeared on the surface. Almost two-fifths of the delegates held post-graduate degrees; about a third had incomes that placed them among the most affluent 5 percent of Americans.[10] For all its diversity in some respects, the dominant presence at this convention was the culturally liberal, intellectual elite that would define the Democratic Party in the public mind for years to come. And while the numbers of blacks and women increased so remarkably, white ethnics were largely absent from the convention of a party they had called home since the days of FDR. The same was true of organized labor. For the first time in its history, the AFL-CIO refused to endorse any candidate for president.

In the process of reorganizing their party to make it more inclusive, Democratic reformers had excluded from their convention large segments of the party's traditional constituency. Another of the destructive effects of the Vietnam War on Democrats became more visible. At Chicago in 1968, the party had split down the middle, mostly over the war. When the antiwar faction found itself in control four years later, it sought to hold an "anti-Chicago" convention and establish an "anti-Chicago" party. This process included the denial of power—and usually of seats—to those associated with the urban machines, such as that of the villain of the 1968 convention, Chicago Mayor Richard J. Daley. Those who should have been united on economic issues allowed themselves to be divided over the war and cultural disagreements.

The 1972 Democratic convention appeared to be almost completely lacking in organization. Presidential nominee McGovern gave his acceptance address in the wee hours of the morning, when no one but Hawaiians, insomniacs, and those, like myself, whose wives were in lengthy labors in an era when fathers were not yet permitted in delivery rooms, was awake to watch it on television. This disarray confirmed the image of liberal Democrats as inept idealists and, since it denied McGovern his chance to define himself before a national audience, made it easier for Republicans to shape public perceptions of the nominee and his party. In his little-noted nor long-remembered acceptance speech, McGovern called upon America to "come home." This obviously meant that the United States should extricate itself from the war in Vietnam. Less obviously, however, it was interpreting that war as a deviation from traditional American ways. This approach had the potential to win over a majority of Americans, including those working- and middle-class people who opposed the war but did not want thereby to condemn their country and its history.

Unfortunately, George McGovern was not the man to carry this message successfully. Surely as good and decent a man as any who has ever been a major party presidential nominee, this son of a Methodist minister came across as being gullible. When he spoke, he looked like he was afraid his teeth might fall out if he opened his mouth too wide. He seemed to have been chosen by central casting for the milquetoast role opposite Richard Nixon's "real man/real American." We learned only later that Nixon's Committee to Reelect the President *had* chosen McGovern as the ideal opponent for their purposes and played a major clandestine role in trying to assure his nomination.

With the actor they wanted playing the leading man on the opposing playbill, and the apparent eccentricities of the Democratic convention providing excellent props, Nixon and the Republicans proceeded to write a script in 1972 that would characterize Democrats as the party of "Acid, Amnesty, and Abortion." Nixon was a man who could never *win* an election; he always depended upon making his opponent the issue, thus causing him or her to lose. Dressing up Democrats in the way that Nixon and his people did in 1972 was the beginning of a long-playing and highly successful Republican production about Democrats, one that might be called, "Abnormal People," which the Republicans try to run in a perpetual double-feature with their own self-styled (but highly deceptive) "Ordinary People." Newt Gingrich made this theme explicit in 1994, when he declared that the Democrats are not the party of "normal people."[11]

Goldwater's themes in the mid-sixties sound very contemporary in the mid-nineties. He wanted to end the welfare state, repeal the progressive income tax, shrink the federal government, and return power to the states. In lieu of federal programs, he proposed to combine federal funds into lump sums to be sent to the states and localities to spend as they saw fit. He suggested making Social Security voluntary, but retreated when he realized just how popular the old-age pension system was. He opposed federal aid to education and the use of the federal government to bring about integration. The only reason that he did not speak out against such programs as Medicare, Medicaid, affirmative action, food stamps, and environmental protection is that they did not yet exist. He campaigned on the issues of morality and ethics, denouncing President Johnson and some of his top aides, who had been caught in financial and other misdeeds, and charging that the welfare state was the basis of the nation's moral deterioration (and this at a time when the welfare state as we know it today was but a twinkle in Lyndon Johnson's eye). Especially notable in terms of foreshadowing the future direction of the Republican Party was a half-hour television film commissioned by Citizens for Goldwater that used such material as pornographic magazine covers, striptease bars, a woman in a topless bathing suit, and scenes of blacks rioting in city streets to depict the United States as a modern Sodom and Gomorrah. When Goldwater saw the film, he concluded that it was racist and would not allow it to be aired.[12]

Although almost all of this sounds like nothing has changed in "conservative" thinking in three decades, it should be noted there are two principal differences between Barry Goldwater and Newt Gingrich. The 1964 Republican presidential nominee had too much decency to use the "Sodom and Gomorrah" film, but decency has apparently never been an issue for Speaker Gingrich, especially when it comes to tactics that might gain him a political advantage. In addition to possessing an ethical core that seems to be missing in Gingrich, Goldwater lacked one characteristic that Gingrich exhibits in abundance: *hubris*. Goldwater was a man totally convinced of the rightness of his views, but otherwise not deficient in modesty. He even remarked to a reporter in 1963: "You know, I haven't got a really first-class brain."[13] As far as policy is concerned, however, Gingrich's 1994 "Contract with America" is almost identical to the proposals that Goldwater made thirty years before. An overwhelming majority of American voters at that time had no trouble seeing this as a contract *on* America, and they voted accordingly.

WAVING THE TIE-DYED SHIRT

Timing may not be everything in politics, but it is of crucial importance. Goldwater made the Republican Party the "anti-sixties party" at a time when the decade was still essentially the "good sixties." He was campaigning against the times, and he was crushed. He understood this. Early in the election year, Goldwater commented: "A lot of people may not be ready to be conservatives yet."[14]

George McGovern made the Democrats the "pro-sixties party" at a time when the decade—finished on the calendar, but still going strong in a cultural sense—had become the "bad sixties." In running *with* the sixties in 1972, therefore, McGovern was running as much against the wind as Goldwater had been in running against the sixties eight years earlier. Although both identifications have ebbed at times, the images of Republicans as the anti-sixties party and Democrats as the pro-sixties party have continued to shape American politics ever since. And as the "bad sixties" image came to take precedence in the public mind, Republicans have benefitted enormously from this association.

In fact, the Grand Old Party has done something very similar in the late twentieth century with memories of the 1960s to what it did in the late nineteenth century with memories of the 1860s. Look at how closely the following description of post-Civil War Republican tactics sounds to a summary of post-1960s Republican tactics: "The closest thing to a subject that really separated Republican from Democrat was also the most meaningless," historian John Garraty has written. "It involved refighting the Civil War—the Republican argument that the Democrats were 'the party of treason' and thus unfit to govern the country." The basic Republican campaign strategy was "to try to revive past animosities." "This dead horse was beaten repeatedly," to great effect.[15]

What Republicans could be counted upon to do in every election a century ago was called "waving the bloody shirt," which meant telling voters that Democrats represented the "wrong side" in the Civil War of the 1860s and were responsible for all that tore the nation apart during that decade. (The term came from an action on the floor of Congress in 1866, when Rep. Benjamin Butler of Massachusetts held up the blood-stained shirt of an Ohio man who had been beaten in Mississippi, to demonstrate to his colleagues that Southerners were still recalcitrant about accepting the outcome of the war and so must be dealt with harshly.[16]) In the post-1860s era, "the bloody shirt" was a shorthand way of saying: "While all Democrats may not have been [Southern] Rebels, all Rebels were Democrats." Now, in every election Republicans can be counted upon to wave what might be called "the tie-dyed shirt," which means telling voters that Democrats (or "liberals") represented the "wrong side" in the cultural civil war of the 1960s and were responsible for all that tore the nation apart during that decade. In the post-1960s era, "the tie-dyed shirt" is a shorthand way of saying: "While all Democrats (liberals) may not have been blame-America-first, flag-and-bra-burning, pot-smoking, free-loving, cultural rebels, all blame-America-first, flag-and-bra-burning, pot-smoking, free-loving, cultural rebels were Democratic liberals.

Making "which side were you on in the sixties?" the central political question of the last third of the century proved marvelously effective for the GOP in both the late 1800s and late 1900s. Waving the bloody shirt from the physical Civil War of the 1860s, Republicans won five of the six presidential elections from 1868 through 1888. Waving the tie-dyed shirt from the cultural civil war of the 1960s, Republicans won five of the six presidential elections from 1968 through 1988.

To the extent that the associations of the sixties are still shaping political attitudes, the trouble with conservatives and Republicans is that they are, as Goldwater was even at a time when the "bad sixties" were still embryonic, against the "good sixties" as well as the "bad"; the trouble with liberals and Democrats has been that they have been perceived to be, as McGovern at least seemed to be, for the "bad sixties" as well as the "good."

WATCH WHAT WE DO, NOT WHAT WE SAY

It was during the presidency of Richard Nixon that the social programs that Republicans of the nineties most castigate took off. This was both because Democrats continued to control Congress, and because Nixon was never a full-fledged conservative in terms of economic and social policy. It was during Nixon's first term, in fiscal year 1971, that federal spending on "human resources" exceeded military spending for the first time. In fiscal 1974, which ended a little more than a month before Nixon's resignation, federal spending on human resources was more than twice what it had been in fiscal 1969, during which Nixon took office. This 104 percent increase in five years was the ignition of a continuing explosion in federal social spending. By the time Gerald Ford left office in 1977, human resource spending was at much more than twice the level of military spending, and 234 percent above what it was when the eight Nixon-Ford years began.[17]

Nixon spoke like a conservative but his governing style was moderately liberal. This was but one area in which the Nixon administration disconnected impression from reality. Attorney General John Mitchell's famous statement, "You will be better advised to watch what we do instead of what we say,"[18] became the ultimate definition of an administration that essentially took the position that "what sells," not what is true, is what determines what a politician should say. Mitchell was being frank in saying that nothing that he and his colleagues in the Nixon administration said could ever be considered frank. This set the tone for American politics in both parties, adding to the growing cynicism that was already dangerously prevalent due to the lies that people had come to expect from advertisers and President Johnson.

Richard Nixon frequently moved his lips with a similar result to that reporters had detected when Johnson moved his. Indeed, in his administration truth ceased to matter. It was replaced by "credibility." As the Watergate scandal unfolded, the White House floated various stories, hoping that one of them might prove believable. When any official account of events was shown to be untrue (and, more important, unbelieved), it would be proclaimed "inoperative," and a new version would be trotted out.

Although a majority of Americans now has only a vague notion of what "Watergate" was all about (when I asked a college American history class in 1995 what they thought of when they heard the word *Watergate*, several students volunteered: "I think of *Forrest Gump*!"), nothing other than the Vietnam War did more to undermine confidence in and respect for government—and so to weaken a party that believes in the capacity of government to improve people's lives.

Much more than "a third-rate burglary," the Nixon scandals constituted an assault on the integrity of the American government and political system. The fact that the whole sorry affair came to be called by the name of the building housing the Democratic headquarters in which agents of Nixon's reelection committee placed bugging devices, led to many people thinking that the break-in and its cover-up by the president and his men were what all the fuss was about.

Many of the misdeeds of Nixon's Committee to Reelect the President—such as "dirty tricks" committed against Democratic candidates that were considered to be formidable opponents, and collecting and laundering illegal cash contributions and spending the money on plots to disrupt the Democratic convention—were part of an attempt to subvert the electoral process by manipulating who the opposing candidate would be. When Nixon declared "I am not a crook," most Americans knew that this was but another lie. Accepting that their president was a crook did not add to people's faith in their government or its leaders. Coming at a time when the American people were also confronting the uncomfortable facts that they had lost a war and that cheap, unlimited energy was not an American birthright, the impact of Watergate on Americans' thinking about their government was especially detrimental.

By the time Nixon resigned, Americans' faith in their government leaders had been severely shaken. Contrary to popular belief, Lyndon Johnson did far more to undermine Americans' trust in government through his lying than he did through any of his "big government" policies, which remained popular long after LBJ himself had come to be despised by a large percentage of his countrymen and -women. Similarly, Richard Nixon did much more to advance the antigovernment objectives of the conservative movement through his failures than he ever could have done by succeeding.[19] Between them, Johnson and Nixon virtually destroyed the confidence Americans had held in their government.

One of the great ironies of the second half of the twentieth century is that Lyndon Johnson and Richard Nixon, two hugely insecure, extremely ambitious men with apparently congenital needs to lie and abuse power, neither of whom was himself a "conservative" in the meaning that word has come to have since the sixties (one, in fact, an unabashed liberal and the other a man without any clear ideology), probably did more, through their misdeeds that discredited government and fostered cynicism, to advance the conservative antigovernment agenda than have such right-wing heroes as Barry Goldwater, Ronald Reagan, and Newt Gingrich.

Jimmy Carter was elected president in 1976 largely on the basis of his promise, "I'll never lie to you." But government and politicians have never regained the trust that they lost during the Johnson and Nixon administrations. The dark clouds of Vietnam and Watergate hang low over our system still and over the Democratic Party. "People turned against government because of Vietnam, Watergate, and other scandals," as Tom Daschle said to me, "and Democrats were more closely associated with the government, so we paid the price."[20]

THE GREAT DEMOCRATIC DECLINE

It seems almost certain that it was only under the peculiar circumstances of 1976, an election year bobbing along in the wake of Watergate, but also of the Arab Oil Embargo and the final American escape from a collapsed South Vietnam, that a man like Jimmy Carter could have been elected president. Mastering the nuances of the party's newly reformed delegate-selection rules and benefitting from the facts that he was a moderate southern alternative to George Wallace and that there were several liberal candidates to split the votes that normally dominate Democratic primaries, the almost unknown former governor of Georgia won the nomination. (This is to say that Carter won as the conservative alternative in the North and the liberal alternative in the South.)[21] Carter began the general election campaign with a large lead, as have all but one (Walter Mondale in 1984, when a majority of voters believed that it was "morning in America") of the Democratic challengers over the years of mostly Republican presidential victories. Like the others, he lost support as the campaign proceeded.

The fact that Jimmy Carter in 1976 and 1980, Michael Dukakis in 1988, and Bill Clinton in 1992 all began their general election campaigns with much higher percentages of the vote than they finished them with must say something. *What* it says is not entirely clear. It might mean that Democratic nominees have been weak candidates or poor campaigners. It might mean that the Republican nominees have been strong candidates or good campaigners. It might mean that Democrats have been presenting an unpopular message or that Republicans have been offering an attractive message. It might mean that the Republicans are more skillful at hitting the "hot buttons" of the electorate.

Two examples of the repeated falloff in support for Democratic nominees are particularly interesting. Carter began his 1976 campaign with an extraordinary 33-point lead over President Ford, who had been tainted by his pardoning of Nixon. Less than four months later, Carter won by only 2 points. Dukakis emerged from the 1988 Democratic convention with a 17-point lead over Vice President George Bush, but lost by 8 points in November. These plunges in Democratic support, 31 points in 1976 and 25 points in 1988, are similar in magnitude to the 23.5-point difference between Johnson's vote in 1964 and McGovern's in 1972. If part of the explanation for that earlier decline in Democratic support is that Johnson was seen as representing a still good sixties in 1964, but McGovern became the symbol for the bad sixties in 1972, it may be that the later losses of support for Democratic nominees indicate that there is a reservoir of support in the electorate for the good sixties (and especially for the Democratic economic policies associated with them), that usually gives a Democratic nominee a large initial base of support. As the campaign progresses, however, the Republicans generally succeed in branding the Democrat as a representative of the "bad sixties" (and the cultural issues associated with them).

This analysis might also help to explain the continued Democratic success in congressional elections, down to 1994, even while Democratic presidential nominees were being clobbered by their Republican opponents. Democrats—especially incumbents—were often linked in their constituents' minds with the economic liberalism of the good sixties (and before) and could not readily be redefined by the Republicans as agents of the "bad sixties."

Each presidential election year has seen the Republicans bring forth symbols of the "bad sixties" to pin on the Democratic nominee. Often the symbols were handed to them by the Democrats. In 1976, for example, there was Jimmy Carter's *Playboy* interview, in which he proclaimed that he had "committed adultery in my heart many times."[22] In 1988, it was Dukakis's membership in the ACLU, his veto of a bill that would have required school children to say the pledge of allegiance, and his prison furlough program, which had allowed convicted murderer Willie Horton to get out on a weekend pass and rape a woman.[23]

(As I see it, though, the most devastating blow to Michael Dukakis was neither the pledge of allegiance nor Willie Horton. What hurt him the most was another self-inflicted punch. It came during his second debate with George Bush, when Bernard Shaw of CNN asked him how he would feel about capital punishment if someone raped and murdered his wife. "Bernard," began the candidate, "I think you know I've opposed the death penalty [pause] all my life. . . ."[24] The proper response would have been, as Mario Cuomo once said to me, "I'd want to kill the son of a bitch! I'd tear him apart with my bare hands!" Then, after showing that he was a human being with normal emotions, the candidate could, as staunch death-penalty opponent Cuomo said, turn to the arguments that the state should not act the way a vengeful husband would. If Dukakis still had a chance to win, he lost the election at that moment when he confirmed just how much he disproved the stereotype about hotheaded Mediterranean people.)

In between these landmarks, Ronald Reagan was able in 1980 to use Carter's "malaise" speech of the preceding year to indicate to voters that the incumbent president was someone who, like the liberals linked with the bad sixties, thought America is a sick society. "They say that the United States has had its day in the sun, that our nation has passed its zenith," Reagan asserted in his acceptance address. "I utterly reject that view."[25] This has been a particularly effective charge over the post-sixties decades. It was given its most potent rendition in 1984 by former Democrat Jeane Kirkpatrick, when she said the sort of Democrats who had taken over the party "always blame America first."[26] Many mainstream Americans have come to believe that there is a sickness in American society. Indeed, conservatives constantly say just this. But, as with their feelings about Vietnam, they don't like to hear anyone suggest that the current sickness they see is true of the American way of life in general. They want to think it is a temporary aberration, and they will listen to politicians who tell them that, yes, things *are* bad at the moment, but this is abnormal and I have a plan to restore things to the way they should be in America. And, no matter how "mad as hell and I'm not gonna take it anymore" people are, they generally want to blame someone else. If there's a malaise, they usually don't want to be told, as Jimmy Carter did in 1979, that it's *their* fault. Carter had understood and used this to his advantage in 1976, when he kept repeating that we need "a government as good as the American people," thereby implying that Nixon and the horrors that went with him were not representative of America—that they were the fault of Nixon, not the American people—and that he, Carter, would restore America to the way it ought to be.

The combination of a critique of current problems, the offering of a scapegoat to blame those problems on, and the promise of a cure is a winning one. "This country doesn't have to be in the shape that it is in," Ronald Reagan proclaimed in his 1980 debate with President Carter. "We do not have to go on sharing in scarcity."[27] That's the sort of thing voters like to hear, especially when it is clear that the speaker believes what he is saying, as Reagan did, even if he had no rational basis for his conviction.

JIMMY CARTER'S MISSED OPPORTUNITY

It is interesting that the only two Democrats who have managed to win the presidency in the post-sixties era are Southerners who have held some appeal for party liberals, but whom liberals have been reluctant to embrace fully. It is, in fact, not much of a stretch to argue that four of the five Democrats who have won presidential elections since the end of World War II fit this description.[28] Harry Truman was from a border state, but, like Lyndon Johnson, he had trouble with liberals over style and culture, despite the fact that by any objective standards Truman and Johnson were more liberal on economic issues than had been their sainted predecessors who were so revered by liberals, FDR and JFK.

It would not seem that the same could be said of Jimmy Carter. Yet a strong case could be made that Carter was, on a host of issues, more liberal than John Kennedy. The conventional wisdom that Carter is probably the best ex-president in American history, but was an inept president is well captured in the quip: "It's too bad Jimmy Carter couldn't have become ex-president without being president first!"

There is, sad to say, a good deal of truth in this popular wisdom. Jimmy Carter won the presidency by reassembling a rough facsimile of the New Deal coalition: the blacks and intellectuals who had stayed with the party even in 1972, most of the college-educated youth that had joined it in 1972, and enough of the white South and blue-collar and middle-class whites who had deserted the Democrats when they nominated McGovern. He was able to do this by being all things to all potential Democrats. A 1976 *New York Times*/CBS poll found that Carter was like a mirror to his supporters: liberals identified him as a liberal, moderates saw him as a moderate, and conservatives called him a conservative.[29] This can be wonderful in an election, but it is an asset that can easily become a liability for an officeholder. Not long after Carter took office, events twisted the image he had had during the campaign and Americans began to see in Carter, not themselves, but "the other side." Now when liberals looked at Carter, they saw a conservative; when conservatives considered him, they saw a liberal.

The fact is that Jimmy Carter was a virtual embodiment of the Democratic Party of the 1970s. "Carter's contradictions," E. J. Dionne has neatly pointed out, "were, in many ways, those of his party."[30] Like the party (and, alas, like the next former governor from the South—and the next Democrat—to occupy the White House), Carter often seemed unsure of where he stood on issues and philosophy. "His administration became," as Dionne puts it, "a battleground in which all the tendencies of the Democratic Party, and all the wings of liberalism, struggled for influence."[31]

Add to this uncertainty at the core a series of problems that were largely beyond his control, including double-digit inflation spurred on by soaring oil prices and the seizure of American hostages in Iran, and you have not only a prescription for defeat at the polls, but a further decline in confidence in both Democrats and government. When a few Arab leaders can make a decision that does more to alter the way we live—waiting in line to buy gasoline, seeing the prices of everything we buy shoot upward—than all the laws enacted by Congress and the president, it is not surprising that popular belief in the government as "part of the solution" dwindles.[32] (Of course, it could be argued that such ramifications of the actions of minor foreign potentates actually demonstrate how interdependent we have become and how much we need to utilize government to defend us from potentially disruptive foreign deeds. If the government fails to protect us from such actions, can anyone seriously contend that we would be better off trying to meet the power of OPEC on our own, as separate individuals?)

In the end, the combination of foreign-caused disasters and the falling out between Carter and the liberals destroyed both, closing out the best chance Democrats had to revive themselves between 1972 and 1992.[33]

SWEEPING, WRENCHING CHANGE

The election of Ronald Reagan brought to power the worldview that Barry Goldwater had enunciated in 1964. Reagan's election hardly constituted a mandate for the "movement conservatism" he faithfully followed. Rather, it plainly was a repudiation of Jimmy Carter and the weakness he seemed to show in the face of American economic problems and Iranian clerics alike. Indeed, despite Carter's unpopularity at the time, it is unlikely that Reagan would have won had he talked the way Goldwater had sixteen years before.[34] Reagan put a smiling face on the harsh dogma of the Right and won people over. Once in power, however, Reagan was able to proceed with the first steps in the conservative plan to sabotage the welfare state and restore trickle-down economics, especially after his good cheer at surviving a serious wound during an assasination attempt greatly increased his popularity.[35]

President Reagan and those behind him disguised their new incarnation of trickle-down economics by calling it "supply-side economics." This is, of course, the name I have given to the modern economy in which the production of vast supplies of "goods" necessitates the stimulation of mass consumption, and it is interesting to examine the connections between these two uses of this terminology.

The basis of the argument of the supply-siders who clustered around Reagan was condensed by George Gilder (borrowing from Jean Baptiste Say) to "supply creates its own demand."[36] Were this true, our economy would not be subverting our values by using any means necessary to stimulate consumption. The actual basis of the supply-side, consumption-ethic economy in which we have been living throughout the twentieth century is that this assertion—"Say's Law"—is wrong. The correct law of our supply-side economy is this: *Supply necessitates the creation of demand*, which is almost the reverse of what Gilder and the so-called supply-siders maintain.

Although some of the supply-siders apparently believed that cutting taxes while increasing spending, particularly on the military, could magically result in balancing the budget, others had not forgotten the simple arithmetic they had been taught in the lower grades. (Budget Director David Stockman had calculated that massive budget cuts of $100 billion per year would be needed to offset the deficits created by increased military spending and decreased tax revenue.[37]) That they did not believe in what George Bush aptly characterized as "voodoo economics" during his 1980 primary campaign against Reagan, did not mean these people did not believe in anything. They sought two other objectives from the Reagan fiscal program: to reduce taxes on the wealthy and create a deficit so large that it would provide them with a future justification for vastly reducing social spending. Both objectives were achieved. Reagan was so wildly successful at creating a massive debt that he ran up more in eight years than FDR and Truman had in winning World War II.[38] In fact, Reagan oversaw the accumulation of more debt than the net of all his predecessors combined. It was a truly historic accomplishment.

Stockman's description of what the Reagan deficits were designed to do is worth quoting at some length, since the Republicans in the mid-nineties are attempting to put the culmination of that design into effect. The plan hidden behind the deceptive advertising of the magic of painless budget balancing through tax cuts was "a blueprint for sweeping, wrenching change in national economic governance," Stockman said. He admitted that it would "hurt millions of people in the short run." None of those suffering this "short-run pain," it might be added, would be rich. The contribution the rich would make to the plan would be to get large tax breaks. But that was OK, since it was the nonrich who would eventually benefit from "abruptly severing the umbilical cords of dependency that ran from Washington to every nook and cranny of the nation."[39] If we are to judge by the budgets proposed by Republicans in 1995, the scheme was so pro-poor that it would deny the benefits of severing federal umbilical cords to all corporations receiving largesse from Washington.

Reaganomics did what it was designed to do: It redistributed income and wealth to those at the top, and it created unprecedented deficits that served the triple purpose of creating a Keynesian boom in time for Reagan's 1984 reelection campaign, keeping up interest rates (to the benefit of those with money to lend), and, of course, building a rationale for cutting social spending.[40] The message that the adoption of this policy sent was clear, said Nobel Prize-winning economist James Tobin: "Inequality of opportunity is no longer a concern of the federal government."[41]

THE DEMOCRATS SELL THEIR SOULS

The popularity of Ronald Reagan left Democrats in even greater disarray than they had been in before. Some wanted to resist by forcefully defending the New Deal/Great Society tradition. Others thought that "me, too, but not so fast" would be the best approach. Still others, such as Gary Hart in 1984, called for "new ideas" to compete with Reaganism.

The latter approach seemed to be the most popular. It was the one endorsed by the Governor of Arkansas. "He's giving us the opportunity to purge ourselves of some of the jackals of the past that we need to shed, without giving up our values," Bill Clinton said of Reagan in a 1986 conversation with me.[42]

But lack of unity continued to characterize the Democratic Party throughout the eighties. Having no agreed-upon message to sell to voters, some congressional Democrats decided to sell themselves—or at least their party's traditional principles—in order to survive in the hostile political environment of the Reagan years. This was the last major strategic error of the post-sixties era that so weakened the Democratic Party and its message.

Despite their lack of success in national races, Democrats continued to reign in Congress, and so they saw little reason to change their ways. The congressional party became something quite distinct from the national, or presidential, party. While the latter had, with the post-Watergate exception of 1976, quadrennial reminders (usually unheeded) of the need to alter some of its habits, the congressional Democratic Party, particularly the House Democrats, got increasingly comfortable—and arrogant. They believed that majority status in the House (and the committee and subcommittee chairs and staffs that went with them) were theirs in perpetuity. It was not that congressional Democrats did not change over the seventies and eighties. Change they did—for the worse.

(This is a good place to pause and remind the reader of the necessity of simplification when conducting analysis. I do not mean to make any blanket condemnation of congressional Democrats, many of whom are, in my view, outstanding, dedicated public servants. What I am addressing here is an unfortunate, utilitarian turn that the party as an institution took.)

At the urging of Representative Tony Coelho, who headed the Democratic Congressional Campaign Committee from 1981 through 1986, Democrats began to bid for contributions from corporate political action committees, on the argument that Democrats would control the House—and its dispensing of favors—forever and so corporations needed to have friends in high Democratic councils. "But understand something here," former Coelho aide Martin Franks says Democrats would tell corporate leaders. "We're in power. And I'd suggest you deal with us. Or at least . . . cover your tail." This pragmatic approach to the problem of a seemingly perpetual Republican advantage in contributions seemed to work. Money began to flow into Democratic campaign coffers. But the contributions were not given out of the goodness of corporate hearts; it was money spent with the expectation of receiving something in return. Coelho answered the question of what the donors got in return by saying, "Access. Access. . . . We sell the opportunity to be heard."[43]

What the Democrats who solicited big corporate contributions were actually selling, it turned out, was their party's soul—or, for those who prefer a different sort of metaphor, the Democrats' *cojones*: "What it did," Paul Wellstone said to me, "was it neutered the Democratic policy performance."[44]

Such, to be sure, was not the initial intention of Coelho or other Democrats. While he was in the midst of his corporate shakedowns, Coelho told me that the Democrats who had lost House seats in 1984 were almost all conservatives and "the reason they lost is that they apologized too much."[45] But if Democrats accepting funds from special interests in business did not have to apologize for past progressive stands, they did begin to see the practicality of toning down their current progressive rhetoric and policies. "Coelho," Ruth Shalit of *The New Republic* has said, "aggressively marketed the once pro-labor Democratic Party as increasingly pro-business."[46] The means Coelho persuaded Democrats to employ subverted the ends the party had traditionally sought.

Coelho was adopting marketplace values as the basis of Democratic politics. Discounting the importance of issues and ideas, he echoed the attitude of the Nixon White House by taking the position that the only relevant political question is: Will it sell?[47] Thus did Coelho and the Democrats who followed him add to the rampant cynicism that so plagues our society.

The price Democrats paid for the short-term benefits they got from the money they obtained from corporate PACs proved to be very large and long-term. When the contributions dried up rapidly following the Republican takeover of the House in 1994, many Democrats in Congress felt betrayed. They found themselves still paying for an automobile that was already in the junkyard. They did not understand that the business interests were just renting them until the product they really desired to purchase—conservative Republicans—was available in large enough quantities to bring about the results they sought. Influence peddling no longer works when you have no influence to peddle. But, having cast aside many of their most basic populist principles in order to solicit and maintain business contributions, Democrats found that they would, in public perceptions, "stay bought" long after the Special Interests halted their installment payments. With nothing left to sell, many Democrats find they have sold out the principles that might win back the constituency that they have lost.

Paul Simon summed up the situation well: "If we pander to those who make campaign contributions rather than standing for what we ought to stand for as a party, we are going to lose more, and, in that event, we should lose."[48]

"This should be a time when Democrats should feel liberated," Wellstone says of the precipitous fall in corporation PACs' giving to their party of non-choice. "They should feel free to really go back to when economics and politics could connect with ordinary people."[49] This much can be said for Tony Coelho: If he played a large part in the neutering of his party, at least he had the decency to make a substantial personal contribution to the potential reconstructive surgery. Called in to advise the Clinton White House, the Democratic National Committee, and the party's congressional campaigns in 1994, Coelho pushed the strategy of nationalizing the congressional elections and turning them into a referendum on Clinton economics versus Reagan economics.[50] This strategy failed miserably, opening the door for Democrats to escape the clutches of the business Special Interests to whom Coelho had sold them a decade before.

It is just possible that the combination of a wake-up call defeat in the 1994 congressional elections and the consequent loss of so much financial backing from big business may prove to be the proverbial blessing in disguise for Democrats. If they are wise, they will be able to take advantage of this painful but needed liberation.

6

"Both Sides Now": Bill Clinton and the Democrats' Direction

Please Please Me

"He spent time trying to be all things to all people, one way guaranteed not to be successful or respected in the lion's den. You can't just play around with all those big cats. You've got to take somebody on."[1]

Thus did the home-state poet that Bill Clinton had chosen to recite a new composition at his Inauguration summarize the first two years of his presidency. Maya Angelou was exactly right in her assessment—as the fact that she felt free to make it of a president with whom she is friendly, confirms. For all his extraordinary abilities, Bill Clinton suffers from three major political handicaps: he wants everyone to like him; he appears to be flexible in his beliefs (or, as Thorstein Veblen once said of college presidents, Clinton seems to have a "versatility of convictions"[2]); and his personal life presents too many opportunities for his enemies to attack him.

Here is another telling list of presidential shortcomings: "dilatoriness, two-sidedness (some would say plain dishonesty), pettiness in some personal relationships, a cardinal lack of frankness . . . , inability to say No, love of improvisation, garrulousness, amateurism."[3] It is quite a damning inventory. Yet, while it seems to have been custom-sewn by Bill Clinton's personal tailor, this garment was actually stitched together by John Gunther in 1950 to fit Franklin D. Roosevelt, the man who is generally acknowledged (even by Newt Gingrich) to be the greatest president of the twentieth century.

Then there is the unkind joke that was told (by conservatives) during the 1980s: "It's not that Ronald Reagan lacks principles, it's just that he doesn't understand the ones he has."[4] Yet many observers rank Reagan as the standard against which late twentieth century presidents should be measured. By the spring of 1995, Bill Clinton felt it necessary to state at a news conference that he was still relevant to the American governmental process. It seems that there is a fine line between political greatness and the appearance of insignificance.

Like FDR (and more than a few other politicians), Bill Clinton wants everyone to hold him in high regard. Almost anyone who has known Clinton will confirm that he "clearly wants to be liked; and seeks approbation in virtually every encounter."[5] In his case, the constant need for approval may be the result of having been brought up in a household headed by an alcoholic stepfather.[6] Whatever its source, Clinton's desire to please everyone is his greatest strength as well as his greatest weakness. He is said by friends to be "genuinely curious about nearly every individual he meets."[7] His ability to remember people is astounding. I experienced this myself in the summer of 1988. More than two years earlier, I had had an interview with Governor Clinton, which lasted about an hour. I had met him briefly once before that. In 1988, I was invited at the last minute to a conference in Washington at which Clinton was to be the main speaker. My name was not on the list of attendees, and I was not wearing a name tag when the Arkansas governor walked, by himself, into the crowded meeting room. He looked across the room, spotted me, and came over. He not only knew my name, but began talking about our conversation two years before and about my book, which he had obviously read. I was amazed. He must be able to do this with thousands and thousands of people he has met. This may be the most important ability for a politician.

The mind that allows him to remember so many people provides Clinton with other political advantages. "Bill gives me a headache," home-state Senator Dale Bumpers told me. "He is an absolute—not exactly a stream-of-consciousness—but a stream-of-ideas. And you know, I'm climbing just one, and he's two ahead of me. [He has] the most incredible political mind I've ever known in my life."[8]

More importantly, Clinton's desire to be approved by everyone leads him to bring people together, to bridge differences, and to be a mediator, as he had to be at an early age in his own family, attempting to bring peace between his parents. He tries to avoid the usual binary political thinking, the idea that there are just two sides and everyone has to divide up and associate wholeheartedly with one or the other. This can be very much to the good.

But Clinton's desire to please everyone also results in a presidential agenda that has been well described by Robert J. Samuelson: "Mainly, he favors everything that might make people feel good and opposes anything that might make them feel bad."[9] Although this is just an exaggerated form of the agenda of most successful politicians, it is no way to run a country.

WAFFLES—PART OF A BALANCED DIET

Those who contend that President Clinton has turned the White House into the Waffle House (as in Garry Trudeau's use of a waffle icon to represent the President in *Doonesbury*) have a great deal of evidence to support their contention, much of it dating back to the 1992 campaign and earlier in Bill Clinton's life. During that campaign, President George Bush relentlessly hammered away at his challenger for the latter's penchant for straddling issues. The incumbent directed the voters' attention to his chief opponent's statements at the time of the vote on the Persian Gulf War, to his agonizing over the draft during the Vietnam War, to his positions on middle-class tax cuts, the North American Free Trade Agreement (NAFTA), environmental protection, and many other issues on which the Democratic nominee had refused clearly to take sides.

The theme song of the Bush campaign might have been the 1930s union ballad from the coal fields of Harlan County, Kentucky: "Which Side Are You On?" The Clinton campaign could have responded with one of the best songs by their friend Judy Collins, "Both Sides Now."

One difficulty with this line of attack by Bush was that it could be contended that he had already turned the White House into the International House of Pancakes by flipping on numerous issues—abortion, voodoo economics, and taxes, to name a few. A strong case can be made that in the realm of political leadership waffles are preferable to pancakes—that not taking sides is better than flipping on issues for reasons of political expediency.

But I would go farther and argue that refusing to identify wholeheartedly with one "side" in every controversy is praiseworthy. Certainly the time comes, for presidents and the rest of us alike, when (to quote the Lovin' Spoonful) it is necessary "to finally decide, to say yes to one and let the other one slide." But every issue should not immediately be reduced to an either/or choice. There is much to be said for the need, which Clinton feels, "to weigh the options to the last possible moment."[10]

Surely some matters should not be compromised, but most issues must be. Diplomacy is almost always preferable to war. Conciliation is usually better than conflict. The essence of democracy is compromise. Ours is a moderate nation; moderation is much more built on "yes-and-no" than "yes-or-no." Extremists are dualists and dualists are duelists. Moderates are blenders. Moderates sometimes waffle; extremists are too often pancakes who flip to the opposite side without ever being in the middle.

Most Americans are wafflers. Certainly most of us yearn for a middle ground on such vexing issues as abortion. We do not want to have to side with Phyllis Schlaffly *or* Madonna, Pat Robertson *or* Larry Flynt, the Islamic Republic of Iran *or* Sodom and Gomorrah.

Balance is the key to effective governmental policy. Blending thinking creates balance, but binary, either/or thinking produces imbalance. Would we not prefer to balance economic recovery with deficit reduction, to balance social responsibility with fiscal responsibility, to balance compassion with common sense, to balance environmental protection with job protection, to balance revenues with expenditures?

Prior to the beginning of the Clinton administration, America went through twelve years of egoism and trickle-down economics. What is less apparent, but at least as important, is that these were also a dozen years of strictly dualistic thinking. Ronald Reagan and his followers saw the world in simple black-and-white, either/or terms. Either you were for government or against it. They were against it. Either you were for taxes or against them. They were against them.

The same is true, and to a higher power, of the Gingrich radicals who took control of the House of Representatives in 1994. To them, *compromise* and *moderation* are four-letter words.

This is foolish. We ought not to be for or against government. We should see it neither as constant friend nor intractable foe, but as something to be favored for those tasks that we can do better together than separately, but also something that has a clear potential for mischief if it is depended upon in matters that are better left to individuals.

There is a time for people who say they are "one thousand percent" for their "side." But more often we are better off with people who are 60 to 80 percent for one side of an issue.

A nation with the diversity of the United States *has* to compromise and conciliate if it is to survive. Either/or thinking leads to exclusion: "us" versus "them." In order to bring the nation together across racial, ethnic, religious, sexual, and value lines, we need to have the sort of both-and thinking that produces inclusion.[11]

Some of our most successful presidents have been wafflers. Franklin Roosevelt is, as the assessment by Gunther suggests, the best example. During the 1932 campaign, Roosevelt's adviser, Raymond Moley, brought the candidate two proposals on tariff policy, one calling for protection, the other for free trade. FDR looked at them and said to an astonished Moley: "Weave the two together."[12] Late in the same campaign, Roosevelt said he would bring bitterly disagreeing "farmers' leaders together, lock them in a room, and tell them not to come out until they have agreed on a plan."[13]

So, rather than reflexively condemning waffles, we should appreciate that they have an important place in a well-balanced political diet.

The Cold War was a time of full-blown either/or thinking; there was no place for neutrality. "If you're not with us, you must be against us" was the motto. Now that that dualistic struggle has ended, we should try to get away from the polar thinking that accompanied it. The end of the bipolar world should allow us to move away from bipolar thinking. To the extent that Bill Clinton has done that—as he has on such issues as the place of religion in schools and of violence in the media—we should all thank him for putting waffles back on the White House menu.

Pass the syrup.

TOO MANY WAFFLES

But.

The *Talmud* says: "These things are good in little measure and evil in large: yeast, salt, and hesitation." We might add waffles to the list. It is, as they say, possible to get too much of a good thing. Excess is to be avoided and, paradoxically, even moderation can be carried to excess.[14] All waffles and no red meat does not make for a balanced diet. There are times when it is essential to come down firmly on one side of an issue. Bill Clinton has done this too rarely. His instinct for compromise and blending leads him into bad actions as well as good. He wavers between opposing factions, ideas, and proposals, giving him a reputation for either insincerity (the essence of the "Slick Willie" label) or indecisiveness. Neither, obviously, is a political asset. A moment during the president's September 1995 *Air Force One* "funk" interview seemed to capture this trait: A reporter asked whether he intended to keep up his recent travel pace through the coming campaign. "Clinton nodded yes but said, 'No.'"[15]

Twice in a period of just over two weeks in the fall of 1995, President Clinton seemed to confirm that his convictions resemble a weathervane more than they do a compass. First, addressing a wealthy audience in Houston, he spoke of his 1993 budget and proclaimed: "You think I raised your taxes too much. It might surprise you to know that I think I raised them too much, too." This astonishing reversal on the hardest-fought, most successful legislation of his first two years justifiably left Democratic progressives in one of two seemingly opposite but actually quite similar conditions: speechless or screaming. Several Democrats who had become *former* members of Congress as a result of heeding their president's pleas for support on this bill saw this instance of Clinton flip-flopping as a betrayal.[16] What makes it all the more bewildering is that increasing taxes on the richest 1.2 percent of Americans had been the one small but significant step Clinton had taken toward addressing the fundamental problems facing America in the nineties.

The chorus of progressive outrage that arose following the tax apology led Clinton to apologize for the apology, claiming that it was just a slip made because he was very tired. (It subsequently came to light that he had made similar statements twice in the days before the Houston gaffe. Maybe he had been tired for a long time.)

Then President Clinton promptly fell back into criticism of his first two years. In a telephone conversation with Ben Wattenberg, the president said that he had "lost the language" of the moderate "new Democrat" that he was in 1992. He said that he had been "so anxious to fix the economy" that he "changed philosophically and missed the boat" and "let Democrats down." He even declared that he had become "a cardboard cutout" of himself. He vowed to change back to his moderate definition.[17]

It is obvious that the fall 1995 Clinton apologies were the handiwork of Dick Morris, the mostly Republican hired gun upon whom Clinton calls whenever he gets desperate. Morris's basic strategy for Clinton's 1996 reelection was "triangulation": positioning the president in the middle, tacking back and forth between the right-wing congressional majority and liberal Democrats in Congress. In conjunction with this, Morris would reprise the "I'm very sorry, ashamed, I know I did wrong and I'll never do it again" strategy that had worked so well in Arkansas in the corresponding period after Clinton's 1980 defeat. "You have to recognize your sins, confess them, and promise to sin no more and then sin no more," Morris had counseled then.[18] (Clinton had used this strategy again after the nominating speech fiasco in 1988. More about that shortly.[19]) But while "triangulation" *might* be politically smart for Clinton; apologizing certainly was not. Despite the surface similarities (repudiation at the polls after two years; another election two years later), Clinton's situation following 1994 was fundamentally different from that following 1980. His major problem in his first two years as governor was almost the opposite of that after his first two years as president. In the former case, he had been perceived as arrogant and patronizing. The cure was a dose of humility. But Clinton may have inhaled too much of this Morris advice. The "tell-me-where-I-went-wrong; I'll-change-it" persona that emerged from the 1981–82 Morris makeover achieved its immediate purpose. In the longer run, though, it apparently helped to construct the wishy-washy Clinton that turned voters off in 1993–94. Apology makes sense when voters think you have been too unbending and sure of yourself. When the problem is the reverse, however, and people think your main fault is that you are always changing your mind and your position, apologizing and promising to change is exactly the wrong course. It only serves to reinforce all the doubts people have.

Prominent Democrats I interviewed for this book repeatedly pointed to a seeming unwillingness to make a clear decision and stand behind it as their president's chief flaw. Paul Wellstone said that Clinton's fundamental problem "has never been a position on an issue." Rather, it is that people ask, "Where is the conviction? What does he stand for?"[20] "I think Bill Clinton's instincts are good, but he ought to get rid of the pollsters. He's got to follow his instincts," Paul Simon said to me. He spoke of his own campaign in 1990, when he was expected to lose because he did not take the popular position on several major issues. "I remember running into this guy in the streets of Chicago who said, 'I think that I disagree with you on every issue, but I trust you and I will vote for you.' People want conviction and I think that's the weakness right now of Bill Clinton. What does he stand for? Where is he in his gut? We all like to please people—the vulnerability we all have in politics. He's got to move away from that. He has to stand for something. He's got to show that he really believes something."[21]

One Democratic leader who asked not to be identified complained that Clinton and those around him "basically are in sync with the Wall Street crowd on trade—the investing community. And it's not our natural constituency. The message is contrary to what our constituency needs or wants to hear. And, as a result, I think we have given up a nice slice of our arsenal of political weapons." At other times, though, Clinton seems to side with more traditional Democrats, as he did when he attacked "greedy" pharmaceutical companies early in his presidency. A White House insider said to me in a not-for-attribution interview that Clinton's populist advisers, such as James Carville, Paul Begala, and Mandy Grunwald, persuaded him to do this, but that "it wasn't really Clinton." When others in the administration, such as Robert Rubin— "the Wall Street crowd," as their populist rivals call them—told Clinton that this was wrong and would turn big business against him, the president backed off.

Mr. Clinton continually vacillates between the politically wise "class warfare" issues and his inclination to conciliate. He is pulled in different directions by competing groups of advisers. More surprising than what some Democrats were willing to say in the background about their president's inconsistency was what others, even those high in the administration, would say on the record. Particularly startling was what an apparently disenchanted George Stephanopoulos said to me in a June 1995 interview, shortly after the rise of Dick Morris to prominence in Clinton's counsels had challenged his own influence. "I think that they [Republicans] have found that it's very effective to simply raise the 'class warfare' flag whenever we've struck a nerve. Either we've got to say we're going to absorb that blow and push on for a larger debate, or let it go; but trying to have it both ways doesn't work." "What we've tried to do instead of taking them on," Stephanopoulos continued, "is that we've tried to reach out to Wall Street, as well, and, you know, an awful lot of the Democrats' funding comes from big business interests. So we're stuck in a contradiction. We're stuck trying to argue for and against, and what comes out is *mush*."[22]

The fact that a leading presidential adviser could say something like this, on the record, while sitting with the door open in a room just down the hall from the Oval Office, suggests another of Mr. Clinton's problems. "There is no penalty for stiffing this administration," Charles Krauthammer has remarked.[23] The analyst was speaking of foreign policy, but the comment applies equally to the domestic front.

A DIFFERENT KIND OF DEMOCRAT

How did Bill Clinton become only the second Democrat since 1964 to win the White House? This is a question of obvious import in any assessment of where the Democratic Party needs to go.

Part of the answer, surely, is good fortune. He had a weak opponent in President Bush, a man who did not even seem like he really wanted a second term and had no rationale for why he should be given one. He had the on-again-off-again third-party candidacy of Ross Perot, a man who first provided a resting place for those who wanted to defect from Bush, then dropped out during the Democratic convention, so that his supporters were left to look for a new candidate at just the moment when Clinton held center stage. Most of those who had decided they did not want Bush concluded that they had no other place to go but to Clinton. When the mercurial billionaire reentered the race, many of his earlier supporters stayed with Clinton and Perot further split the potential Republican vote. And Clinton had in President Bush an opponent who nauseated the right-wing base of his own party, many of whom concluded, as David Frum notes, that it might be better for the "conservative movement" if Bush (whom Frum characterizes as a "pantywaist") lost: "Do us a world of good, get out of office, think things through, recharge our batteries, let the Democrats worry about the deficit."[24]

But luck, while it is always nice to have, is of little interest in an analysis of what Democrats need in order to win in the future. Bill Clinton managed in 1992, despite all the personal baggage he carried with him, to get over a few hurdles that had tripped up several other Democratic presidential candidates. One group of Clinton advisers argues that he took two key symbolic steps during the campaign that made him acceptable to the major part of the New Deal coalition that had defected from Democratic presidential candidates from 1972 onward: the working-class whites who had come to be known as "Reagan Democrats." To make himself acceptable to these voters, Clinton—or any other Democrat—had to show that he would not follow the "no enemies on the left" practice that had led so many Democrats to accept whatever kookiness might emerge from cultural radicals. He would also have to show that he was not beholden to the leaders of high-profile interest groups and that he truly cared about middle Americans. Bill Clinton achieved these objectives in 1992 through two (uncharacteristically) daring steps.[25]

First, and most importantly, when he spoke to Jesse Jackson's Rainbow Coalition in June, Clinton denounced a rap singer named Sister Souljah, who had addressed the meeting the night before. Speaking of the recent Los Angeles riots, she had declared: "If black people kill black people every day, why not have a week and kill white people?" It was precisely the sort of outrageous remark (like, from the other extreme, G. Gordon Liddy's declaration that people should aim for the heads of federal agents) that ought not be tolerated from anyone, but generally had not been condemned by Democrats in the past two decades, so long as they were made by people "on our side." The opportunity it presented Clinton was like a hanging curveball served up to Hank Aaron, but it was the sort of fat pitch that pusillanimous Democrats had taken with their bats on their shoulders for two decades. The stakes were high, and Clinton was reluctant to upset Jackson, but George Stephanopoulos and Paul Begala persuaded him to seize the opportunity. He declared that Souljah's comments "were filled with hatred." "If you took the words 'white' and 'black' and reversed them, you might think David Duke was giving that speech," the soon-to-be Democratic presidential nominee rightly said. Jackson was irate about Clinton's condemnation of one of his guests, which also redounded to the candidate's advantage.[26] The simple message that Clinton conveyed was this: People who suggest that killing folks is OK are *not* on our side.

The second key step Clinton took to show that he was different from previous Democratic presidential nominees was choosing Al Gore as his running mate. Gore's strong environmentalism made him acceptable to the cultural and intellectual liberals who remain an essential part of the Democratic coalition.[27] But Clinton's selection of Gore sent a signal that was, in its own way, almost as dramatic as that Franklin Roosevelt had sent sixty years earlier, when he flew from Albany to the Democratic convention in Chicago to accept the nomination in person. His action was "unprecedented and unusual," Roosevelt told delegates in 1932, "but these are unprecedented and unusual times." The message was clear: "Let it be from now on the task of our Party to break foolish traditions."[28]

Clinton's selection of Gore, a fellow Southern Baptist from an adjacent state, carried four important messages: First, *This shows that I am unconventional; so you can be reassured that I am not a conventional Democrat.*[29] Second, *I really do believe in change; tickets have always been "balanced" in the past, but I'm changing that and picking someone like me.* Third, *You can count on me to do what I say, since I'm not mixing the message by picking someone different from me.* Fourth, *I don't need to balance the ticket with someone from the other side of the party, because I'm already "balanced"—I'm in the middle, just where most of you voters are. So is my running mate.*

Perhaps best of all, while making it possible for Clinton to send all those messages by seeming not to be someone who was balancing the ticket, the fact was that Gore *did* provide an unspoken balance for Clinton. Given all the doubts about Clinton's character, connected principally with marital infidelity, Gore, with his "picture-perfect family,"[30] provided the ideal balance. Clinton's greatest need for equilibrium on the ticket was not to balance himself as a southern moderate with a northern liberal; it was as an accused philanderer with someone who had a Boy Scout/dedicated-family-man image.

Voters were sufficiently reassured by these messages (and were sufficiently disenchanted with President Bush) that Clinton was able to do what only one other Democrat had done since he reached voting age: win a presidential election.

A RISING STAR OF DESTINY

"One of the things that Reagan understood, one of the things that Kennedy understood, one of the things that Roosevelt understood, is that you have to represent something in order to be president," Bill Clinton said to me six years before he was elected to the office himself.[31] It is a lesson that Clinton seemed to forget in his first two years as president. During his 1992 campaign, he said he stood for something: change. (Contrary to popular belief, the sign that James Carville hung in the campaign "War Room" in Little Rock did not just say "The economy, stupid." It actually read: "Change vs. more of the same. The economy, stupid. Don't forget about health care."[32] Change was always the primary message.) That's almost always helpful in winning an election, especially at a time of discontent such as the Psychic Crisis of the Nineties. The reason "change" is such an effective campaign theme is that it is an empty vessel that can be filled with each voter's favorite potable. (This may begin to sound similar to the mirror image so effectively used by the last successful Democratic candidate, Jimmy Carter.)

Change, however, is meaningful only if it eventually takes on a specific content. With Bill Clinton, the general impression has been that this did not happen, at least not before late 1995, when his backbone appeared finally to stiffen a bit. Two issues seemed partially to reverse Clinton's image as an irresolute leader at that time: Bosnia and the budget. Polls indicated that sending American troops to help enforce a peace agreement in Bosnia would be very unpopular. But it added to Clinton's popularity. Much as apologizing and promising to change is not the thing for Clinton to do when people think his problem is that he changes too much, he is in the paradoxical position of becoming more popular by taking an unpopular decision. Going against character is a good thing to do when your character is questioned. Standing up against Republican extremists in the budget battle at the end of 1995 added to the public perception that, just maybe, Bill Clinton believes in something, after all.

Some would not believe it even then. "One thing will not change," wrote William Safire that fall. "This president, who ran on the promise of change, will keep changing his mind."[33]

Yet even if Clinton has not managed to represent something in the way the three presidents he mentioned to me did, he does have something very important in common with them: genuine optimism, about both himself and the nation. Unlike any of the nineties crop of Republicans, in Paul Begala's view, Clinton has Reagan's optimism. "He is utterly confident. You get him privately, you get him alone, he's totally certain that America is at least going to kick ass in this world economically. He is very excited about it. . . . He, like, totally celebrates all of these changes."[34]

Much like Franklin Roosevelt, who had so much personal confidence that he did not allow polio to stop his belief that he was destined for the White House, it is Bill Clinton's unbounded personal optimism that has allowed him to continue to expect to achieve his highest ambitions, no matter how great the odds against him seemed to be. Like FDR, Clinton seems to believe that he is following a star of destiny that can suffer occasional eclipses, but will never stop rising. This unadulterated optimism is what accounts for many of the remarkable events in Clinton's career. It is undoubtedly what led Clinton to believe from an early age that he could—that he *would*—be president. It enabled him to recover from his humiliating defeat in his first attempt to be reelected Governor of Arkansas in 1980. That recovery took a little while. His defeat that year was the most catastrophic he had suffered. "His reaction, biographer David Maraniss writes, "characteristically, was of two parts. Here he was whining, feeling sorry for himself. There he was resolved, plotting a comeback course."[35] Over the ensuing months, Dick Morris recalls, Clinton "would very often be soulful: 'Gee, do you think I can come back?

Do you think I've had it?' . . . He was like a patient afflicted with cancer wondering if he had any chance of survival."[36] Soon enough, however, this malignancy in his career was, in his own mind, in complete remission.

The faith in his own future that is so characteristic of Bill Clinton made it possible for him quickly to come back from the disaster of his interminable speech nominating Michael Dukakis in 1988, which had briefly made him a national joke. Most people have forgotten just how big that calamity was. I was in the Omni in Atlanta that night and I can testify that the reaction was not quite that for which an orator hopes. A few minutes into the speech, loyal Democrats stopped listening, began talking with each other, yawning, reading newspapers (the house lights had not been turned down). As it dragged on, delegates shouted "Enough," "Shut up," and "Get the hook!" When the governor finally said "In closing," the arena burst into applause. The next morning when NBC newsman Tom Pettit was asked on the *Today* show how Clinton could have been seen as "someone to watch" as a future presidential candidate, his simple reply was devastating: "Now we know better." Things were no better for Clinton on *The Tonight Show* than they had been in the morning. Johnny Carson declared that the Surgeon General had approved Clinton "as an over-the-counter sleep aid." But while this painful episode left such longtime Clinton aides as Betsey Wright in tears, to the governor himself it was merely another minor setback from which he would quickly recover on the road to the White House.[37] And recover, of course, he did.

It must have been his unshakable faith in his own destiny that led Clinton to go ahead with the presidential race even though he knew that philandering and the draft would be potentially lethal issues that could not be kept under wraps. After Gary Hart was done in on the infidelity issue in 1987, Clinton was persuaded to back off from his intended 1988 presidential run,[38] but he convinced himself that he could survive the scandals four years later, arguing that "the adultery question would prove to be 1988's passing fad. In 1992, the economy would matter," he reassured friends (and himself).[39] Subsequently, Clinton's self-confidence helped him to believe that he could still win in 1992 after he was hammered by the character questions in New Hampshire. Clinton's support plunged by between fifteen and twenty points after the Gennifer Flowers and draft stories came out. His initial reaction was denial. "This goddamn fucking middle-class tax cut is killing me," he told a group of aides, all of whom knew that his plummet in the polls hadn't a thing to do with taxes.[40] Quickly, though, he was out fighting to reverse the seemingly irreversible reverses to his campaign. Then his blind faith in his own destiny helped Clinton to believe that he *had* won the New Hampshire primary when he had actually finished second. It enabled him to believe that he could win the general election when he was running third in the polls, behind Ross Perot as well as George Bush, in the spring of 1992.[41] Later, after the usual brief period of confusion and anxiety following the Democratic debacle of 1994, which had been made largely into a referendum on him, Clinton's indestructible belief in himself led him to conclude that he could come back again and win reelection in 1996.

Richard Nixon had his *Six Crises* before he became president (and many more after); Clinton had that many during the first half of the 1992 election year alone: Gennifer Flowers, the draft manipulation, the "didn't inhale" marijuana story, the release of his letter thanking an ROTC official "for saving me from the draft,"[42] the first revelations about Whitewater in the *New York Times*, and Ross Perot's entry into the race. "Somewhere along the way," as Elizabeth Drew writes, "Clinton seemed to have become convinced that he was indeed 'The Comeback Kid'—the title Paul Begala had coined to magnify Clinton's second-place showing in New Hampshire (after the Gennifer Flowers and draft episodes). Clinton was a truly resilient man. He had come out of more corners fighting than most people had ever been in at all."[43]

Bill Clinton seems to have taken to heart the beer commercial that asks rhetorically, "Who says you can't have it all?"

OPTIMISM WITHOUT DIRECTION

And yet there is something odd about Bill Clinton's optimism. Ronald Reagan had both convictions (whether or not he fully understood them) and optimism. Clinton appears to have only the latter. He may not be sure exactly where we are (or he is) going, but he's completely confident both that we'll get there and that it will be good and we'll like it. People love optimism in a leader, but they also want direction. It's wonderful that our captain has complete self-assurance that he can get us to our destination, but it would be helpful to know where that port is located and what climate we might expect to find upon our arrival.

In one sense, Bill Clinton has always known his direction: up. But we live in a three-dimensional world, and his bearings along the other two axes have never been certain. His generally upward trajectory has wavered from side to side, from left to right. He seems to suffer from an intermittent ideological dyslexia. Thus his upward path has been that of a rising, irregular corkscrew.

Surely part of the reason for Clinton's wavering is that his widely different experiences have contributed to the building of a multifaceted person, whose sides often seem to be at war with each other. Clinton is, as Elizabeth Drew has said, "a complex mixture of the southern boy who grew up poor white, the young man who matriculated at Georgetown

University, Oxford, and Yale Law School, and the adult who traveled in sophisticated intellectual and moneyed and international circles—but had not lost his good-old-boy, down-home southern core."[44] "Mixture" is the correct term. Bill Clinton is not a chemical compound in which the elements are blended into something different, but uniform. Rather, "several Bill Clintons" exist simultaneously: "the populist and the wonk, the poor southern kid and the well-read, well-connected networker, struggling for his mind and his voice."[45]

Another portion of the reason for Clinton's irregular movements on his way up is that they are ingredients in a strategic recipe devised by Dick Morris, which came to be known as "triangulation." Morris had advised Clinton following his 1980 defeat that he must learn how to sail into the wind. "You don't abandon where you want to go, but you have to tack to get there. You have to one minute go right for the objective, and then at some point when you find the boat about to tip over, you steer in another direction until the boat regains stability, then once more head toward the objective. You approach it in a series of triangular moves, instead of head-on."[46]

Perhaps another part of the explanation of why Clinton has often been unsure of his lateral direction is that his optimism was never simply his own. "For most of his life," Maraniss points out, "people had been talking about how he would be president someday. Those great expectations had both carried him along and circumscribed his path. He often seemed to be doing things because they were what someone who might be president should do. Occasionally, in rebellion," Maraniss writes, Clinton did things "because they were precisely what a future president should not do."[47] Sometimes Clinton apparently wonders: Who says *I have to* have it all?

The combination of his belief in his own rising star with his sporadic rebellion against a personal destiny that he has completely internalized but is not entirely self-chosen may help to explain more than Clinton's wavering convictions. It may also be at the root of his lapses into such fate-defying, self-destructive behaviors as his notorious womanizing. "Bill has always been someone who has lived on the edge, politically and personally," one of his friends accurately said to Elizabeth Drew.[48] Much like the strain of Calvinist who would sin in order to prove his utter faith in predestination and his own status as one of the Elect (God would not change his heavenly destination, no matter what he did), Bill Clinton may be attracted to political sins as a way of rebelling and simultaneously proving his faith in his unalterable destiny as a member of the political Elect at the highest level.

THE IMITATION OF JFK

Since Bill Clinton had long been told that he was a future president, that is the role he tried to play. Like many another ambitious Democratic politician of his generation, Clinton chose John F. Kennedy as the model for his political persona. In the eighties, both Gary Hart and Joseph Biden tried to take on the Kennedy role. Both adopted Kennedy's speech patterns and mannerisms. Hart even attempted to adopt the late president's private lifestyle and saw his political career ruined as a result. Playing "JFK" in productions of their own (not to be confused with that of Oliver Stone) did not work for either candidate, because their role-playing finally led the public to see them as unreal. Senator Bob Kerrey auditioned for this role in 1992, with similar results. The echoes of a distinctly un-Nebraskan Kennedy cadence were unmistakable in many of Kerrey's speeches. (Kerrey seems now to have put this thespianism behind him.)

One suspects that Kennedy imitation may have been part of the motivation for Bill Clinton's womanizing, as it probably was for Gary Hart's. But, to his credit, Clinton avoided overplaying the Kennedy role during his 1992 campaign. His inauguration, however, made the temptation too great for him to resist. (Willpower in the face of temptation does not seem to be Clinton's forte.) There was much that was good about Clinton's inaugural address. But too much of it was too clearly patterned on the Kennedy model. There were the echoes of the torch being passed to a new generation and asking what you could do for your country: "My fellow Americans, you, too, must play your part in our renewal. I challenge a new generation of young Americans to a season of service"; "this is *our* time; let us embrace it." A few days earlier, Clinton had made it plain that the torch that he wanted passed to him was the eternal flame at the JFK gravesite, which the president-elect visited for a much-photographed "private" moment of prayer and reflection.[49] More troubling to me as I watched were Clinton's hand gestures and physical bearing while delivering his speech. These were close enough to the original to have landed Clinton a gig on *Saturday Night Live*, playing JFK.

Trying to do *some* of the things that John Kennedy did and attempting to revive the spirit of the early, "good" sixties are worthy objectives. But trying to *be* Jack Kennedy is something else altogether. We had enough of presidents trying to play roles during the eighties.

No historian can fully endorse the refrain of Clinton's campaign theme song: "Yesterday's gone; yesterday's gone." In fact, yesterday is never wholly gone. We are very much connected to the past, and we must seek to understand those connections. We should learn from the past; but we should not worship it. Too much admiration for the past—or a person from the past—can condemn one to repeat its (or his) mistakes as readily as can ignorance of the past. The frontier we face today is very different from the "new" one Kennedy called upon us to find and confront at the beginning of the sixties.

Playing someone else is never a reassuring activity in a leader. It suggests that he is unsure of who he is. The whole fascination with Kennedy on the part of a generation of liberals is a reflection of their uncertainty about who they are. The best advice for Clinton may be: *Let Clinton be Clinton.*

BILL CLINTON—THE EARLY SUCCESS

Bill Clinton realized during the Reagan years that what he hoped to do if—no, in his mind, it was *when*—he became president would be much tougher than what Reagan had done. "Actually getting something done [is difficult]—anybody can give a speech that sounds good,"* he said to me six years before his election, "—but what we are arguing for is still *con*structive. When you try to construct something, it is a very complicated world, and it is very difficult. It was easier in a way for Reagan and his program because what he wanted to do was to *un*do. He wanted to lower taxes, he wanted to reduce government spending. Sure, there were a lot of interest groups opposing, but none of them were responsible for his election. He wanted to increase defense spending in a way that didn't require any major tough choices that we would be advocating if we were in control of the government. So I don't want to minimize the difficulty of the [constructive] role."[50]

Despite all of the difficulties inherent in pursuing a positive, constructive program, and despite all of his personal problems, Bill Clinton had some notable successes in the first years of his presidency. He stood up to the National Rifle Association and won passage of the Brady Bill and a ban on some types of assault rifles. The Clinton administration significantly reduced the size of the government, although one would never know it from listening to its opponents. In his first two years in office, before the Republican victory in the 1994 congressional elections, Clinton cut 71,000 federal employees, and put in place programs that would yield by the end of his first term the lowest percentage of federal employees in the

* The comment on good speeches was meant as a dig at Mario Cuomo, whom we had just been discussing and whom Clinton obviously considered to be his major rival for the Democratic presidential nomination. Two years before, when Cuomo had burst on the national scene with his keynote address at the 1984 Democratic convention and Colorado Governor Richard Lamm told Clinton that he was moved by it, Clinton shot back: "Come on, what did it really say about the issues we're trying to raise?" (Maraniss, *First in His Class*, p. 417).

civilian workforce in thirty years. During the same period prior to the electoral rebuke of 1994, the Clinton administration lowered federal spending as a percentage of Gross Domestic Product to below its level under either President Reagan or President Bush. AmeriCorps, the Family Leave Act, the National Voter Registration Act (Motor Voter), the restoration of democracy in Haiti, assistance in achieving agreements between Israel and the Palestine Liberation Organization and Israel and Jordan, and a budget that significantly reduced the federal deficit and helped produce a substantial economic recovery are among the other achievements of Clinton's first two years. The passage of the North American Free Trade Agreement (NAFTA) and the new General Agreement on Tariffs and Trade (GATT) are other accomplishments, although ones that many progressives would classify as negative.

In this brief discussion of aspects of the Clinton presidency as they relate to the direction of the Democratic Party, I want to focus on two areas of legislative success: the 1993 economic plan and the double-barreled blast of free trade, NAFTA and GATT.

Clinton's economic plan was much watered-down as the administration made deals and compromises to obtain support. An initial example of this provides an interesting comparison between the courses of the Carter and Clinton administrations. Both had great troubles stemming from an early mistake involving members of Congress from western states. The mistakes, however, were of very different, almost opposite, sorts. In his first month in office, President Carter alienated Democrats in Congress by canceling some nineteen water projects in western states, saying that such "pork-barrel" spending must be cut. Democratic leaders rebelled and Carter wound up with both the water projects and the ill will of his own congressional leadership.[51] Perhaps hoping to avoid a Carter-like mistake that would lose critically needed Democratic support in Congress, Clinton caved in to western senators in March 1993 by removing from his budget grazing and mining fees on federal lands. Clinton actually gave the senators more than they had asked for.[52] This action certainly avoided the danger of alienating members of Congress, but it showed them that this president could be "rolled." It was a devastating message with which to begin an administration.

Most revealing in the subsequent struggle over the economic program was the fate of Vice President Al Gore's ambitious "BTU tax" to encourage energy conservation. After assuring House Democrats that it would not be traded away and getting several of them to agree to "walk the plank" by voting for it, the administration agreed to let it be dropped in the Senate. The conference committee finally returned a bill with a 4.3-cent-a-gallon tax on gasoline, a far cry from what Gore—and, presumably,

Clinton—had sought. The major reason for all of the retreats was that Clinton had displayed great ambivalence about aspects of his program.[53] Without the president's driving, committed leadership, interest groups got the upper hand in Congress.

Also dropped by the wayside as the economic plan made its way through Congress were most of Clinton's plans for investing in children, training, and "infrastructure." The final product did reduce the deficit significantly, but, as Senator Wellstone laments, "Clinton once upon a time called for the need to attack both deficits—the budget deficit and the investment deficit."[54] Addressing the latter, critical to the needs both of the country and the party, was sacrificed.

Relatively mild though it became, the Clinton economic plan did not win the support of a single Republican in either house of Congress. It appears to be unprecedented in American history for a major piece of legislation to be enacted without *any* votes from the opposition. It was a foretaste of the extreme Republican partisanship that would be more evident after the Republicans won control of Congress in 1994.

As for how onerous the tax increases on the rich were, Warren Buffet, at the time listed as the wealthiest man in America, had the best comment: "If anybody tells you that it's going to be a hardship for them, advise them to lower their salary to $200,000 a year and buy stocks in companies that don't issue dividends, and it'll be just fine."[55]

For all the compromising, the economic plan had tangible good effects on the nation. There were aspects of it that might call for apologies, but the modest tax increase on the richest 1.2 percent of Americans was not one of them.

MORE JOBS AT LOWER WAGES?

Bill Clinton said to me in 1986 that trade policy is an area where Democrats have to be careful, because it is very difficult and all Democrats would not be in agreement as to the right course. "What kind of trade policy are we going to have?" Clinton asked. Many people in this country, he noted, "are the casualties of worldwide economics. So in those areas, it will be more difficult to reach an agreement."[56] His own experience when he became president showed how right Clinton had been in predicting intraparty strife on trade.

When it came to the passage of NAFTA and GATT, the party lines that had been so sharply defined on the economic plan were blurred beyond recognition. Congresswoman Rosa DeLauro spoke with me about how troublesome the issue is for Democrats and their constituents. "The core [question for voters] is the standard of living and how are we assisting with that. . . . I can talk about trade to the people of my district *if* they believe that the end result is that we want to create a stronger economy here and create jobs here," she said. But "what they have been shown over the years is that that is not in fact the case. The case is—one more time—it increases the corporate bottom line. They get a lower wage and jobs go overseas. And therefore there has been nothing shown to workers that says, 'Trust us, we are going to help you in this process. We understand that wages are so low overseas and we may even want to take advantage of that, but we are not going to put you in jeopardy.' That has not been the case," the Connecticut progressive continued. "We now have a Mexican economy that may or may not be able to buy what we sell. I'm not opposed to trade. But, we have not made good faith with the workers in this country to let them know that we have their interests at heart when we are doing something."[57]

Paul Wellstone puts the problems of free trade pointedly: "More jobs at less wages is not the answer from most people's point of view." "All this stuff with NAFTA and GATT and this notion that our economics will be based upon the global economy, which is run by global corporations—frankly, it's not very reassuring to the people of this country. And frankly, our present course hasn't served them very well."[58]

Progressive Democrats were especially upset by the contrast between Clinton's efforts in pushing NAFTA and what they saw as his less forceful effort on other matters. "We failed in our first legislative initiative, the stimulus package," Rep. Nydia Velazquez said to me. "We failed because the president was not there putting the kind of enthusiasm and energy that he invested in getting NAFTA passed."[59]

"I regret that we're not talking the language of [angry white males] on trade—because of the White House," David Bonior states. "I think the trade issue has been a lot bigger part of losing that group than any other thing [has]." Bonior does not think the damage to relations between Democrats and workers is irreversible. He suggests that the Clinton administration could recover from its losses with working people on free trade "if they take on some trade policy with the Japanese, who have been screwing us for a while, and the Chinese as well, in some respects."[60]

Early in 1996, however, it was Pat Buchanan, not the Democrats, who took up this issue.

THE HEALTH CARE DEBACLE

President Clinton's early successes were much greater than he got credit for, but it is clear that the failures eclipsed them. The administration had three major objectives when it took office: a national health care program, welfare reform, and political reform (to eliminate or greatly reduce the influence of moneyed interests in government decisions). Had these three goals been achieved, it is highly likely that the middle class would have been cemented into a new majority Democratic coalition. It is beyond question that the Republicans would not have won control of Congress in 1994 had Clinton and the Democrats delivered on these three promises. But when November 1994 arrived, the Clinton administration had struck out on the central features of its program: three swings, three misses.

Polls indicated that the promise of national health care was one of the main reasons people had voted for Clinton in 1992.[61] The time was so ripe for this long-sought reform that in the fall of 1993, Charles Murray stated in his article calling for the abolition of welfare that national health insurance is an idea whose time seems to have come, so even he would stipulate that this should be provided for everyone.[62] In December, Newt Gingrich himself spoke of those who said that the Republican position on health insurance "should be against everything." "That's nuts," the rising star of the Right declared.[63] A year later national health insurance appeared to be an idea whose time had gone. Those that even Gingrich had categorized as "nuts" had opposed everything and won. Blowing this opportunity is the most unforgivable thing that the Clintons have done. Democratic House Whip David Bonior captures the enormity of the loss: "Most [Democratic] members who were in the Congress—senior members, I'm talking about—had come with the vision of providing health care. That's why a lot of us came here. And it was a window of opportunity to get it done. It was the first time that we had Democrats running the government at all levels, and we thought we could push it through."[64]

The greatest mistake was not having a plan ready to go when President Clinton took office. Indeed, most of the administration's early problems were largely the result of the failure to have *anything* ready to present when they took office. The day after the 1992 election, the *New York Times* found that Democrats in Congress were moving quickly "to commit the 103rd Congress to fast action on President-elect Clinton's legislative plans." They said that "the election results assured him of effective support on Capitol Hill." The story, reported by Adam Clymer, went on to say that Democrats on the Hill were hungry for legislative success and had assured Clinton that they would "be able to pass his main proposals, *once he tells them what they are*, in the first months of his Administration. That is when unity, rather than political agendas, will matter most politically."[65] The italicized words proved to be crucial. Democrats were said in the story's headline to be ready to pass *a* Clinton plan. The indefinite article was suggestive. Clinton had no clearly formulated plan when he won the election, and that unfortunate condition had not been remedied when he took office eleven weeks later. Congress was ready to pass Clinton's top priorities, but he was not ready to tell them what, in specific terms, they were.

The traditional presidential honeymoon was frittered away because there were no goods ready to sell to a public and a Congress that would have been eager to buy from a new presidential salesman. Washington and the media abhor a vacuum, and the void that Clinton's unpreparedness left was quickly filled with such "issues" as gays in the military. This, in turn, gave a substantial portion of the public the mistaken idea that promoting homosexual rights was Bill Clinton's number one priority. Right-wing radio did nothing to disabuse people of this notion, and in many quarters Clinton has remained defined by this early impression.

An important member of the administration who does not want to be identified suggested in an interview for this book that the early prominence of the "gays in the military" issue may have hurt Clinton more because of the last three words than the first. The controversy reminded people of Clinton's avoidance of military service and so was much more damaging to him than it might have been to a president who had a strong military record.

The key question is *why* it took so long to develop a health-care reform proposal. A large part of the answer seems to be the enormously complex mechanism that Ira Magaziner, the friend whom Clinton placed in charge of the process, set up. (A major reason that Clinton put Magaziner in charge, despite opposition to this step by many of his advisers, was probably that Magaziner, unlike most others who looked at health-care reform, was saying what Clinton wanted to hear: that large savings could be effected at the same time that coverage was being extended to the uninsured.[66] Magaziner's health-care reform arithmetic sounded a lot like that Ronald Reagan's "supply-side" fiscal plan: "Voodoo health care." But candidates and new presidents often seem to prefer pleasant fairy tales to more painful reality.) Magaziner formed a "working group" of some 500 experts and broke that up into 34 subgroups and . . . . There is no need to go further into the details. There was little chance that this process would produce a politically viable plan—and no chance that it would produce anything quickly. One administration official stated the problem succinctly: "You had five hundred people with every wacky idea that had ever been suggested in health care."[67] And they were meeting in secret. It was a recipe for disaster as well as delay.

When Clinton gave the opponents of national health insurance time to organize, they hit the plan with a massive propaganda fusillade. Over time they were able to persuade people who had recently been demanding national health insurance that they were better off without it. "I think one of the mistakes we made, tactically, was that we did NAFTA instead of doing health care, which was a terrible, terrible thing," David Bonior told me. "Now you can't get anyone to admit that. I tried to convince the First Lady and the President to set it [NAFTA] aside and do the health care: do it the way that Gingrich has run through this 'contract.' Get it done. Use your capital, your goodwill, your honeymoon and do it. I told him, you let these committees get a hold of this thing and they will strangle the son of a bitch to death. And that's exactly what they did."[68]

"The reason we didn't get health care is because the president was trying to accommodate too many different interest groups instead of going out there to the public and making his case," Rep. Velazquez says. "So we lost the battle."[69]

Senate Democratic Leader Tom Daschle has a similar explanation for the health-care reform fiasco. "We were out-organized and out-communicated on health-care reform," he said to me. "We came in with a 1300-page, very specific proposal and then left it out there for nearly a year before we tried to pass it. Everybody could take their shots at it and weaken support for it. And, then, I don't think the Democrats in the House and the Senate were convinced that this was something we really needed to work at to get it done."[70] (The latter problem was a reflection of the general "we're in the permanent majority" attitude of Congressional Democrats. That should not be a major problem in the wake of the 1994 election. Now that they have seen that they can lose, it should be easier for Democrats to get together and work hard for their objectives.)

"Bill had a chance to cut a deal with John Chafee at one time and he should have done it, but he kept holding out," Dale Bumpers said to me. "I imagine that Magaziner and Hillary wanted him to hold out." The moderate plan the Rhode Island Republican was presenting "would have been less dramatic, less revolutionary than what Bill was trying to do, but it would have at least started us on the road towards national health care," Bumpers continued. "But because of the time involved and not having seized that opportunity early on, and continuing to hold out for a plan that people didn't understand, therefore, the detractors could say almost anything they wanted to and people thought it [was true], because they didn't understand what Bill was trying to do." Bumpers believes that the insurance industry did not realize at first what the reform would mean to them. Then "they got all their little agents in every small town in America—a massive mailing campaign—and then they came up with 'Harry and Louise.' And 'you can't choose your doctor' and all that sort of thing, so by the time they [the Clinton administration] began to really focus on the genuine fears that people had, it had just caught on like that and the plan was dead."[71]

Paul Simon spoke of the effects of the campaign against the Clinton plan. "[Something like] $400 million was spent to defeat it. I would have town meetings where people would get up and say, 'well, I really like the idea of health care, but I really like the doctor I have and under the Clinton program, I can't keep my doctor.' You, know. This thing was distorted."[72]

Another problem with the Clinton health-care reform proposal is one that is intrinsic to his approach. Clinton, following his usual split-the-difference politics, as Representative Bernie Sanders said, "tried to balance large insurance companies against the needs of people without health insurance and comes up with some convoluted concept called—whatever it was called— 'managed care,' and the result was enormously complicated."[73] It was the president himself who had made this decision during his first week in office. According to one of the members of the original health-care policy-making group, "the president made a decision early on that he wanted managed competition. He didn't want to go back to single payer. He said no to broadening the discussion."[74]

"The president should have been a little more up front about the revenues," Senator Simon said. "To say we are going to pay for this out of cigarette taxes is just not realistic. I think people want gutsy leadership. And I think that if the president said, 'Here's what we are going to do and it's going to add 2 percent onto your income tax,' I think the American people would have bought it."[75]

Bonior also sees the flaws in the product as well as the process. "We didn't build on a national constituency base that was already out in the country—for a single-payer system," he said to me. "So we kind of left all the natural base that we had and tried to create something new and different, which was a mesh between that and the mess we have now. And it was a hybrid of it and it pleased nobody. It was overly burdensome, complicated, done as one piece instead of segmented. We misread it terribly on the political front. The other side pumped [in] tons of money and tainted it before we could [defend and promote it] because we didn't know what the hell it was. And we made about every mistake you can imagine."[76]

Clinton not only came up empty-handed on this top priority of his administration, but in the process, he delayed movement on the other major goals, including welfare reform, lobbying reform, and campaign finance reform. The last two were introduced so late in the congressional session that Republicans were able to block them. After two years, the promise of the Clinton administration was largely unfulfilled and the Republicans had a series of issues—some real, some phony—with which to attack the president and his party in the midterm elections.

There is, in fact, a school of thought that holds that the basic mistake was putting health-care reform first. "I think in retrospect it's clear that we would have been better served by a strategy that first tried to redeem the campaign pledge to end welfare as we know it," former White House domestic policy advisor Bill Galston told me, "and then moved on to political reform, and finally, to the problem of health care." [77]

The failure to move more quickly and decisively on political reform was particularly egregious. "Clinton had devoted half of his Inaugural to this,"

Senator Wellstone said with only a little exaggeration, "but he didn't push it hard." The removal of improper influence by moneyed interests is one of the greatest demands of the public. It was a major part of the appeal of Ross Perot in 1992. But many Democrats refused to believe how potent this issue is. "Democrats have made a huge mistake in being so far behind the curve on the political reform agenda," Wellstone rightly says.[78] Democrats' failure to deliver on this was, in Paul Begala's view, a bigger reason for their defeat in 1994 than was the botching of health-care reform.[79]

Then there was—or, rather, *wasn't*—welfare reform. Along with health insurance and political reform, the enactment of a genuine welfare reform plan that focused on enabling people to help themselves and get off welfare would have convinced much of the middle class that the Democrats were once again on their side. But the only significant progress that was made on this front in the first two years of the Clinton administration was the granting of waivers to about half the states, letting them experiment with reforms.

A LIKE/HATE RELATIONSHIP

The public reaction to Bill Clinton is curious. It has been suggested that his "stature gap"—the feeling that he does not quite measure up to what people expect a president to be—may be simply "the baby-boomer curse, the price of coming of age in a generation that took no form of authority—not even its own ascension to power—quite seriously."[80]

Be that as it may, about one-fourth of respondents to polls that include the question indicate that they "hate" or intensely dislike Clinton. That, in itself, is not what is surprising. A similar percentage of Americans probably would have been found to have despised FDR, had such a question been asked in polls of the time. But a much larger percentage of people in the 1930s would have said that they "love" Roosevelt. Who would say the same of Clinton? The best reactions are likely to be something tepid; perhaps: "Yeah, I think he's all right. He's doing a pretty good job now."

Opinion on Clinton shows that "bipolar" is not the redundant term that it appears to be. Opinion on Clinton is "unipolar": there is one extreme and a middle, but no opposite pole. The temperature range on Clinton should ease fears of global warming. It is frigid to lukewarm; there is no torrid zone. The American people seem to have a like/hate relationship with their chief executive.

This is difficult to explain. There is nothing new about it, though. The first time Bill Clinton sought public office, when he ran for Congress in 1974, the intensity of feeling against him was greater than normal, even in Arkansas's no-holds-barred politics. "There was something in his personality and style that engendered that kind of passion on the part of people who wanted to keep him from being elected," recalled Doug Wallace, who worked on that campaign.[81] Dale Bumpers made the same connection. He told me that the public's uncertainty about Clinton "is exactly what happened in Arkansas the first time he ran for governor. He was young, attractive, articulate, said things that they liked. But there was something about him that made what he was saying and what they really felt about him a contradiction. But they elected him with the idea that 'We are going to give him a chance. We're going to test him and see if he is what we think he is.' That's exactly what the American people did in 1992."[82]

During his presidency, the loathing of Clinton has been strongest in his native region. This suggests that part of the cause is the reaction toward one who is seen as a traitor or apostate. It's bad enough when "one of them" does things we abhor; but that is to be expected. When "one of us" is perceived to have gone over to the other side, it is intolerable. Clinton is the Southern Baptist from Arkansas who does not condemn homosexuality, apparently has extra-marital affairs,* is pro-choice on abortion, pushed through mild gun regulation, and believes in multiculturalism to the point of leaving important government posts vacant for months in order to fill them with minority or women appointees. To many southern white men, this is insufferable behavior from one who shares much of their background.

Some of the antipathy toward Clinton is plainly of his own doing. Whatever the merits of his positions on cultural issues (and I agree with most of them), the prominence given to his stands on such matters as gays in the military, abortion, and gun control combined with the Clintons' proclivity for hobnobbing with Hollywood figures, such as producers Harry Thomason and Linda Bloodworth-Thomason (who are old friends from Arkansas) and Barbra Streisand, vacationing at trendy resorts, and having their hair styled by men with one name and three-figure prices[83] tended to reinforce the links already established in the public mind between Clinton and the "bad sixties"—pot, protest, promiscuity. All of this stamped the young president as a liberal cultural elitist.

Then, in an attempt to regain the center, Clinton retreated from his on-again/off-again economic populism, which was his strength, not his

* This may not in itself be a subject on which many men in the region have room to be critical, if testimony about Hot Springs, Arkansas, while Clinton was growing up there is to be believed: "The men got away with anything they wanted to," a prominent woman of the city told David Maraniss. "They had no respect for women. They all had mistresses. They all beat their wives. It was a tradition of this city" (Maraniss, *First in His Class*, p. 35).

weakness, and has never been the Democrats' problem. By allowing himself to be identified with the cultural elite and fitfully abandoning economic populism (hence not drawing a clear line between himself and the economic elite), Clinton got the worst of both worlds—and secured the contempt of many Americans.

But some of the hatred for President Clinton is the result of planning by his opponents. A steady torrent of vilification of Clinton has streamed from the overwhelmingly right-wing voices of talk radio since before he was elected. For those whose idea of independent thought is to say "dittos, Rush," hatred is highly contagious. Then there is the not-so-Reverend Jerry Falwell, who is shamelessly marketing a videotape that accuses Bill Clinton of complicity in murder.

Paul Begala forcefully maintains that the plotting to destroy Clinton with personal attacks went on at higher levels than those of Limbaugh and Falwell. Begala gave me the company line as we sat in his Washington office in March, 1995, charging that at the end of 1993 Republican leaders decided that their only hope was to destroy Clinton with personal attacks: "All of the '93 fights were about Clinton's policies. And we won. Just barely, but we won. They said his budget was tax, spend, send us into recession, blah, blah, blah. We won. They fought against the Brady Bill, Motor Voter, NAFTA. Clinton won, won, won, won, won. So he goes into Christmas, '93 with the highest rating of his presidency. The highest in office. Sixty-five percent job approval. Higher personal favorability. You can plot it on a chart," Begala said. "From that point on, the Republicans switched their strategy. And they said, 'We can't let this guy have the stage. He's just too good. He's just too talented. His stuff is working. We're going to rip him apart.' You bring down Clinton—you know, you chop the head off, you kill the snake. You bring down Clinton, the whole progressive movement is dead. They went after him personally."

Warming to his subject, Begala said to me that media went along with the Republicans because they will put out anything that is sensational, regardless of whether there is any reason to believe it. The Republicans used "these lying, thieving state troopers—they were just lying—who get huge, huge play," he points out, referring to the Arkansas troopers who alleged that they acted as procurers for Governor Clinton's affairs. The Republicans "pump Whitewater up into the single biggest political governmental story of 1994. In the national data base of all papers in 1994, there were 19,555 stories on it. There were 2,700 on Clinton and his health-care bill. There were eight stories on Whitewater for every story on the most important piece of social legislation since the New Deal."

After pointing out that polls show that only a small percentage of the public believes these stories, Begala said: "So conventional analysis would be that the whole Whitewater-trooper-Paula Jones (who is a pathetic, scumbag liar)—all of that—the conventional wisdom would be that that failed. Right? Because it didn't move Clinton's poll numbers." But, while Republicans certainly would have welcomed a sharp drop in Clinton's popularity, that would just have been icing on the cake. The real purpose of the attacks, Begala insists, was to occupy the public's attention with diversions. That way most people would not know that Clinton had decreased the deficit; they wouldn't have any understanding of what his health-care reform was trying to accomplish. "There's no room for that in the newspaper. It's just another hearing on Whitewater, another allegation from some liar."

"There is a bias [in the media] toward the sensational or scandalous and Republicans understand that bias. They picked up on the fact that the press will run just about anything now; there are no more standards."

Begala told me that he *knows* that his charge about the Republicans plotting all this is true, "because, you know, Carville is married to a Republican strategist [Mary Matalin] and I know this. When they sit around, they talk about Clinton's great political abilities" and what they can do to win on their issues. "I feel bad, I guess, for him as a human being, because they are really trying to rip him apart. Literally destroy him and his family." Then he offered me a final piece of evidence that the ulterior purpose of the attacks on Clinton was to defeat his programs. "James [Carville] did a thing on *Nightline* when they were pressing Whitewater and Rush Limbaugh was on and at one point Rush just popped out and said: 'This isn't about Whitewater; this is about health care.' And he was right."[84]

There are serious flaws in the argument that the trooper allegation was cooked up just because Clinton was high in the polls in December 1993. The *American Spectator*, which broke the story, is a monthly magazine and the story had to have been in the works long before anyone knew that Clinton's numbers would be up in December.[85] But there can be little question that political motivation has played an important part in the pushing of various Clinton scandal stories. However, this does not mean that there is no truth in them. At this writing, no significant wrong-doing by the Clintons in Whitewater has been proved—or even seriously alleged—but their persistence in acting like they have something to hide is troubling. As Gloria Borger of *U.S. News* said, Whitewater appears to be "a cover-up without a crime."[86] As for the sex charges, many of the details may be exaggerated and some wholly fabricated, but there can be little doubt of their general truth. Clinton had said in his infamous tape-recorded telephone conversation with Gennifer Flowers, "They don't have pictures. If no one says anything, then they don't have anything."[87] It is difficult to conjure up an interpretation of this statement that does not mean that there was something to take pictures of and that people could talk about.

WAFFLING ON CLINTON

As the reader has probably noticed, I am a waffler when it comes to Bill Clinton. Like him, I tend to see both sides of an issue, and I can see—and at different times, agree with—both sides of the Clinton issue. From my limited contacts with him, I like him personally. I certainly like what he usually says about where the country needs to go. But I cannot help but wonder whether he is the person to do it.

On the one hand, he has frequently laid out a course that is very close to the new progressivism that I believe the Democrats and the country desperately need. I was struck by this when I first met and interviewed then-Governor Clinton in 1986. He stated it brilliantly in a 1991 speech to the Democratic Leadership Council: "Our burden is [to] give people a new choice rooted in old values. A new choice that is simple, that offers opportunity, demands responsibility, gives citizens more say, provides them responsive government, all because we recognize that we are a community. We're all in this together, and we're going up or down together."[88]

It would be hard to improve on this as a capsule statement of the ideals upon which a progressive Democratic vision of the future must be based. Bill Clinton has moved in his personal career in much the way the party needs to. He refashioned himself from being a state coordinator for George McGovern in 1972[89] to the candidate who was elected president twenty years later with a campaign that he could summarize on election night by proclaiming: "it was a victory for the people who work hard and play by the rules, a victory for the people who feel left out and left behind and want to do better, a victory for the people who are ready to compete and win in the global economy, but who need a government that offers a hand, not a handout."[90] This was a statement of almost exactly what the party—and America—needs.

Having a man in the White House with this understanding of where we need to go should be a blessing to the nation and progressive Democrats alike. But Bill Clinton's flaws, which I have outlined in this chapter, have made it difficult for him to accomplish the great things that his words indicate he should. It is, as he said to me, easy to "give a speech that sounds good," but it is very difficult "when you try to construct something."

It is difficult for someone who so often seems unsure of his own direction to lead the nation in a new direction. "Triangulation" may be acceptable when the goal toward which one is moving through tacks to the port and starboard is a vision for genuine improvement in most people's lives. But when the objective becomes merely winning, as too often seems to have been the case with Bill Clinton since he adopted the strategy in 1981, the result is to advance the worst tendencies in our supply-side society, so well stated by football owner Al Davis: "Just win, baby!"

The biggest problems with Bill Clinton trying to lead us out of the wilderness in which we are lost, though, stem from the character issues, particularly the philandering charges. These are, to say the least, inconvenient when Clinton attempts to use the "bully pulpit" to preach "old values." If Ben Wattenberg is correct in saying that "values matter most" (even if, as I argue, the ultimate source of our decline in values is to be found in our supply-side economy), it is very difficult for someone with the character questions that plague Clinton to deal with our immense national problems. David Frum puts it directly: "Who could keep a straight face if President Clinton delivered an address about the sanctity of the family?"[91] Indeed, his attempts to address moral questions tend to reinforce the very cynicism that is a major component of the national crisis that a new progressive vision centered on values seeks to solve. It increases the distrust in government and politicians, which is exactly counter to what our society needs.

Clinton overcame the public's doubts about his character in 1992 by arguing that there are two economic sides in America, and he is on the side of ordinary Americans, and saying to the voters, in effect: "Look, you have to decide. Is this going to be your election or theirs? Is it going to be about my personal life or *your* personal life?"[92] It's a good argument, but it would be nice if his personal life were not at odds with his professed goals for the nation. What focusing separately on economic questions (which Clinton can, at times, do quite well) ignores is the basic point I am trying to make in this book: that the three sides of the crisis America faces today—moral decline, a two-tier economy, and virulent cynicism—are interrelated. A self-inflicted incapacity to address one aspect of the national predicament necessarily thwarts a leader's attempts to progress on the other two fronts.

Bill Clinton knows where we need to go as a nation. He has enormous skills and abilities; but he also brings much ballast to the American sailing vessel as he tries to tack back and forth toward a better future. "Among Clinton insiders," Walter Shapiro reported in mid-1995, "there is a poignant sense that though reelection may be won, the promise of his presidency has been irredeemably lost."[93] If this is so, it constitutes a genuine tragedy for the United States. In the mid-nineties, progressives have little choice but to accept that we have to live with both sides of Bill Clinton and hope that the huge potential for achievement will, in the end, outweigh the flaws, and that the great promise of his presidency might yet be redeemed.

7

A Fourth American Revolution?: States' Rights and States' Wrongs

The Revolutionary "Conservative"

"I am a genuine revolutionary; they [the Democrats] are the genuine reactionaries. We are going to change the world," Newt Gingrich boldly proclaimed to a meeting of the Republican National Committee shortly after he became Speaker of the House in January 1995.[1] Plainly this was yet another demonstration that Mr. Gingrich is a living embodiment of the words *hubris* and *megalomaniac*. He would do well to remember Sophocles' dictum: "Every man will fall who, though born a man, proudly presumes to be a superman." Beyond this, Gingrich's statement seems an odd declaration from a man who constantly professes to be a "conservative." Most of the leading conservatives of the eighties made no such claims. Ronald Reagan, an occasional reference to remaking the world notwithstanding, usually indicated that his goal was the plainly reactionary one of bringing back the days of Calvin Coolidge.

"There hasn't been so much loose talk in Washington about 'revolution,'" Hendrik Hertzberg noted in *The New Yorker* early in 1995, "since Abbie Hoffman and Jerry Rubin hit town." Hertzberg found that a Nexis search for "articles containing the words 'revolution' and 'Gingrich' immediately yields a warning that there are more than a thousand."[2]

If we take the Speaker at his word, the time has come to stop calling him and his followers conservatives and label them instead as radicals. The question is whether we should believe Gingrich's proclamation that he is a revolutionary.

Surely there are grounds to suspect the reliability of some of what the Speaker says. It is prudent to doubt the candor of anyone who punctuates his comments with the word *frankly* as often as Gingrich does. I counted thirteen "franklies" during the Speaker's June 1995 hour-long town meeting with President Clinton in New Hampshire. (One suspects that a person's honesty is inversely proportional to the number of times he or she utters "frankly.")

One reason that Gingrich has chosen to call a return to the past a revolution is that he is a salesman. He understands how attractive the concept of novelty is to Americans. "Americans always want something new," the then-little-known Georgia Congressman said to columnist Richard Reeves in 1986. "We don't buy last year's soap."[3] Gingrich is trying to sell, not last's year's, but the last century's soap—or patent medicine—in new boxes saying it contains the "revolutionary" new ingredient X-498. A large part of the talk of a revolution is pure commercial hucksterism of the kind that has become so central in our supply-side economy.

Since their major objective is to increase the power of those who already dominate our society, not to shift control from one class of people to another, the Republican "revolutionaries" of the 1990s fail to meet one of the most basic definitions of *revolutionaries*. Yet they do seek a fundamental change in the nation's direction. If they really are, in this sense, revolutionaries, they are not really conservatives.

I shall return to Gingrich's assertion that he and his followers are revolutionaries in a moment. First, though, let us examine what has happened to a conservatism that claims to be revolutionary.

REFLECTIONS ON THE REVOLUTION IN CONSERVATISM

This decade is an appropriate time to take a look at how the modern brand of conservatism stacks up against its progenitors. Two hundred years ago the most important book in the history of conservative thought was published. For more than a century after its appearance, Edmund Burke's *Reflections on the Revolution in France* defined conservatism. But that definition bears scant resemblance to the beliefs of most of those who call themselves "conservatives" today.

The practices of those who have taken up the conservative name in recent decades are in fact, as I pointed out in Chapter 3, among the major forces undermining traditional values. It was those traditional arrangements for which Burke stood. The basis of Burke's conservatism was the long, connected view he took of society. In this perspective, people have responsibilities to one another. Society, he maintained, is "a partnership not only between those who are living, but between those who are living, those who are dead, and those who are to be born." Burke was dismayed to see around him people who would "not look forward to posterity, who never look backward to their ancestors." He remarked that "duration is no object to those who think little or nothing has been done before their time, and who place all their hopes in discovery."[4]

Here Burke was quite accurately describing the modern mentality. What is most peculiar is that it is also the mentality of the late twentieth-century "conservative." It is a hallmark of many modern "conservatives" to claim that they are doing things that have never been done before. One thinks of Richard Nixon discussing his personal finances in his 1952 "Checkers" speech, proudly claiming that "this is unprecedented in the history of American politics." Indeed, *unprecedented* was one of Nixon's favorite words. He was forever asserting that things that happened while he was in office, such as the moon landing, were "unprecedented." In truth, some things that occurred during the Nixon administration *were* unprecedented, but that is a strange boast for one professing to be a conservative (almost as strange as Gingrich's affirmation that he is both a conservative and a revolutionary).

But if Nixon's sort of "conservatism" was far removed from the Burkean definition, Ronald Reagan's and Newt Gingrich's are much more so. President Reagan once went so far as to admiringly misquote Thomas Paine to the effect that "we have it in our power to begin the world over again." Since Reagan was not much of a student of history, someone should have pointed out to him that Paine and Burke were on opposite sides of most issues and the side taken by Paine was not the conservative one. Dr. Gingrich, the holder of a Ph.D. in history, lacks Reagan's excuse. He must have been taught the difference between Paine and Burke—and which one was the conservative.

Bad as Burke thought the understanding of connectedness was in 1790, it has gotten far worse over the ensuing two centuries. Yet most "conservatives" today accept the idea that each individual is independent and should pursue his or her own self-interest with little or no regard for the well-being of others. If it is possible to secede from the society of one's contemporaries, it follows that one can also secede from the flow of time (history), abandoning ancestors and descendants alike. The effects of our modern failure to understand that we are part of the flow of history can be seen all around us, from environmental damage through corporations principally concerned with the quarterly profits report, to our national practice of consuming with funds that our children will have to repay. And "conservatives" have been prominent in all of these imprudent practices. Prudence, Burke asserted, is "the first of all virtues." This point must have been discussed during a history class that Ronald Reagan cut. What is Gingrich's excuse?

The essence of Burkean conservatism was balance and moderation. On reflection, it appears that the origins of the revolution in conservatism can be traced to 1964. The year that made Ronald Reagan a national political figure was also, as I have discussed, the year in which Barry Goldwater uttered the immortal words, "Extremism in the defense of liberty is no vice! ... Moderation in the pursuit of justice is no virtue!" Here, masquerading as conservatism, was the antithesis of Burke's thought. Goldwater and his followers reversed Burke not only in their extremism, but also in their insistence that unrestrained individual liberty is an absolute good.

Burke made it plain that, to him, extremism in the defense of liberty would be among the worst vices. "But what is liberty without wisdom and virtue?" he asked. "It is the greatest of all possible evils; for it is folly, vice, and madness, without tuition or restraint." "The restraints on men, as well as their liberties, are to be reckoned among their rights," he declared. Left to itself, Burke warned, "the spirit of freedom" would lead "to misrule and excess." Accordingly, it had to be "tempered with an awful gravity."[5]

Many present-day conservatives have nothing against employing awful gravity to temper liberty in such areas as artistic expression, but most want no part of even modest restraints on the liberties of the marketplace.

Neither making a government nor granting freedom was difficult, Burke said. For the latter, all that was required was "to let go the rein." But what is needed, he wisely said, is "to form a *free government*, that is, to temper together these opposing elements of liberty and restraint in one consistent work."[6] This was an admirable goal, but it is to be doubted that many of those who now wear the conservative label are willing to join in an effort to achieve the sort of balance that Burke had in mind.

Burke believed that responsibility went with privilege, and that those who enjoy disproportionately large holdings in the social corporation thereby incur special duties to the society. What, one wonders as so many Republicans make it their highest priority to defend the wealthy from fair taxation, has become of this notion among today's "conservatives"?

REVERSING THE SECOND AND THIRD AMERICAN REVOLUTIONS

The truth is that Newt Gingrich's claim to be a revolutionary must be taken seriously. There have been three revolutionary transformations in American political, social, and economic structures: the War for Independence, the Civil War, and the New Deal. When Gingrich says he wants to conduct a revolution, it is not merely a matter of rhetorical excess or pretentiousness. Were he and his followers to succeed in accomplishing what they have in mind, the changes would indeed be on a scale with those of the last two American revolutions.

In fact, what they are trying to do is to reverse major parts of both of those revolutions. It is obvious that they want to dismantle much of the New Deal. (In this, they go well beyond their Reaganite precursors. "The press is trying to paint me as now trying to undo the New Deal," President Reagan wrote in 1982. "I remind them that I voted for FDR four times. I'm trying to undo the 'Great Society.' It was LBJ's war on poverty that led us to our present mess."[7]) What has been less noticed by most observers is that these radicals in conservatives' clothing also seek to reverse one of the most revolutionary changes produced by the Civil War. It may be suggestive that the Republicans wanted to include in their proposed constitutional amendment requiring balanced budgets a "three-fifths" requirement to raise taxes. The only place this odd fraction appears in the Constitution is the infamous "three-fifths compromise," whereby the Founders agreed, in effect, that African-American slaves should be considered three-fifths human. Of course, this does not mean that any of the current "radicons" (save perhaps Charles Murray) subscribe to that view; but the number carries connotations that remind us of the time before the Civil War, a time to which these "revolutionaries" would like, at least in some respects, to return.

Next to ending slavery, the greatest importance of the Civil War was to establish that the United States is *a* nation, not a confederation of sovereign states. That war determined that "United States" is a singular, rather than a plural term; an "it," not a "they"; *the* United States, not *these* United States. "Up to the Civil War," as Garry Wills has put it, "'the United States' was invariably a plural noun: 'The United States are a free government.' After Gettysburg, it became a singular: 'The United States is a free government.'"[8] The plans of the new Republican leadership in the House (all of the major figures in which, it may be worth pointing out, represent states that were part of the Confederacy) to transfer much of government back to the states would reverse important legacies not only of the New Deal, but also of the Civil War.

In his dissent in the 1995 Supreme Court decision striking down state-imposed term limits on members of Congress, Justice Clarence Thomas made it clear that among his "conservative" objectives is to reverse one of the principal outcomes of the war that was won under the leadership of the first president of his party, Abraham Lincoln. Thomas argued that the union is not one of the people, but one of the (sovereign) states. In his minority opinion in *U.S. Term Limits* v. *Thornton*, the right-wing Justice correctly noted that throughout the Constitution "United States" is used "consistently as a plural noun."[9] What Mr. Justice Thomas is overlooking is that, three-quarters of a century after the Constitution was written, there was a war fought over that issue and that the side favoring the singular won out over those supporting the plural. "The results of this victory are priceless," George Templeton Strong wrote of Gettysburg, "Government is strengthened four-fold at home and abroad."[10] If the Thomas view prevails, the federal Union will become a Confederacy. This is not what Mr. Lincoln, who had the motto "One country, one destiny" written on the silk lining of the overcoat he used for his second inauguration,[11] had in mind. It is clear that the Republicans are the party of Lincoln no more.

The right wing's ambivalence toward Lincoln, the Union, and the second American Revolution is evident in the response of the organizer of a "second amendment rally" in 1995 to the question of why the demonstration was held at the Lincoln Memorial. "He led the people for freedom," Ron Long said of the sixteenth president. "Even though he did do more to damage states' rights than any president in history. But, heck, it's a nice location. Lots of trees."[12]

So far, the Gingrich revolutionaries have not suggested reversing the first American Revolution by rejoining the British Empire. Perhaps such a "Contract with Britain" will be a highlight of a future Hundred Days under a President Gingrich?

STATES' RIGHTS AND STATES' WRONGS

One of the most popular parts of the program of the Gingrich Revolution is the one that would reverse a portion of the second and third American revolutions: the promise to reduce the federal government by transferring powers and responsibilities to the states. People distrust distant government and are attracted by the idea that state government would be closer to them and more familiar with their needs and concerns. Progressives must understand this desire and respond to it. This means that we should react to these calls in a selective manner. People do not like impersonal government; but they must realize that a government in Sacramento or Springfield, Austin or Albany, will not be appreciably "closer" to the people than is that in Washington.

Various Republicans have been talking about a "New Federalism" at least since the presidency of Richard Nixon. *Federalist* is a word with an interesting tradition in this country. The dominant sentiment in the new, scarcely United States was certainly for state and local control. Americans had gained their independence in a war against a (very) distant, centralized government. *Federalism* referred to a division of powers in which most authority rested with the states; it implies that the United States *were* more of a federation (as in the Articles of Confederation) than a singular nation. The supporters of the Constitution, which would substantially increase the powers of the central (somewhat misleadingly called "federal") government, realized that federalism was a popular concept, so, in a late-eighteenth-century example of deceptive packaging, they adopted the name *Federalists* for themselves. (It is for the same sorts of marketing reasons that antiabortion crusaders now call themselves "pro-life" and supporters of legal abortion term themselves "pro-choice.") This seizure of a name meaning almost the opposite of what they actually stood for by proponents of the Constitution, left their opponents, who really believed in federalism, to be known as *Anti-Federalists*. This confusion continued as the first political parties in the new nation arose. The followers of Alexander Hamilton, who were actually strong nationalists, took up the popular *Federalist* label.

The New Federalism called for by Republicans in our own time is not, unlike the old, nationalist. It actually *is* federalist, although it is not new. It is, perhaps, fitting that the economic descendants of Hamilton in the twentieth century have concluded that the Hamiltonian goal of encouraging and protecting the concentration of wealth is now best served by shifting power to the states—the federalism whose name Hamilton appropriated, but which he opposed in practice.

Progressive Democrats should be both more radical and more discriminating than the Republicans have been in their approaches to "devolution." "I think we all have to be strong decentralists," Paul Wellstone said to me. "Decentralization is critically important [for progressive goals]."[13] People desire a sense of participation in the decisions that affect their lives. This can be had only at a much lower level than the states. Where appropriate, Democrats should propose moving powers and decision making from Washington, beyond the state capitals, to the local level where people can exercise a degree of control over their own destinies.

States' rights do exist; they are an important part of the American system. But any call for states' rights makes many people uneasy, because this terminology has so often been used in the past as a cloak for evil practices. White supremacists from John C. Calhoun through the Civil War used the cry of "states' rights" as a cover for their defense of slavery. Even today, those white Southerners who want to maintain respect for the Lost Cause comfort themselves by insisting that "the War" was not about slavery, but about "states' rights." The question that must be asked of the advocates of the position that the Confederacy's purpose was to defend states' rights is the following: "Just which rights of the states were so important that they were worth dividing the nation and fighting a terrible war over?" Can anyone seriously contend that the tariff or any other matter of disagreement between the states and the federal government other than slavery would have produced majority sentiment for secession anywhere, with the possible exception of South Carolina?

The *only* "states' right" that the southern states were sufficiently intent on perpetuating that they would destroy the Union and fight a war over it was the right to hold human beings as property—and that is not a right, but a wrong. Indeed, a favorite southern name for the Civil War, "the War for Southern Independence," has the matter just backward. It was actually the War for Continued Southern Dependence (on slave labor).

In the twentieth century, "states' rights" has usually been used as a smoke screen by those who wanted to maintain segregation. It was the rallying cry for Strom Thurmond's "Dixiecrats" in 1948, for Ross Barnett when his attempts to block the integration of the University of Mississippi in 1962 led to a riot in which two people were killed, for Birmingham's Eugene "Bull" Connor when he used dogs and water cannons on children the following year, and for George Wallace when he preached "Segregation forever."[14] The reason for such opposition to the federal government in the South, Bill Clinton said to me before he became president, "is that white folks think that the federal government caused all these racial problems. Busing and stuff like that—in the poor southern states." In the wealthier southern states, he argued, there is another factor. "The reason the Republican argument has such appeal is we knew we were paying taxes that were lower than the national average because of the natural resources that God put here. And so the government was a problem." But it was clear that Clinton attributed the greater part of southern white antipathy to the federal government to race.[15] For most of the history of the Republic, the concept of states' rights has been tightly tied with slavery, segregation, lynching, and racism, all of which are actually *states' wrongs*. The use of "states' rights" to describe these wrongs has tarnished a central concept of federalism.

We have to remember why many powers were taken over at the federal level in the first place. The federal government "didn't get involved in these things because we were eager for power," as Paul Simon said in our interview.[16] If the states had been doing an adequate job of protecting civil rights, the environment, working conditions, and other vital areas, the federal government would not have had to step in. It is unclear how various states would act now if these responsibilities were returned to their jurisdiction. "When you're talking about income maintenance for poor people," Barney Frank contends, "devolution to the states is just a way to make sure that the poor people will get screwed."[17] "Why do Republicans want to block grant welfare and school lunches?" Paul Begala asked rhetorically. "Answer: because they're not really for them. They say, 'Oh, no, no, no.' They're such pathetic liars."[18]

It is only in areas they do not care about that much that conservatives are urging that power be returned to the states. You don't hear conservatives arguing that abortion should be left up to the states. They don't even want to leave that up to the Congress. This is something they consider to be very important, and they want a constitutional amendment that would prevent state and federal government alike from deciding to allow abortions. What would be the reaction to letting states decide whether to permit slavery (as had been the case prior to the Thirteenth Amendment)? Most conservatives (although perhaps not some of the kooks on the right-wing fringe that they tolerate these days) would join with everyone else in rejecting this idea as absurd. How about basic civil rights? Only three decades ago leading conservatives (including Barry Goldwater, the man most of today's "conservatives" revere as their founding saint) were arguing that whether to allow segregation was a matter that should be left up to each state. It is essential that on issues of major national concern, federal standards be maintained.

"The president believes that a reconfiguration of the federal system is, within limits, positive and long overdue," Bill Galston said to me. "On the other hand, he has to draw the line at such things as the notion that there will be no federal safety net for children. [There are] truly national commitments that cannot be left to local discretion."[19]

Whenever conservatives suggest that something be turned over to the states, they are thereby saying that they do not consider it an essential national concern. An example: House Republicans voted in 1995 to end national standards for nursing homes, enacted eight years earlier, when investigations had found that many states were not protecting their elderly citizens from unscrupulous nursing home operators. It was a classic instance of why the federal government steps into an area being neglected by several states. And the federal regulation of nursing homes has worked well. There was no pressure from the major nursing home organizations for the lifting of federal standards. But the GOP ideologues believe in "states' rights," so they pushed forward (or, rather, backward) anyway.[20] They place a higher priority on their philosophy than on the interests of the nation's elderly citizenry.

A similar question arises over education. "The national government has never fully embraced any responsibility in terms of preparing the next generation of children in the country," Rep. Chaka Fattah said to me. "And this is in our *national* interest. This notion that education is a local prerogative and that people in some township can figure out how smart or dumb they want their children to be, and that it should be nobody else's business, is a notion that is not responsive to what we see in terms of our economic competitors abroad."[21]

There are, to be sure, states' rights ideologues who are even more extreme than those who let ideology stand in the way of assuring decent living conditions for Grandma. George Will uncovered a group called the Southern League, whose more than one thousand members are dedicated to "the cultural, social, economic, and political *independence* and well-being of the Southern people." They maintain that Woodrow Wilson's concept of "self-determination of peoples" should apply within the United States, and that states or regions should have the right of secession. Members and sympathizers are instructed to say "divisible" as loudly as they can when they reach the "one nation, indivisible" part, if they "absolutely must recite the 'Pledge of Allegiance' to the flag of our Yankee conquerors." The organization hails the dissolution of the Soviet Union and Yugoslavia and cheers on the Quebec separatists.[22]

Obviously it would be unfair to judge more mainstream "devolution" advocates on the basis of the kooky goals of this Southern League. It is fair to wonder, though, how many of the more extreme foot soldiers of the Republican Revolution in the House would refuse to repudiate this and similar groups. "No enemies on the right."

Do we really want to look forward to the day when, like "the former Soviet Union" and "the former Yugoslavia," we will hear people speak of "the former United States"?

THE DEMOCRATIC RESPONSE TO "DEVOLUTION"

In those domains where it is now decided that the federal government can step back out, it will be necessary to keep a watchful eye to be sure that the states do not once again abandon their less powerful citizens in order to aid Special Interests. If such care is taken, there is much to be said for transferring *some* powers and responsibilities back to the states. They can, after all, be used (as they were during the Progressive Era at the beginning of the twentieth century) as experimental laboratories to find better ways to solve problems. The Clinton administration is already encouraging this. It has provided waivers for more than half the states to try innovations in welfare.

The benefits of having government genuinely close to the people cannot be denied. Madeline Kunin told me that every time she returns to Vermont, she notices that "there is less anger and skepticism there. Predominantly because it's a scale thing. So there are people who don't feel this sense of being disconnected from their government to the same degree. I think when people feel that they understand the government and that they can have input into the decisions and get a response, then the political process obviously has much more of a chance of working," she said. "I think somehow we've got to get that [feeling] on the national level, and I don't know exactly how you do that, except maybe to build up from the grassroots."[23]

Secretary of Education Dick Riley said to me that, while he and President Clinton, as former governors, "have a very strong belief that education is a state responsibility and a local function," they also recognize that it is "a very important and serious national priority." He suggested that there are responsible and irresponsible kinds of block grants, and that the Goals 2000 Educate America Act "is what I call a responsible block grant." He explained that Congress adopted eight broad goals and "the funds go down for education improvement—not for basic education costs like teachers' pay; that is a state and local function—but for education improvement reform. And the states, then, to qualify for the money, just have to develop their own plan, their own standards, their own system aligned to those standards and then the accountability is the testing that takes place on the state and local level. And then parents can know whether the money is being spent properly or it is not." The critical thing that differentiates a "responsible" block grant from a foolhardy one, Riley said, is "accountability and broad standards or purposes for the funds, as opposed to just sending a check to the state, which is kind of what these folks [Republicans] are interested in and saying, 'spend it on education.' That's not enough. In my judgment, the federal government that taxes the people and takes the money here, should, where possible, be very supportive of money going down to the state and local government to get close to the people to perform the function, but to send down with it clear goals or purposes that the money has to be spent for and then some significant accountability of results."[24]

Senator Simon offered other examples of how and why federal standards are set. "We had a lot of public schools that said, 'If you're blind or deaf or in a wheelchair, sorry. We can't help you.' We had a majority of mentally retarded not getting help. So we said, 'you have to help everybody.' I am not about to hand this money back to the states and say, 'you just do what you want, whether it's that or school lunches or other things.'" "I am not an enthusiast for block grants and I will give you a practical example [of why]," Simon said. "We did block grant a few educational programs including school libraries. In the state of California, within the last few years half of the libraries have closed. During the whole Depression, not a single library in the nation closed. You withdraw that federal support and, even though it's not a huge amount of the total, it is enough to hurt, and it signals that this is not a priority."[25]

Paul Wellstone told me that he is convinced that the Republicans have tapped into a "mood piece" in the nation with their talk of devolution. "It is genuine, legitimate, and I think that it is a thoughtful and important critique." But he said that what the Republicans are doing with it is "a con because it's a bait and switch. What they actually want to do is move the federal government out of setting any kind of standards, so that they can take issues of race, gender, and poverty and make them a matter of local option as to whether anything is done or not. That's not acceptable," he rightly declared. "They also want to take out the revenue. They want to cut federal taxes dramatically. That's the con. It will get shifted to property taxes. It's fine to say 'streamline; get it closer to the people; get the people more involved.' I think that should be our language, too. But it's quite another thing to emasculate Medicare or Medicaid or nutrition programs. Some states may say, 'fine,' but other states are not going to walk away from those people, in which case, they are going to have to pay for it."[26]

"I think we have to be selective," was David Bonior's response to a question about what attitude Democrats should take toward transferring powers to the states. "I think this wholesale shift is crazy. I think it runs over basic standards that are important to have. I mean, the children in Michigan should have just as good an opportunity as a kid in Texas and vice versa. And that is all going to go by the wayside," the House Democratic Whip contended. "In some areas, we need to do that experiment and try and see what happens, but I think this wholesale return to the states thing is too much, too fast."[27]

Several Democrats with whom I discussed this matter said that the corruption and inefficiency that people complain about in Washington will only be worse if money and power are transferred to the states. "The ethical standards up here [in Washington] are much higher than they are in 'most any state capital. It's just the nature of the scrutiny," Paul Begala maintained.[28] "People tend to talk about corruption in government, but if you want to see corruption you just send all this money back to the states and you are going to see another level of that," Bonior said. "We are also going to see another level of bureaucracy in the states."[29]

Begala said that the sort of anecdotes that Republicans have used with such effect to discredit the federal government are far more plentiful at the state level. "In one state, they used a block grant to teach braille sculpting. You know, rub each other's bodies to learn how to sculpt. In another state, they used black crayons to study why prisoners want to escape from prison. Now these are the sorts of anecdotes that used to fuel Republican antigovernment sentiments for Reagan. There's another one they found in Delaware County, Pennsylvania, which is an all-Republican machine. They took the block grants and they were using it for banquets and trips to Broadway shows, and you know, it was supposed to be to feed the poor. You see, I worked at the Texas legislature, and I know a little bit about how state government actually works."[30]

Besides the corruption at the state level, Begala pointed to another problem. In their attempts to save money, Republicans want to give out block grants based on the number of people in a state who were receiving a particular service in 1990. "We can't have a block grant which says that according to the 1990 Census, there were *x* number of learning-disabled children in Florida, so we're going to give you that much [each year until the next census]," Begala contends. "I just got a letter from a woman who teaches disabled kids in Florida. She says, (and she was the teacher of the year in Florida), 'Look, if they block that, my program is dead. Tallahassee is growing by leaps and bounds. They want to block according to the 1990 Census. My class is so much bigger than 1990 today, and they want us to operate on an immediate cut. Can you imagine what it will be like in 1999, and they wouldn't change the block until 2003, 2002—something like that. It's impossible.' She would be out of business. And these kids. You know that's why they are trying to do it, though. Because they want to cut it."[31]

It should be noticed that the argument that it is the intervention of the federal government in areas that once were reserved for the states that has messed America up is a not-too-subtle appeal to latent (or nonlatent) racism. Mississippi Governor Kirk Fordice made this clear when he told the Republican Governors Association that the message of the 1994 elections was that "voters longed for the calmer days of the 1950s."[32] Those days may indeed have been calm, "Happy Days" for some of us, but the allure, conscious or otherwise, that the fifties hold for many is that it was a time when blacks—and women—acted as if they knew "their place."

The days of states' rights were not as wonderful as the doctrine's advocates would have us believe.

The key to achieving the ideal of keeping as much government as close to the people as possible is that states' rights must finally and decisively be detached from states' wrongs.

A REVOLUTION WITHOUT A CAUSE

Newt Gingrich is *both* a genuine revolutionary and a genuine reactionary.

But what he and his followers envision is a tall order. The previous American revolutions were based upon highly disruptive events. The War for Independence was the culmination of more than a century of *de facto* self-government for the colonies, followed by more than a decade of affronts to the independence to which the colonists had become accustomed. And then it took a war against the greatest military power in the world to accomplish the changes of the first American Revolution. The second and third American revolutions were achieved through the two most massive upheavals in American history: a fratricidal conflict that killed more than 600,000 Americans and an economic collapse that left a quarter of the workforce unemployed and many more in deprivation.

What contemporary disruption has occurred to provide the basis for another revolutionary metamorphosis? The Republicans have done a great job of disguising the fact that the electoral "earthquake" of November 1994 actually consisted of a 51–49 percent national margin of victory in the House of Representatives. This electoral "landslide" would not seem to be on quite the same scale as the monumental events of the Civil War or the Great Depression. (In fact, the 1994 nationwide House vote was only marginally different from that of ten years before, when the Democrats won slightly more than half the Congressional votes while Ronald Reagan was sweeping to a massive reelection victory. The principal differences between 1984, when the Democrats won a comfortable majority in the House, and 1994, when the Republicans did the same, was not to be found in the national vote itself, but in the distribution of that vote and the drawing of congressional districts.) And just after the conclusion of the miraculous Hundred Days of the Republican "Contract with America," a national poll found that 48 percent of Americans identified themselves more with the Democrats and 43 percent more with the Republicans. Those numbers swung more in the Democrats' direction as 1995 progressed.

Relatively few of those who voted Republican in 1994 were thereby endorsing the Gingrich contract. "I don't think that the people voted Republican last time," David Bonior said in a 1995 interview. "I think that they voted against Democrats. They didn't have any idea what the hell was in the contract. They were just mad at us—and justifiably so, because of health care."[33] Even after the House had passed most of the Republican contract, more than 50 percent of the American people said they had never heard of it.

Newt Gingrich may be a genuine revolutionary, but he does not have a genuinely revolutionary situation in which to bring about the dramatic changes he envisions.

THE REPUBLICAN VICTORY IN 1994

The question remains as to why the Republicans did as well as they did in 1994. One reason, surely, is that mentioned by Rosa DeLauro: "We got very comfortable; we didn't ever think we would lose the majority. We've got to face that." The conservative Republicans, she points out, had spent "the last forty years going through a philosophy and coming up with the words that they could use to quickly explain it to you." Democrats, meanwhile, were acting more and more like holding the majority in the House was their birthright. Because they have developed a philosophy and have been on the outside for so long, Republicans are Delauro says, "also willing to drive an agenda and do it with more discipline than we have done."[34] Many Democrats in Congress forgot that "there is a lot more to this than just eating right and exercising if you want to be chairman one day," Paul Begala says. "You've got to work for it. Too many of them did, in fact, become irrelevant."[35]

Another important factor in the Democratic debacle of 1994 was that, as Marcy Kaptur said to me, the gains that had been made by Democrats over their long control of the House "had come to be taken for granted by many voters."[36] Democrats, moreover, had for so long been warning Americans that Republican control of both houses of Congress would mean the end of Western civilization—or at least of Social Security, Medicare, and common decency—that many voters built up an immunity to such arguments. The Republicans gave people "a theory," Begala says. "We ran around in the end of the '94 campaign. All of our folks are running around saying, 'You let them in here. They're going to cut Medicare, Veterans, student loans, just like chicken liver.' I had these candidates come and say, 'pour it on, pour it on.' I'm looking them in the eyeballs and saying, 'you're not winning.' They don't believe me. They don't think it's going to happen. It was just like when George Bush waved his wallet and said, 'Let the Democrats come in, they'll tax you.' The voters response was: 'We'd like to change. We're willing to take that risk.'" Begala contends that voters suspended their concerns about Democrats in 1992 and did the same about Republicans in 1994. "Now," he told me in the spring of 1995, "they're saying that Chicken Little was right."[37]

Principally, the Republican victory in 1994 was caused by the same thing that led to the Democratic victory two years before: the Psychic Crisis of the Nineties. People are extremely anxious about their jobs, their wages, their health insurance, their retirement, their children. "There is no doubt that populism is in the air and that people feel kind of ripped off by both the economic and political system," Senator Wellstone said in a 1995 interview. "And people in the last election were in a downright anti-status-quo mood, a real change mood. But that begged the question of what kind of change." He made the point that "if you feel ripped off, if you're convinced that your children won't do as well as you and all of that, which is the truth if we keep going on the current path; if you feel the real squeeze and you just plain don't have a good feeling about your family's situation or where the country is going and the president is a Democrat and the majority of both houses are Democratic and you have a sort of politics of anger as the central dynamic of American politics, then the logical decision is to throw the bums out, right?"[38]

"That frustration is out there," agrees David Bonior when asked to explain the Democratic defeat (for such it clearly was, rather than a Republican victory) in 1994. "We didn't address it. We had a chance to deal with that on the trade issue, but we pushed it away. And we didn't address the income issues on the tax side in the first two years. You know, we said we were going to do a middle-class tax cut and we didn't do it. And they were looking forward to it. They wanted it. We said we were going to do a stimulus package. Well, we didn't do that either. Then we went out and we told them, we created four and a half million jobs. Well, they didn't believe us. Sixty percent of them thought that they were in a recession. And they were right, because their incomes were standing still."[39]

Prior to 1992, the issue had been gridlock, Congressman Joe Kennedy maintains. With Republican presidents and Democrats controlling Congress, "nothing got done. And finally the American people gave the Democrats the triple crown. They sort of said, 'fine; here's your day in the battle.'" Congressional Democrats and spokespersons for the Clinton administration "will go through a litany of accomplishments in that two-year period that will go from the Brady Bill to assault weapons to the fact that he got the budget reduced by 500 billion dollars and created 5 to 7 million new jobs, 90 percent in the private sector, was able to reduce the size of the federal government down to the level of the early 1960s," Kennedy said to me. "The litany of accomplishments goes on: a new crime bill, one hundred thousand new police officers, and the new education bills setting standards for American students."[40]

The list of achievements can sound impressive, but we need to remember that man (and woman) does not live by legislation alone. Most Democrats kept talking about economic issues, which are certainly of critical importance when people are terrified about losing their jobs. But a most interesting survey was taken for the *Wall Street Journal* and NBC a little over a month before the 1994 elections. It asked whether people thought that "the social and economic problems that face America today are mainly the result of" a) "a decline in moral values" or b) "financial pressures and strains on the family." Fifty-four percent said the problems were more caused by the decline in moral values, and thirty-four percent leaned toward financial pressures.[41] Even many of those who might have been pleased with what Clinton had done for the economy were focusing on other areas that gave them cause to be unhappy. "The trouble is people are sitting in their homes and they're watching as kids their children's age—my son's age—are being wheeled in and out of the city hospital every single night—and it's fifteen minutes every night at 6:00 and 11:00

on the news," Joe Kennedy said to me. "They know their kids are not getting educated in the school system. They watch as some mother drowns her children, and they watch O. J. Simpson and they watch a federal building being blown up. They look at that TV between 9:00 and 11:00 in the morning, and they watch mothers say they are sleeping with their daughters and fathers are sleeping with their sons, and they just go, 'This whole thing has gone cuckoo. The country is in chaos. Government can't do anything.' Then Gingrich comes along and says, 'This is a really bad, ugly picture and I can give you your ticket back; you can leave the theater and you can get your money back on the way out.' And people go crazy. He comes up with all of his programs, which nobody reads—I bet *nobody* could tell you what's in that 'contract.' He comes up with this agenda, but [the details] didn't make any difference."[42] People are just seeking something different.

PLAYING THE OTHER SIDE'S GAME

Beyond all this, the election of 1994 was a referendum, not only on the two years of Democratic control of all three legs of the legislative stool, but also, and first and foremost, a referendum on Bill Clinton. It was not Newt Gingrich and his contract that made it so; this undoing of Democrats was the doing of Democrats—in particular, Tony Coelho. "Tony . . . was the first person to urge strongly that we take a hard look at the Republican contract and use it to frame the elections as a collision between Reaganomics and Clintonomics," according to Deputy White House Chief of Staff Harold Ickes. "He was our key to focusing on it."[43]

It had been Newt Gingrich's idea to "nationalize" the 1994 congressional elections. (This is another odd thing for a "conservative" champion of states' rights to do.) No congressional elections in American history had really been nationalized before, although one party or the other had tried it from time to time. The foolish attempt of Woodrow Wilson to turn the congressional elections of 1918 into a referendum on his peace plan and League of Nations had backfired. "There's no question the strategy of trying to nationalize the election was a mistake," Democratic pollster Mark Mellman says of 1994.[44] The fact seems to be that it takes two to nationalize an election. Two parties, that is. Gingrich would not have been able to do it if the Democrats, at Coelho's behest, had not gone along. Most voters were clueless as to what Gingrich's contract really meant. If that had been the only national issue, politics would have stayed local and the Democrats would have retained their House majority, although with reduced numbers. But, while people didn't know what they thought of the Contract with America, they *did* know what they thought of Bill Clinton. When the Democrats said, in effect, *Yes, it is a national referendum, and we're putting up Clinton against the Contract*, a majority of the minority of Americans who voted opted for the pig in a poke. Disregarding the advice many of them had received at their mother's knee, they decided to take a chance on the devil they didn't know, rather than the one they felt they knew all too well. Clinton had not only appeared uncertain and without real convictions; he had also not delivered on any of the major promises that had gotten him elected: health insurance, welfare reform, and political reform. Some "Reagan Democrats" thought it was worse than that. "When Democrats of my stripe think of the Clinton presidency," Ben Wattenberg says, "a single word comes to mind: 'betrayal.'" The major reason why these people felt betrayed by Clinton was, I think, that he had allowed himself to be reidentified with the cultural elite and the "bad sixties." As Wattenberg sees it, in 1993–94 "Democrats, led by President Clinton, not only failed, but betrayed their promise."[45] From my perspective, this conclusion is too harsh, but I have a somewhat different philosophy from Wattenberg's. The fact that we both feel that Clinton strayed from what we expected of him speaks not only to Clinton's shortcomings, but also to the fragility of the Democratic coalition that he briefly and partially reassembled in the summer and fall of 1992.

Coelho, Clinton, and company helped the Republicans to make the 1994 elections a choice between "something (undefined) different" and "more of the same." Clinton should have known from his own experience two years before when he had been wearing the other ("something different") label, which way that decision goes in times of discontent.

Paradoxically, some Democrats may have lost this referendum on Clinton because they tried to run away from him—to distance themselves from their president. That had often worked in the past, when congressional elections were usually decided on local issues and personalities. But with a largely nationalized election in 1994, Democrats running away from Clinton were essentially saying to voters who had been persuaded that Clinton and their local Democratic candidate were on the same team: *Our team is wrong. I condemn our captain.* The logical thing to do, then, was to vote for the other team.

Paul Begala points out that Georgia Governor Zell Miller refused to abandon Clinton or deny his friendship with him and won, while across the South Democrats who tried to avoid any association with Clinton were dropping like roaches in an insecticide commercial. Begala contrast's Miller's victory with Jim Cooper's Senate race in neighboring Tennessee. Cooper ran away from—virtually *against*—the Clinton administration in the home state of Vice President Gore and wound up being crushed. Cooper got about 39 percent of the vote in a state that Begala correctly characterizes as "much more progressive than Georgia."[46]

A CHOICE, NOT AN ECHO

A related foolish tactic used by some Democrats was not only to denounce their own president, but also to repudiate their own beliefs and pretend to be "conservatives." In Mississippi's first congressional district, a seat that had been occupied by Democrat Jamie Whitten since 1941, a progressive state legislator, Bill Wheeler, won the Democratic nomination. As it happens, Wheeler is a former student of mine and a good friend. I know what he actually believes. He tried to reinvent himself to suit what he thought voters wanted, painting himself as a social conservative, while maintaining his genuine economic populism. He proclaimed himself pro-life and, although he had been very active in the 1992 Clinton campaign, declared that he did not think President Clinton deserved reelection on the basis of what he had done in his first two years. Wheeler lost by about as much as it is possible to lose by, getting only about 31 percent of the votes against Roger Wicker, who would go on to be the head of the soon-to-be-notorious freshman Republicans in the House. Surely Wheeler could not have done worse by saying what he believed. Voters do not always spot a phony, but pretending to be what you obviously are not does not usually win elections; it only makes another contribution to cynicism.

That there were so many Democrats cross-dressing as Republicans accounts for some of the party's losses in 1994. Give the voters a choice between two Republicans, as the saying goes, and they're going to pick the Republican every time. Voters want, as Barry Goldwater and his backers used to say from the other side, "a choice, not an echo." Most of the Democrats who lost their seats in 1994 were the ones who most closely echoed Republican themes. Progressive Democrats generally held their seats while the conservative flood was washing away many of their moderate-to-conservative colleagues.

Part of the explanation both of the progressive Democrats doing better than moderates and of the large loss of Democratic seats when the national vote was so close is redistricting. The maximization of minority representation in the House by concentrating minority voters in districts that are 60 percent or more minority drained normally Democratic voters from other districts and left many white Democratic representatives, especially in southern states, with new constituencies with Republican-leaning majorities. The consequences of this race-based redistricting are evident in several southern states. The case of Georgia is most dramatic. In the 101st Congress, the Georgia delegation to the House consisted of eight white Democrats, one black Democrat, and one white Republican (an impudent, heavyset young man named Gingrich). In the 104th Congress, Georgia sent three black Democrats and eight white Republicans to the House (even while reelecting Democratic Governor Zell Miller). The composition of the North Carolina House delegation changed over the same period from eight white Democrats and three white Republicans to two white Democrats, two black Democrats, and eight white Republicans.

The massacre of the moderates (and conservatives) in the Democratic congressional ranks in 1994, whatever its cause, furthered the polarization of the parties. It came exactly twenty years after a similar phenomenon occurred in the Republican ranks. The post-Watergate election of 1974, in which the recently resigned and pardoned Richard Nixon played something of the nationalizing role that Bill Clinton did in 1994 (although Republicans at that time were not foolish enough to add to their troubles by agreeing that the election was a national referendum on their disgraced president), "cost the Republicans virtually every congressional seat in which there was any sprinkling of liberal voters—finished off what remained of the party's moderates." This left a desolate, depopulated Republican landscape in Congress that archconservatives could (and did) occupy later in the decade.[47] Much the same prospect confronts progressive Democrats in Congress after the party's 1994 catastrophe.

THE DEMOCRATIC FUTURE

The consequences of the 1994 election remain unclear as I write this a little more than a year later. They do not seem entirely bad for Democrats. "From a purely Clinton perspective," Begala maintains, "losing the Congress was a liberating thing."[48] This comment suggests two troubling points: First, it seems that Clinton may be looking at Democrats in Congress much the way some of them looked at him in 1994: as a millstone best discarded before facing the electorate. The second troubling implication of Begala's comment is that it suggests that the only pure perspective Clinton and his advisers have is winning reelection. That goal may well have been advanced by the loss of Congress. Surely progressive policy objectives—the sorts of things that would help the American people—were not at all helped by the Republican victory; not, at least, in the short run. In order to succeed at the polls, Democrats need to come together, and they need to focus on philosophy and policy, not on polling booths.

The good that can blow for Democrats and progressives from the ill wind of the Republican victory in 1994 is that it can help to wake them up, unify them, and force them to develop new ideas and a new vision that can help both the party and the nation. The Republican takeover has certainly made plain to Democrats and the general public what the stakes are. There can no longer be any doubt that it *does* make a difference which party controls Congress. (Amidst the flood of polling numbers, one will occasionally jump out that is very significant. One that may fit that category is the finding by the Times Mirror Center that "the percentage of Democrats saying that there are real differences between the two parties rose from 28 percent in 1994 to 41 percent" in late 1995.[49]) The Republican agenda also shows Democrats what can be accomplished when a party holding the majority unifies around a set of objectives. And it makes it easier for Democrats to achieve some degree of unity, at least while they are in the minority. "Blocking, rather than creating, tends to be, at least mechanically, easier to do," as David Bonior pointed out.[50]

A year after the 1994 elections, polls indicated that a growing majority of Americans realized that they had made a mistake when they cast their ballots. But the psychic crisis was, if anything, deepening, and politics continued to be extremely volatile. No one could say with any assurance in which direction the loose cannon of public opinion might fire for the remainder of the decade.

What we *can* say, though, is what the "revolutionaries" of the Grand New(t) Party would do if given the opportunity. It is to those contours of the proposed fourth American revolution that I shall turn in the next chapter.

8

It's the Same Old Meaning with a Different Song: The Grand New(t) Party's Vision

Big Business Strikes it Rich

"Anybody who thought the greed decade ended several years ago hasn't yet had time to study the new balanced-budget proposals put forward by the U.S. Senate and the U.S. House." Thus did Republican political analyst Kevin Phillips, the man who defined "the emerging Republican majority" in 1968, castigate the new leadership of his party in May 1995. If there really were a budget crisis, Phillips pointed out, "we'd be talking about shared sacrifice, with business, Wall Street and the rich, the people who have the big money, making the biggest sacrifice." But that's not at all the way the Grand New Party proposed to deal with the budget crisis. "Instead," as Phillips said, "it's senior citizens, the poor, students, and ordinary Americans who'll see programs they depend on gutted, while business, finance, and the richest one or two percent, far from making sacrifices, actually get new benefits and tax reductions."[1]

"Businesses struck it rich during the first 100 days [of the new Republican Congress]," the *Wall Street Journal* reported in April 1995. "They're just not sure how rich."[2]

If that sounds a lot like the old Republican ideal of redistributing income from the poor and middle class to the affluent, it is for good reason. What the Republicans' allegedly new ideas amount to is the same old meaning with a different song.

The tune was the same as that the Reagan administration had sung in 1981. Then, Budget Director David Stockman had admitted that the tax reductions for the middle class were "a Trojan horse to bring down the top rate."[3] The objective of Republicans in the mid-nineties is to use the genuine need to reduce budget deficits as their Trojan horse. Phillips rightly identified his party's putative concern for deficit reduction as "a pretext for fiscal favoritism and finagling," aimed at "further upward income distribution." This, of course, is just the goal that "conservatives" from Alexander Hamilton through Ronald Reagan had sought. The new GOP plans amount to more of the same. "In short," Phillips concluded, "aid to dependent grandmothers, children, college students, and city dwellers is to be slashed, while aid to dependent corporations, stockbrokers, generals, and assorted James Bond imitators survives or even grows."[4] Mario Cuomo put it succinctly when he termed the Gingrich agenda "déjà voodoo."[5]

Small wonder that the Republican leaders tried to rush their budget through so quickly that few people would comprehend what was going on. Giving no time for examination, serious discussion, or deliberation on a proposal that they said would revolutionize America by reversing policies and trends built over decades, House Republicans voted their approval of the budget only eight days after it was introduced. The Senate took barely a week longer. The Republicans held one hearing on their plan to perform radical surgery on Medicare.

How does the pell-mell pace of the revolution guided by self-styled "conservatives" square with the fact that, in the words of Harvard sociologist Daniel Bell, "the oldest piece of conservative wisdom is to do things slowly"?[6]

HAMILTON LIVES!

"There are two ideas of government," William Jennings Bryan contended a century ago in his famous 1896 "Cross of Gold" speech. "There are those who believe that, if only you will legislate to make the well-to-do prosperous, their prosperity will leak through on those below. The Democratic idea, however," Bryan continued, "has been that if you legislate to make the masses prosperous, their prosperity will find its way up through every class which rests upon them."[7] No clearer statement of the most fundamental difference in the philosophies of the two major American parties has ever been made. There can, moreover, be no serious question that the basic Republican outlook remains the same in 1996 as Byran described it in 1896. We know it today as "trickle-down economics." There was nothing new about it in Bryan's day, let alone in Ronald Reagan's or Newt Gingrich's.

"The Republicans have for generations been the party that did not support the right of ordinary people to advance themselves—they opposed

Social Security, unemployment compensation, unions, work-study, and so forth," Marcy Kaptur reminds us. They haven't changed: "They want to put people into a free-market sea, without a boat to sail on."[8]

It is worth demonstrating just how "un-new" the "revolutionary" program of the Republicans is. A little more than two hundred years ago, in 1791, Treasury Secretary Alexander Hamilton issued the capstone of his fiscal program, the Report on Manufactures, which provided a rationale for the policies he had promoted over the previous two years.[9] Hamilton was clearly the American author of what later came to be called "trickle-down" economics. The idea that the central objective of government ought to be to make the rich richer has been the basic thrust of conservative political parties in this country from Hamilton's Federalists through Henry Clay's Whigs and William McKinley's Republicans of Bryan's era down to the present. The Reaganites gave this hoary theory a new name when they spoke of "supply-side economics," and Gingrich and his followers now dub the same idea "revolutionary." Nothing has changed today except the populist lyrics that right-wingers now sing in order to obscure the fact that their basic intentions still have the same old meaning.

Hamilton's intention was to promote economic development; his method was to concentrate wealth and income in the hands of the rich. The justification for this policy was—as it has remained ever since—that if money were spread out among the masses of people, they would use it for such unproductive purposes as eating and paying the rent. But additional income directed to those who were already wealthy would not be needed for such functions and so could be used for investment.

It is clear that the "modern" Republican economic programs, from Reagan to Gingrich, have been based upon precisely the same assumptions as those that guided Hamilton two centuries ago. The tax cuts of the eighties (like those proposed by Republicans in the nineties) were directed toward the upper-income brackets, with very Hamiltonian results. While the rate of federal taxation on the richest one-fifth of Americans fell by 5 percent during the eighties, for the poorest one-fifth, the rate rose by 15 percent. As I noted in Chapter 1, between the beginning of the Carter administration in 1977 and the end of Reagan's second term in 1989, the richest one percent of American families received 70 percent of all the gain in income, and the top 20 percent received 100 percent of the income growth, leaving *nothing* for the remaining 80 percent of American families—all of middle-class and poor Americans. The lower 40 percent actually saw their incomes decline, after adjustment for inflation.[10]

Unfortunately, the increased productive investment that both Hamilton and Reagan had promised as a result of making the rich richer was not forthcoming from the Reagan upward redistribution of the eighties. Instead, America's wealthy used their soaring incomes to support ever more luxurious lifestyles and to make short-term profits from paper manipulations that produced no genuine wealth.

All of this has come to be widely recognized, but there is a much clearer indicator of the triumph of the thinking of Alexander Hamilton among late-twentieth-century Republicans. The unprecedented federal deficits of the eighties and early nineties made debt service the fastest-growing segment of the federal budget. Interest payments have surpassed military spending to become the largest portion of federal spending that is supported by general revenues. (This excludes Social Security and Medicare, which are financed by separate taxation.)

There should be no confusion about where the bulk of these interest expenditures go—or about where they have always been *intended* to go: to the same worthy beneficiaries that Hamilton sought for federal spending in his day. Hamilton wanted debt service to be the major item of federal spending, since interest payments would go mainly to the wealthy people he sought further to enrich. Most of interest spending still goes to such people. While unscrupulous politicians try to turn the middle class against the poor by telling the former that their taxes are going into welfare payments to the latter, the fact is that the largest area of government spending has been what amounts to transfer payments from the middle class to the rich, both at home and abroad. Republicans complain about foreign aid, but we spend more on interest payments to wealthy foreign investors than we do on foreign aid for all other purposes.[11] In Hamilton's budget plan, interest payments on the federal debt constituted a whopping 80 percent of federal expenditures. We have not gotten to that point, but it is not for lack of effort on the part of the Republican representatives of bondholders. By the end of the Bush administration, debt service had increased as a percentage of federal spending (exclusive of Social Security) from less than 13 percent when Reagan took office to more than 20 percent.

Of course, the new Republicans of the revolution are trying to balance the budget. That might give the appearance of going against this analysis, but it really does not. Once again, this is part of the falling of the second shoe of what began when the Reagan administration created the massive deficits. It was obvious that the huge deficits could not go on forever, but without them the Republicans would have neither their rationale for attacking social spending nor the huge interest payments to bondholders. Were it not for the debt run up by the Reagan and Bush deficits, the budget would already have been in balance in 1995, when the Republicans began their crusade to balance the budget in seven years.

This is one of those points that has generally escaped notice, but is of enormous importance, so it needs to be reemphasized: *Had Ronald Reagan and George Bush not followed policies that more than tripled the national debt in twelve years, there would be* no *deficit today*. The total annual deficit in the mid-nineties is less than the interest on the portion of the debt that was accumulated under Reagan and Bush, so *all* of the current deficit is being spent on interest payments, most of them going to wealthy investors. But eliminating that part of the budget is not an option. We must meet our obligations. Hence the rationale for cutting elsewhere. As spending in other areas declines, interest payments will not. They *can*not, other than fluctuations caused by changing interest rates, unless the debt itself is decreased, and I have heard no Republican suggestions that we begin running a federal surplus after 2002 in order to pay down the debt. So the share of federal spending going to bondholders will continue to increase. Less and less federal money will go to the poor; more and more will go to the rich. It seems safe to assume that interest will never reach the 80 percent of federal spending mark that was Hamilton's goal, but the trend that his ideological descendants have established in the 1980s and '90s must have the ghost of the Founding Father of American trickle-down economics smiling.

TURNING BACK THE CLOCK?

"There is one thing about those guys," Senator Bumpers said to me of the radical Republicans. "They know exactly where they are going. The chore of Democrats is to tell the American people where they are going."[12] Providing such an itinerary for the journey to the America after the Republican Revolution is the main purpose of this chapter.

The Republican-dominated 104th Congress "is trying to overturn sixty years of people's history," Paul Wellstone said. Their agenda is "much more far-reaching, much more extreme, much more of an effort to turn back the clock" than was Ronald Reagan's program.[13] There can be no question that in many areas, they *are* trying to turn back the clock. "The Republicans are always talking about how great it was fifty years ago or twenty years ago—let's go recreate that," Joe Kennedy said in our interview.[14] This argument tries to take advantage of the human tendency toward nostalgia. The past usually takes on a glow as it recedes, and Republicans are trying to identify themselves with those fond memories. But there may be a little more to it than just exploitation of nostalgia. They may be, as I suggested in discussing "states' rights" in the last chapter, making a subtle appeal to something else, as well. There is always a constituency in America for turning the clock back on race relations to a time when blacks "knew their place" and were kept in it, and that constituency becomes larger if the appeal to racism is made subtly.

Yet in one sense, the Republicans are not trying to turn back the clock. In some ways, they really are trying to do something never before done in this country. "We don't just *call* these people extremists; they *are* extremists," Bumpers rightly maintains. "They have values that if we had accepted them throughout our history—as the president says, if our leaders had tried to divide this country for the past two hundred years like they are trying to do now, we'd be a third-class nation. And so we are now in a position of constantly calling to the attention of the American people that these people really do look out for the rich and they don't care about you."[15]

The Republican Revolution is bloodless for some, but quite bloody for others. Under the GOP plans, everybody gets cut, but only the poor and the middle class will bleed. The cuts they receive are in programs they need; the rich get cuts in their taxes. One assumes those cuts will not hurt so much. The Republicans maintained that their proposal for a $500 per child tax credit would be a boon to ordinary families. For many, it would be a help. But the wonderful-sounding tax credit would help only those families who make enough to owe taxes. The working poor and lower middle class would be left out. A family of four earning up to about $25,000 a year doesn't pay federal income taxes. What would these struggling families that do not earn enough to pay income taxes—families in which a third of all American children live—receive from the Republican tax cut? Nothing.[16] Well, that's not quite accurate. They would receive *less* than nothing, because another part of the GOP budget proposal was to cut the Earned Income Tax Credit in half. A working family might *lose* nearly $500 per year, while wealthy investors receive a windfall from a cut in the capital gains tax. This is just another example of how, at a time when the United States is already experiencing the greatest income disparity in the industrialized world—a situation that threatens to reduce us to the status of a Third World country—"every single policy the Republicans are championing exacerbates that very problem," Bumpers says.[17]

Ultimately it must be recognized that the Republican Revolution is not a turnaround from the direction we have been going in the last twenty-five years—toward an ever-growing gap between the rich and the rest. Rather, it is a stomping on the accelerator to rush faster in that dangerous and mistaken direction.

WALL STREET SOCIALISM

What the Republicans seek is not, contrary to what they advertise, a weak government. "The Republicans premise their arguments on the idea that government doesn't work," Paul Begala said to me. "But they know that government *does* work; they just want it work for *their* interests. It looks like Carl Lewis in the 100-yard dash—if you're powerful. If you're wealthy, if you're privileged, if you're an S&L that needs bailing out—then it hunts."[18] Republicans seek what they have long sought. To borrow Michael Harrington's wonderful construction, they want "socialism for the rich and free enterprise for the poor." "Who decides to cut nutrition programs for children, but not subsidies for oil companies?" Senator Wellstone asks.[19]

Kevin Phillips's name for the same phenomenon is "Wall Street socialism," under which the risks of the free market are to be borne by workers who lose their jobs in corporate mergers or downsizing (no government help for them; after all, they need to learn to be self-reliant), but when stock- and bondholders (who, presumably, are already admirably self-reliant and so need no more lessons to help them develop this trait) face adversity, say when Chrysler is going under or the Mexican peso collapses, the government steps in to bail them out. *Their* risk is socialized; not so that of ordinary folks.[20] Health insurance? That's socialism! Job insurance? Are you kidding—this is America! Peso insurance for Wall Street? ¡*Si*!

Republicans seek a government similar to what the O. J. Simpson trial (as well as numerous less noticed trials) indicated the justice system is. The "O. J. Government" Republicans desire is one that responds to those who have enough money to hire the best lawyers and lobbyists. Everyone else is on his or her own.

Why, it is reasonable to wonder, are Republicans so intent on *increasing* military spending, beyond even what the Pentagon says it wants, when the Soviet Union has imploded and the United States has no major military rivals on the planet? Why spend *more* on military hardware in the midst of the slashing of domestic spending and when their contention is that their first priority is balancing the budget? The only reasonable answer is that they like defense contractor welfare because they like these big businesses as much as they like other major corporations, especially when they make large contributions to GOP coffers. Thus the Republicans (with the help of some Democrats) voted in the spring of 1995 to build twenty additional B-2 "stealth" bombers, which the Defense Department did not want, at a total cost of $38 billion (nearly $2 billion for *each* plane—or, in the words of Secretary of Defense William Perry, each "white elephant"). But the Republicans decided that Northrup-Grumman is among the truly needy wards of the state and voted to shower billions on this big contributor. Then the House voted a 21 percent increase in the amount the Clinton administration had requested for continued work on Star Wars.[21] (Why the administration wanted *anything* further to be spent on this Reagan illusion is a good question.) The Republicans justified the increases they voted in military spending by saying that it is necessary for "readiness." Representative Patsy Mink asks a relevant question: "Readiness for *what*?"[22] Space invaders, perhaps?

It should not be thought that corporate welfare and other federal goodies dispensed to Republican constituents are an insignificant part of the federal budget problems. A single new federal farm assistance program enacted in the first year of Ronald Reagan's presidency *tripled* federal aid to "farmers" (a term that often means "agribusiness"). This increase alone cost the federal government almost three times as much between 1981 and 1986 as did Aid to Families with Dependent Children over the same period.[23]

CORPORATE WELFARE KINGS

But it should never be forgotten that by far the largest and most sacrosanct federal income redistribution program that Republicans use to transfer income from the middle class to the wealthy is the debt itself. In the mid-1990s, as Senator Paul Simon points out, the gross federal interest expenditure of more than a third of a trillion dollars was twice as much as the aggregate of all money spent on all poverty programs and eleven times as much was being spent on interest as on education.[24] For all the Republican complaints about money going to "welfare queens," the largest share of federal spending was going to those the GOP deems to be the worthy rich—"corporate welfare kings," we might christen them.

The fact is that while the Republicans talk about the necessity of "sacrifice" to balance the budget, the only folks they have in mind to make the offerings are those on the lower rungs of the economic ladder, few of whom voted for their party. Bill Clinton noted this same approach in the Reagan years when he said to me that the Reagan cuts were not tough choices because "there were a lot of interest groups opposing, but none of them were responsible for his [Reagan's] election."[25] In their post-1994 revolution, the Republicans have followed the same course of least resistance: they "have taken care of their own and penalized those who tend to vote Democratic," *Time* noted in its discussion of Gingrich as "Man of the Year" for 1995.[26]

The Republicans are using a time-honored and highly objective way to distinguish good special interests from bad special interests. It involves asking two questions: Did they support us? If so, how much did they contribute? House GOP Whip Tom DeLay "actually keeps a book in his office listing how much the 400 largest special-interest PACs gave to either party in the past two years and makes sure contributors to the Democrats are marked down in his book as 'unfriendly.'"[27] If such an approach was good enough for Tony Coelho . . . . If someone is going to be asked to sacrifice, it might as well be those who oppose us.

In addition to wanting government to help the rich and powerful, but not help the poor, Republicans also want a government that does not bother their big-business friends, but can keep workers from causing any trouble. They want, in short, a government that is weak in controlling the strong and strong in controlling the weak. An excellent historical example of this comes from that similar decade a century ago. In 1895, the Republican-dominated Supreme Court handed down two critical decisions involving the Sherman Antitrust Act, which had been passed five years earlier to calm the public outrage at monopolies. First, in the case of *The United States* v. *E. C. Knight Co.*, the high court ruled against the government's claim that the defendant's virtual monopoly of sugar refining constituted a violation of the act by holding that its provisions applied only to commerce and that manufacturing is distinct from commerce. Then, in a case involving the use of the Sherman Act against the American Railway Union, the court ruled in *In Re Debs* that the government's interest in interstate commerce permitted injunctions against unions whose strikes and/or boycotts disrupted commerce. The net outcome of these two rulings was that manufacturing monopolies were placed beyond the government's power to regulate or break up, while unions were, in effect, held to be labor trusts whose actions could be regulated by the government. This is exactly the sort of government that Republicans have generally sought over the years. Certainly it is the kind they covet today. Then for good measure, the justices ruled in *Pollock* v. *Farmers' Loan and Trust Co.* that a federal income tax is unconstitutional. The next year, the Court upheld state-imposed segregation in the infamous case of *Plessy* v. *Ferguson*.[28] Within a little more than a year, the Court had proclaimed that the Sherman Antitrust Act applies to unions but not to manufacturing monopolies, that the Constitution does not permit a federal income tax, and that the Fourteenth Amendment does not prohibit segregation. *Ah*, many of the Republican "revolutionaries" of the 1990s, must sigh, *those were the days! Forget the 1950s; let's restore the 1890s!*

AMENDMENTITIS

Speaking of the Fourteenth Amendment, it might not seem that today's radical Republicans have much in common with their namesakes from the Reconstruction Era. But there are a couple of similarities. Most important is that both realized the importance of writing their reforms into the Constitution. The Newt Gingrich Republicans of the 1990s, like the Thaddeus Stevens Republicans of the late 1860s, want to write into the Constitution protections for their favorite minority. That favorite Minority is the wealthy. The Radicals who oversaw the Reconstruction that completed the second American Revolution sought to protect the African-American minority with the Thirteenth, Fourteenth, and Fifteenth Amendments (of course, the obliging Supreme Court soon ruled that the Fourteenth Amendment provided little protection for blacks, but much protection for the favorite Republican Minority, corporations).

The wealthy have long realized the importance of writing their protections into the Constitution. The minority whose rights and interests James Madison had been most intent on protecting when the Constitution was drawn up was property holders.

The radical Republicans who now seek a different sort of reconstruction as the culmination of their hoped-for fourth American Revolution are not content with depending on legislation, which might readily be reversed when the majority in Congress changes. Curiously, for people who still call themselves "conservatives," they seem ready to amend the Constitution over anything that troubles them, such as abortion or flag burning. More significant, though, are their proposed balanced-budget amendment and the talk of an amendment to repeal the Sixteenth Amendment, thus making federal income taxes unconstitutional. Such amendments would provide greater protection for the goals of the fourth American Revolution than those of the third American Revolution ever had. The New Deal never placed any of its reforms into constitutional amendments, relying instead on legislation. This made its achievements less secure from assaults by political opponents than they would have been as constitutional amendments. The Republicans today realize this. That is why these self-styled conservatives have "amendmentitis."

The Gingrich radicals have also gone against the Constitution that conservatives generally praise by making—or, at a minimum, *trying* to make—the House of Representatives the center of the government. The Constitution, after all, was designed to quiet the passions of the recent revolution. If not counter-revolutionary, as some critics have charged, the Constitution was at least intended to provide a means of calming and channeling potentially revolutionary passions. The ardor would be allowed to rage in the House, but the Senate was fashioned as the "upper house," where cooler (less revolutionary) heads would prevail. We saw this plan of the Founders operate to some extent in 1995, but Newt Gingrich's intention was clearly to arrogate to the House (and specifically himself) as much power as possible. Again these radicals in conservatives' clothing think that they know better than the Founding Fathers.

THE NEW THEORY OF THE LEISURE CLASS

In an apparent attempt to demonstrate how much the economic system is a meritocracy, the Newt Age Republicans proposed in 1995 to raise the amount exempt from federal inheritance taxes from $600,000 to $750,000, at a cost of $27 billion over ten years. This benefit, like so much else these "revolutionaries" are trying to do, would help only the wealthiest 1 percent of Americans.[29] Actually, many Republicans would just as soon abolish inheritance taxes altogether, as Ronald Reagan had proposed. The Kemp Commission, a group of Republicans appointed by Speaker Gingrich and Majority Leader Dole in 1995 to come up with proposals to change the tax system advocated eliminating all taxes on estates (as well as on all other forms of income for which people do not have to work: interest, dividends, and capital gains).[30] The Republicans clearly feel the pain of the rich, many of whom display the great merit of having been born to wealthy parents. Doing away with inheritance taxes would have the effect of providing more opportunity for these deserving heirs and heiresses who had the superior initiative to chose their parents carefully. (This seems to be the true essence of the "Conservative Opportunity Society" that Gingrich and Associates are always talking about: increasing the opportunities of those who are already well-to-do.) Nothing could be more meritorious than being born into the right level of society. Just ask Malcolm "Steve" Forbes, Jr., who rode his father's millions and his proposal for a "flat tax" from obscurity into prominence in the 1996 field of Republican presidential aspirants. There's conservative opportunity for you! Under the Forbes version of trickle-down economics, wealth would trickle all the way down from Malcolm Forbes, Sr. to Malcolm Forbes, Jr., and then to his children. It is an "All in the Family" trickle-down proposal. Hearing "Junior" Forbes (he might have gotten farther with that nickname; it sounds even more populist than "Steve" does) call for a flat tax reminded me of a comment Senator George Norris, a progressive Republican from Nebraska, made about the 1926 tax cut bill pushed by Treasury Secretary Andrew Mellon, one of the richest men in the nation. "Mr. Mellon himself gets a larger reduction than the aggregate of practically all the taxpayers in the state of Nebraska," Norris remarked.[31] Forbes's plan to eliminate all taxation of income obtained without work is the New Theory of the Leisure Class. While opposing the Earned Income Tax Credit, Republicans are pushing what amounts to a 100 percent *Un*earned Income Tax Credit.

The flat tax is one of the most pernicious of the Republican proposals. Indeed, nowhere are the old objectives of the Republicans clearer in their "new" program than in their proposals for tax "reform." House Majority Leader Dick Armey's call for a flat tax, like that put forth by Forbes, not only would eliminate the fundamental principle of progressivity (the concept of progressive tax rates, by the way, has been so universally accepted that it was even endorsed by Calvin Coolidge), but would tax only *earned* income. Like Kemp, Forbes, and many other Republicans, Armey would not tax unearned income—interest, dividends, capital gains, inheritances—*at all.* (It may be germane to note that since 1979, income from property—dividends, interest, and rents—has risen three times faster than income from work.[32]) Nothing better demonstrates how radical the Republican leaders of the nineties really are.

The widespread support a "flat tax" enjoys in opinion polls as I write this is largely the result of an intentionally produced confusion in the public mind. Of course, most people favor both a simple tax and a fair tax. The radical proponents of the rich have skillfully sold the mistaken idea that *flat* is a synonym for both *simple* and *fair*. A flat tax certainly would be the former, but it is the antithesis of the latter. There is no reason whatsoever why a simple tax has to be flat. If people want simplicity in taxation, what needs to be removed are the myriad exemptions, exclusions, deductions, and so forth, *not* the progressive rate structure. A simple tax with progressive rates could be filled out on a postcard as easily as a flat tax could. Nor is there any connection between flat and simple in the other direction. Remove progressivity and leave the exemptions, incentives, etc., and you will have a flat but complicated tax that could take up as many pages and hours of record keeping and calculation as our current long form does.

Because of all the legerdemain the right wing has employed in retailing the flat tax, the truth needs to be reemphasized: *There is no connection between a flat tax and a simple tax.*

There are, however, connections between a fair tax and both a flat tax and a simple tax. In both cases, the relationship is basically an inverse one. A flat tax is inherently an *un*fair tax, since it is not based on ability to pay. And, sad to say, simplicity is also to a large extent inversely proportional to fairness. The complexity of the tax code is—potentially, at least—what makes it possible to take the various conditions of different taxpayers into consideration in fairly adjusting their tax burden. It is also the complexity (as well as the progressivity) of the tax code that makes it possible to provide incentives for socially desirable goals, such as home ownership or locating factories in areas were there is a great need for jobs.

So, from the progressive viewpoint, the first priority in taxation is fairness and the second is simplicity. From the viewpoint of the radical Right, the first priority is unfairness (flatness or regressivity) and the second is simplicity.

The program of the radical Right is actually that of the radical rich. If the American people let them get away with this transfer of the tax burden from the rich to the middle class, we will deserve what we get (or, rather, what we *lose*). They propose tax *deform*, not reform.

"CLASS WARFARE"–WHO'S ON THE OFFENSIVE?

"The question for both Democrats and workers is how did we allow the Republicans to get so successful in getting people to vote against their interests." George Stephanopoulos rightly says. "Shame on us for letting that happen when it does."[33]

One of the favorite means whereby Republicans have been advancing the interests of the already rich and powerful is to yell "class warfare" whenever Democrats say anything that might lead people to see what the real GOP agenda is about. "I think, basically, if the Republicans scream 'class warfare!' it means your argument is working," is the way Stephanopoulos put a point made repeatedly by Democrats interviewed for this book.[34] "The reason the Republicans squawk so much about 'class warfare' is that they know how effective it is," Barney Frank agreed.[35]

"Biggest crock I've ever seen" was Paul Begala's description of the Republican charges that Democrats are practicing "class warfare." "It's hard for me to believe that a 39.6 percent top marginal [income tax] rate constitutes class warfare," Begala said. "I mean, we ain't talking about no guaranteed maximum income the way Huey Long did." The Republicans "say it's class warfare that we don't want to go down to 17 percent."[36] Frank says that the Republican charge "is the vilest hypocrisy and demagoguery, because they keep trying to woo the middle class by beating up on the poor and helpless in this society."[37]

Begala contends, quite correctly, that it is the Republicans who have declared war on the lower class and much of the middle class. There is indeed a class war going on, but it is the Republicans and the rich who are on the offensive and the Democrats and the poor and middle class who are on the defensive. "The Republicans are the ones engaging in class warfare," Senate Democratic Leader Tom Daschle says. "Look at the attacks on the Earned Income Tax Credit, Medicaid, Medicare, student loans."[38] House Democratic Whip David Bonior points to other examples of class warfare by the Republicans and the rich. "The benefits in this country—the tax expenditures, the subsidies from the government, are going basically to the wealthiest 20 percent. People have to understand that they are not being given a fair shake."[39]

"It's a very good tactic that often works," Bernie Sanders says. "Unfortunately, the Democrats are not guilty of the charge." "The Republicans go on attacking the Democrats for perpetrating class warfare," Vermont's Congressman declares, "while at the same time the Republicans give huge tax breaks to the richest people in America and make savage cuts in dozens of programs which affect the middle class and the poor and the elderly." Sanders neatly characterizes this Republican tactic: "It's like smacking you in the head and saying, 'Jesus, you're a violent person! My hand hurts; what did you do to me?'"[40]

The Republican argument is as follows: When the rich get much richer and others see wages fall and job security evaporate, that does not fit the definition of class warfare. But when somebody points out that this is going on, *that's* class warfare. Cutting the capital gains tax (which benefits only about 7 percent of Americans, almost all of them well-to-do) and the Earned Income Tax Credit is not class warfare, but complaining about the consequences is. "The politics of envy," is another phrase the radical advocates of the rich like to employ in their attempts to dismiss the legitimate complaints about what they are doing. It was remarkable, though, how quickly Republican presidential hopefuls began to practice the same sort of politics when the adoption of class warfare rhetoric by Pat Buchanan seemed to be working early in 1996.

When he became his party's whip at the beginning of 1995, Bonior gave a speech to the House Democratic Caucus in which he told his colleagues: "Republicans are going to do three things: They will be hypocritical on reform; they will be excessive on social policy; and they will be greedy on economic policy. It is just their nature; they can't help it. And it's just going to happen."[41] Bonior was assuming that the "new" Republicans were not much different from the old. He was right.

What the Republicans are seeking to create and maintain is the same goal the party has long sought. James Carville describes it as a "bond market Nirvana, where we have literally no inflation, and an insecure, compliant workforce."[42] His partner Begala expands on the Republican objective: "A huge population of people who have no minimum wage—none whatsoever, who won't have safety requirements, none of that. We won't be able to sue if we get ripped off by a corporation, or if we get our arms chopped off in the hospital. And so, we'll just work cheap, mind our own business, and shut up." "I think that's the kind of world they want," Begala continues, "so there are a few people who are highly educated and highly skilled who can make it and really go to town and can be 'competitive.'"[43]

That's the kind of world a large segment of Republican leaders have always wanted. They are applying the same philosophy to government and people as their corporate allies are to business and people: All that matters is the bottom line; if people are hurt, that is not our concern. Early in his speakership, Gingrich invited small groups of CEOs from major corporations to dinner at the Capitol. The purpose, aside from stroking those who are the real constituency of these counterfeit populists, was to get advice on "downsizing" from executives who had undertaken major reductions in their corporation payrolls. Gingrich sees his goal of downsizing the government as analogous to the mission of the corporate axmen. The consensus of their advice: "when the bloodbath was over, they all wished they had done more."[44]

The only measure of value for the New(t) Republicans, as for most corporate leaders, is money, not human beings—which is to say that Republican values are actually value$.

Their song may sound new, but the meaning is the same as it has always been.

CONSUMPTION-ETHIC POLITICS

The extremism of many of the radical Republicans is hard to fathom. They appear to have adopted the strategy outlined by right-wing guru David Frum in his 1994 tract, *Dead Right*. They have identified themselves firmly with the Right (and almost nothing seems too far to the Right to be acceptable to the new GOP leadership). They shun the moderate positions George Bush and his administration (people Frum characterizes as "almost pathological moderates"[45]) often accepted. Frum criticized the Bush men of 1992 for trying to play both sides. Now the GOP is unmistakably identified with *one* side. With this identification (and with the psychic crisis making people impatient and desperate for change) the party obtained 51 percent of the nationwide vote in an off-year election with a low turnout at a time when an incumbent Democratic president was very unpopular. But that identification with the extreme Right may soon marginalize the Republicans.

Frum ridicules the Bush Republicans for just about every indication of common decency that appeared at their 1992 national convention. Disdainfully pronouncing that they were trying "to pull in every mush-minded voter" in the country, Frum complains about speakers at the convention favoring such silly policies as adequate pay for teachers, spending money for drug treatment, occasionally allowing environmental concerns to take precedence over profit, pursuing alternate fuels, and for supporting such things as civil rights laws, the Clean Air Act, Head Start, and federal assistance for mass transit. (Conservatives, Frum apparently believes, should let the masses transport themselves; the rich do it. *If they don't have a Mercedes, why don't they ride in a limousine?*) Frum also makes clear that he hates "trust-busters" (I guess he's never met a trust he didn't like) and the "meddlers" of the Justice Department's civil rights division, and he is horrified that it was under the Reagan administration that the Equal Employment Opportunity Commission began investigating sexual harassment.[46] What business is it of the government if a man wants to coerce sex from his employees or subordinates? It is—or would be, if the radical Right had its way—a free country—*very* free.

This is a revolutionary program, all right. But if the Republicans continue to follow it, it is likely to return them to minority status and keep them there for as long as they adhere to it. Those Frum considers "mush-minded" for wanting clean air, racial justice, and well-paid teachers usually constitute a majority of the voters. It seems telling that he speaks of "the good old days when conservatives contented themselves with 39 percent of the vote."[47] For those who would rather be Right—extremely Right—than president (or than have a congressional majority), his extremist agenda is just the ticket. After the Republicans had pursued it for a year, the public's response to the question, "Do you have more confidence in Clinton or in the Republican Congress to deal with the major issues facing the country?" had gone from 46–30 percent favoring the GOP Congress to 49–35 percent favoring the Democratic president.[48] Dead Right, indeed.

Although the Republican leadership has adopted most of the Frum philosophy, they generally try to cloak their more outrageous objectives. They cynically seek the support of those they despise as "mush-minded," since they realize they cannot win with only those who agree with their actual philosophy and goals. Much as Willie Sutton said he robbed banks "because that's where the money is," Republicans go after the common folk because that's where the votes are. They are willing to pander to the people who read supermarket tabloids. Hence the pseudopopulist rhetoric of the Right. Like the Whigs in 1840, the Republicans of the late twentieth century strike up poses and utter slogans designed to win over people to whose genuine interests they are, in reality, steadfastly opposed. Today's Republicans employ such symbols as Willie Horton, the Pledge of Allegiance, and affirmative action in much the way that the Whigs used the symbols of a log cabin and hard cider to elect William Henry Harrison in 1840.

It is important to recognize that this is all a matter of marketing, at which the business-oriented Republicans are understandably good. Rush Limbaugh is one of the world's best salesmen. What the Republicans are doing in politics is the same thing that their principal constituents are doing in the economic realm. They sell their product by doing market research and finding out what people will buy. Then they "construct" their products (candidates and positions) in such a way that consumers can be persuaded to buy them. This is exactly the process that was used in developing the 1994 "Contract with America." Nothing was included in it that did not win at least 60 percent approval in advance polling.

Consumption-ethic politics is almost as injurious to the commonwealth as consumption-ethic economics. Plainly it encourages (and often creates) cynicism, division, and strife.

FAIRNESS IS A DEMOCRATIC IDEA

From time to time, however, Republicans cannot restrain themselves and blurt out just what the old meaning of their new song is. "This whole idea of fairness is a Democratic idea; we should be about opportunity," Senator Richard Lugar boldly proclaimed at a January 1996 debate among

Republican presidential candidates.[49] (It provides some measure of how extreme the Republican leaders have become that Senator Lugar was dismissed as too nice to have a chance of winning the party's presidential nomination.) If Republicans really want to say: *To hell with fairness! If you want fairness, vote for the Democrats!* I guess we can live with that.

When we read David Frum listing "federal aid to handicapped schoolchildren" as one of "the things [conservatives] dislike in the contemporary world,"[50] we begin to see just how adamantly opposed to fairness these folks are. *Let the handicapped fend for themselves! If they can't make it, let them die and decrease the surplus population!* I don't want to be unfair (since I happen to believe in the Democratic idea of fairness) in characterizing Frum's unfairness, but this is what he wrote. Surely he and "conservatives" like him prefer Scrooge before the Christmas ghosts visited him to the sappy, "fair," "liberal" Scrooge after his transformation.

Many conservatives rail against biological Darwinism and try to banish it from the schools, but they have fully embraced the crudest form of social Darwinism.

Another area in which the Republicans seem unable to restrain themselves sufficiently to hide their true positions is their assault on environmental protection. House Republican Whip Tom DeLay of Texas set the tone when he referred to the Environmental Protection Agency as "the Gestapo." That this was not an idle comment, but rather one that represents the attitude of most House Republicans is clear from the infamous seventeen riders they attached to the 1995 appropriation bill for the EPA (which cut the agency's funding by one-third, a larger slice than that they sought to take from any other major government agency). In addition to their specific assaults on the environment, the environmental riders point to two other outrageous aspects of GOP policy. First, the use of riders to appropriation bills as a way of enacting policy changes is, as Secretary of the Interior Bruce Babbitt says, "basically a sneak attack, misusing the process to kind of sneak through provisions they didn't have the courage to put into a bill and debate out in the open."[51] Second, this was one of several 1995 examples in which the new Republican leadership actually allowed representatives of special interests to write most of the legislation themselves. (It must be admitted that this is more efficient. Instead of the special interests lobbying members of Congress to try to get them to include what they want in legislation, the middleman is eliminated and the lobbyists just write laws directly, as they want them.) Another example of this unprecedented direct transfer of legislative power to lobbyists was the bill imposing a thirteen-month moratorium on federal regulations. As this bill was debated on the floor, lobbyists sat with their laptop computers, typing out talking points that were handed to the GOP honorables for use in support of *their* legislation.[52] Paul Wellstone offers the reasonable reaction: "What they're doing is outrageous beyond belief. The notion of literally locking the doors and having lobbyists come in and write the bill—have these folks with laptop computers faxing in talking points to them [Republican congressmen] during the debate! I don't know of anything that is more transparent."[53]

The EPA riders, which kept being blocked by the defection of a sufficient number of less extreme Republicans, but kept being brought back by the leadership, would accomplish such noble objectives as forbidding new regulations to deal with toxic air pollution by oil refiners, blocking the enforcement of all wetlands regulations, making it difficult, if not impossible, for the EPA to limit the amount of untreated sewage that may be released into bodies of water, ... The list goes on, but the point should be made.[54]

Nor was the GOP assault on environmental protection limited to the EPA riders. One House leader declared that DDT is "not harmful and shouldn't have been banned." Another rider was attached to a budget reconciliation bill in an attempt to open, without normal debate or a direct vote, the Arctic Wildlife Refuge to oil drilling. Then the Republicans proposed to close up to 100 of the National Park Service's 369 units.[55]

Bruce Babbitt does not exaggerate when he says that these Republicans are "a genuinely radical band of ideologues who were out to systematically take apart the architecture of conservation and environmental laws that had been built up over the last couple of generations by Republicans and Democrats alike."[56]

Patsy Mink may have the best description of the agenda of the House Republicans in the 104th Congress: "The list is Alice-in-Wonderland."[57]

Since their heady intoxication with power in the 1994 election, Republicans have been, as David Bonior said to me, "doing all the things necessary for us [Democrats] to get back in the ball game."[58] They got off on the wrong foot with the public by trying to cut funding for school lunches. "Immediately you see them running into a buzz saw on school lunches, which they consider to be welfare," Paul Begala said. "It was a huge mistake. And it will serve as a touchstone reference, fairly or not. I think very fairly." He saw it as similar to the effect the gays in the military flap had in defining President Clinton at the beginning of his presidency. That, Begala believes, gave an inaccurate impression, "because it didn't illuminate his views on social policy at all. But I think this lunch thing does shine light on exactly where [the Republicans'] economic and social priorities are." The GOP problem was not that they had a poor communication strategy on school lunches, as Speaker Gingrich asserted. "No, Newt, you don't have a good *history*," Begala pointed out. "You have a hundred years of history going into this. I mean, people are not stupid. It's very difficult to convince people that Republicans are for school lunches; it's very easy to convince them that they are against them."[59]

In fact, it is more than two hundred years of history, if we may count the Federalists and Whigs as "pre-Republicans." "As much as Mr. Gingrich wants to talk about his view of the future, I think it's in the past," Rosa DeLauro said to me. "It's a relic of the past. Now what they are doing is saying after forty years, they can't gobble enough up here that they want to try to undo. I believe that this crowd is truly the representative of the past."[60] When they think they are looking at the future, they are really looking in the rearview mirror.

The current "Republican Revolution" certainly is a *revolution* in the sense of the word as going around in a circle and winding up where you started.

THE REPUBLICAN ROBESPIERRE

There can be no question who the central figure is in giving the Republicans the opportunity to try to sell their old wine in new bottles. That Newt Gingrich was the "Man of the Year" in 1995 is as indisputable as that Maximilien Robespierre was the "Man of the Year" in the Year II. (Whether his revolution will do politically to Gingrich what Robespierre's did physically to him cannot be safely predicted at the time of this writing.) I have had—and will continue to have—many occasions in these pages to discuss the head of the Republican Revolution's Committee of Public Safety. But a brief assessment of the man and his motivations seems appropriate at this point.

If there is something about Bill Clinton that leaves people unsure about him, the same cannot be said of Newt Gingrich. To know him seems to be to dislike him. He has been accurately described as "the most disliked member of Congress." As the American people came to know him, they reached a similar conclusion. During 1995, the year that he became a household word, Gingrich's unfavorable rating rose from 29 percent to 56 percent, probably the highest ever recorded for a major American figure not on the verge of impeachment. By the end of 1995, only 24 percent of Americans had a favorable impression of the Speaker. (The same poll found 61 percent had a favorable impression of Bill Clinton, the man whose unpopularity was said to have caused the Republican Revolution a year earlier.)[61]

"Gingrich is a crook. Period," Paul Begala stated in an unsurprising opinion. "I believe that; I really do. It frightens me as a citizen to have him in a position of great power. This guy brings in lobbyists and shakes them down. It's in the paper every day: 'If you don't give me money, I will screw your business. And if you give me money, I will love your business.'"[62]

"I am very pleasantly surprised," says Barney Frank of Gingrich's first-year performance. "He's been much worse than I expected."[63] "Gingrich is mean-spirited and petty. The episode when he said he had shut down the government because he didn't like where the president made him sit on *Air Force One* is just one example of this," Tom Daschle said to me.[64]

Partisan opinions of Gingrich might be discounted, except that the level of animosity runs so much deeper than what might normally be expected. Gingrich himself is the architect of the verbal guillotine that Democrats use on him. He set out to change American politics, and he succeeded in toppling the decorum and courtesy that had generally prevailed in Congress during the twentieth century. In 1978, the then-obscure congressional aspirant declared that "one of the great problems we have in the Republican Party is that we don't encourage you to be nasty. We encourage you to be neat, obedient, and loyal and faithful and all those Boy Scout words, which would be great around a campfire but are lousy in politcs."[65] This is no longer a problem. Not only the Speaker himself, but his handpicked lieutenants, such as Dick Armey and Tom DeLay (to say nothing of the fanatical freshmen of the 104th Congress) are unlikely to be mistaken for Boy Scouts.

Gingrich did not just hope that Republicans would get nasty; he recruited likely candidates and instructed them in the art of offensive speech. He told Republican challengers to call their Democratic opponents "traitors," "thugs," "sick," "corrupt," and "bizarre."[66] His political advice could be summarized in three words: *Screw Miss Manners!* (As Mao Zedung said, "Revolution is not a tea party.")

"We're trying to actually have an adult conversation with the American people instead of a 30-second pandering," Gingrich told *Time* at the end of 1995.[67] This raises the question: Could he be so self-delusional that he actually believes this, or is it all part of his false advertising campaign?

Surely Gingrich has always been prepared to use, as the radicals of the "bad sixties" used to say, "any means necessary" to achieve his objectives. Truth has never been of any more concern to him than etiquette. After two losses in races for a seat in Congress, when Gingrich ran again in 1978, he attacked his female opponent because she said she planned to commute to Washington, leaving her husband and children in Georgia. Gingrich used the slogan: "When elected, Newt will keep his family together." True to his word, he kept his family together until after he won the election, but eighteen months later he paid his now infamous visit to the hospital where his wife, who had seen him through thin, but apparently was not what he deemed suitable for thick, had had surgery the day before for uterine cancer. The family candidate insisted that they discuss terms of a divorce. Six months later he married another woman.[68]

"Just win, baby!"

What Newt Gingrich seeks is not popularity, but fame. He made a revealing comment after he had succeeded in getting Speaker Tip O'Neill reprimanded for calling one of Gingrich's escapades "the lowest thing I've seen in my 32 years in Congress." Gingrich proclaimed: "I am now a famous person."[69]

Gingrich wants a place in history and believes that he can achieve this objective by leading a revolution. Twentieth-century revolutions have given governments more power, so if he wants to be a revolutionary, it must be in the other direction. But one doubts that the direction is of much importance to Gingrich. His destinations are power and fame, and he'll get to them by any route that is available.

Just how inflated his ego is was demonstrated after historian Michael Beschloss pointed out that revolutionary leaders, "even when they are successful, usually flare for only a year or two, and then they fade."[70] Gingrich responded by pointing to Jefferson, Madison, Lincoln, the Roosevelts, Wilson, and Reagan, indicating that this is the company in which he believes he belongs.[71]

Gingrich has followed a long-term plan to gain power for himself (although power was never his ultimate goal; it has always been a means through which he can gain lasting fame). He used people and institutions as props in his stage-managed ascent. The most important event along the way was his bitter, relentless attack on former Speaker Jim Wright. Sometimes, at least, Gingrich has admitted that it was just a stratagem in his larger effort. "Wright's a useful keystone to a much bigger structure," Gingrich told a journalist early in the campaign to overthrow the Speaker. "I'll just keep pounding and pounding on his ethics. There comes a point where it comes together and the media takes off on it or it dies."[72] Some of the pounding got pretty hard. Gingrich called Wright "the most corrupt Speaker in the 20th century" and said he was "so consumed by his own power that he is like Mussolini."[73]

When he became Speaker himself in 1995, Gingrich immediately seized for himself just the sort of personal power he had condemned Wright for trying to gain. He abolished seniority as a basis for selecting committee chairs and chose them instead on the basis of their loyalty to him. With this degree of control, Gingrich was poised to run the House as a personal fiefdom to a degree that no one since "Czar" Thomas Reed at the end of the nineteenth century and "Uncle Joe" Cannon in the early twentieth century had done. Then, when ethics charges were brought against him, Gingrich howled: "They are misusing the ethics system in a deliberate, vicious, vindictive way, and I think it is despicable."[74] Certainly no one would know better than Gingrich how to recognize such a despicable misuse of the ethics system.

THE STUDENTS FOR A REPUBLICAN SOCIETY

The scarcely noticed fact is that Gingrich is, as Hendrik Hertzberg of *The New Yorker* has noted, "the first sixties-style radical to occupy a position of power in Washington."[75] The irony is that, for all their complaints about the ill effects of the sixties on American society ("Since 1965, however," Gingrich wrote in *To Renew America*, "there has been a calculated effort by cultural elites to discredit this civilization and replace it with a culture of irresponsibility"[76]), Gingrich and his cadres are the true heirs to the "bad sixties." Before anyone closes the book with a dismissive laugh, let me explain:

Like the worst side of the sixties, Gingrich is a rhetorical bomb thrower. Like sixties radicals, Gingrich has no respect for institutions or people in positions of authority. The middle-aged rightists of the nineties are convinced that they have, as the young leftists of the late sixties were convinced that they had, solutions to all problems and that those solutions are simple. Both have sought to impose their beliefs on the nation and said they will achieve their goals "by whatever means necessary." Both have disdained civil behavior and believe in extreme freedom (except in areas where they favor authoritarianism). Like the radicals of the late sixties, Gingrich is self-righteous, self-indulgent, and given to self-promotion.

The differences between Gingrich and someone like Jerry Rubin, Mark Rudd, or Eldridge Cleaver are much smaller than one would at first think. The Gingrich followers are the Weathermen of the Right. They think they know which way the wind blows, but they had sense enough to come in out of the rain—and work their revolution from the inside. The far Right has replaced the far Left as the threat, but it is a much greater threat, since the far Left was always a fringe movement, but the far Right took control of the House of Representatives in 1994.

When it comes to the breakdown of civilization (and civility) that conservatives properly lament, Newt Gingrich is not part of the solution; Newt Gingrich is part of the problem.

THE POOR YOU *SHOULD* ALWAYS HAVE WITH YOU

Now that one of the two great post-World War II American struggles, the Cold War against the Evil Empire of Soviet Communism, has been won, the Republicans seem eager to lose the other one: the War on Poverty. Of course, they argue that that war was lost long ago—indeed, that it was unwinnable in the first place. The right wing defines the second postwar war differently. As they see it, the enemy to be overcome in this other war is not poverty, but the welfare state. Gingrich and Company credit Reagan with the defeat of one of their great enemies, but they believe that the

Reagan Revolution will remain unfinished until they vanquish the other Evil Empire in Washington.[77] They are trying to win this one for the Gipper, too.

It may be instructive in trying to understand from whence the persuasions of the radical Republicans come to look at the War on Poverty in conjunction with one of the segments of the Cold War, the war in Vietnam.

Everyone, it seemed, came to oppose one or the other of Lyndon Johnson's wars. Liberals had initially favored both, but soon came to oppose his War in Vietnam; conservatives opposed his War on Poverty from the start. By 1975, liberals had succeeded in ending the Johnson war that they could not tolerate. Conservatives have taken longer, but they are trying in the nineties to end the Johnson war that they could not abide.

As liberals argued that the Vietnam War could not be won and should never have been started, so today conservatives contend that the War on Poverty could not be won and should never have been started. And, as some on the Left finally came to say that the other side *should* not be defeated, even if it could be, so some on the Right now seem to believe that poverty *should* not be defeated, even if it could be. It is, to them, not merely that the poor we shall always have with us, but that we *should* always have the poor with us.

The irony is that the so-called conservatives, who are themselves in many ways the unconscious heirs to the "bad sixties," are attacking the decade's good war, the crown jewel of the good sixties, while justifying their assaults by pointing to some of the legacies (other than themselves) of the "bad sixties."

The Grand New Packaging that Newt Gingrich and Company have given to the GOP is a clever disguise for a party that retains in the second Gilded Age of the late twentieth century the same Greedy Old Priorities that guided it in the first Gilded Age of the late nineteenth century.

9

THE CONTRADICTIONS OF CONSERVATISM—AND OF LIBERALISM

THE INHERENT CONTRADICTION OF THE REPUBLICAN AGENDA

The positions taken by the Republicans may be popular, but many of them are strikingly contradictory. They say, for example, that the cause of social pathology is cultural, not economic. Yet they simultaneously insist that cutting unmarried teenage mothers off welfare—surely an economic approach—will lead them not to have out-of-wedlock babies.

Republicans oppose preventative measures to stop crime. They mock midnight basketball programs that would cost a small amount of money, but are willing to spend huge amounts on prison construction; they prefer the death penalty to a ban on assault weapons, spending on more jail cells to spending on more cops on the street. Yet many of these same Republicans believe that a Star Wars antimissile system can protect us from nuclear attacks. They say we cannot protect or defend ourselves against street crime, but we can block incoming missiles.

Gingrichism is willing to means-test benefits, but not taxes. Conservatives readily say that subsidized school lunches should not go to middle-class children. Many of them contend that Medicare and Social Security benefits should not be going to wealthy people who do not need them, but they argue that very high incomes should not be taxed at a higher rate than low incomes. That, they say, is not fair, and they castigate as "class warfare" the argument that those who enjoy the greatest benefits in society ought to pay at a higher rate.

The rich, these Republicans say, need a positive incentive to get richer, but then they say this will not work for the poor. Instead, we are told that the poor must have a negative incentive in order to make them work.

Gingrich and company have no enthusiasm for day-care programs, which many of them say do not provide good environments for children; yet they have contended that orphanages would provide an acceptable locale in which to place the children of unwed mothers. Apparently they do not notice that orphanages amount to twenty-four-hour day-care centers.[1]

The Republicans say they want to reduce sex and violence on television, but seek to eliminate funding for PBS, one of the few sources of quality programming that does not indulge in gratuitous sex and violence. The Christian Coalition had the audacity to place the elimination of funding for the Corporation for Public Broadcasting in its "Contract with the American Family." Now there's a real "Christian" objective designed to help families.

It is also ironic that the same "conservatives" who constantly call for getting the federal government, and especially federal courts, out of our lives are opposed to the *Roe* decision, which tried to get the government at all levels out of our personal lives.

FREEDOM TO HATE

The debate over hate speech that erupted in the wake of the 1995 Oklahoma City bombing starkly revealed contradictions in the thinking of both conservatives and liberals.[2] For many years, most self-styled conservatives have contended that the depiction of sex and violence on television and in movies promotes antisocial behavior. Now many people identified as liberals are saying that the preaching of hate and division, which is particularly evident on talk radio, contributes to a climate in which insane acts of violence are more likely to occur.

Both groups are correct about the potential effects of the messages that reach us through the electronic media. Yet each side seems willing to see the problem in only one portion of the media. The conservatives who have led the charge against unwarranted violence and explicit sexual content in films, television shows, and song lyrics now react with anger to the suggestion that hate-filled right-wing radio shows might cause some people to engage in violent acts. For their part, many of the liberals who have long defended Hollywood's right to present any images that sell, and have generally insisted that there is no connection between those images and social pathology, have been quick to detect such a connection with talk radio.

One side would have us believe that violent speech and images are dangerous if they come out of a television set, but not if they are emitted by a radio. The other side tries to persuade us that such images can lead to trouble if they issue from a radio, but not if their source is a television.

It is difficult to see how either side can have it both ways. Either words and images can affect behavior or they cannot.

Can anyone who maintains that there is a danger of Ice-T's "Cop Killer" song pushing one sort of unstable person over the edge into an attack on a police officer reasonably argue that something like G. Gordon Liddy's September 1994 radio declaration ("Alcohol, Tobacco, and Firearms agents—don't shoot at their vests; shoot at their heads. Kill them! Kill them!") does not carry the potential of motivating another brand of demented person to assault a federal officer? On the other side, can anyone who suggests that regular listening to Rush Limbaugh's tirades against the government can contribute to an atmosphere in which violence thrives seriously contend that a constant diet of graphic violence in such movies as *Pulp Fiction* and television shows such as *N.Y.P.D. Blue* does not do the same?

For a time, Liddy's radio show began with a recorded introduction that included such statements as: "I know it seems impossible. But I promise you, the day shall come when the Witch and her husband will be gone and you shall be free of the shackles of liberal Democrats." While this was being said, the sound of gunfire, planes, and explosions was constantly heard in the background. Surely this is the sort of thing that an unstable person on the Right might easily take as a suggestion to "free" the nation of its shackles by using violence to eliminate Hillary and Bill Clinton.

None of this is to say that reasonable political debate about the size and role of the federal government is out of place or can plausibly be linked to tragedies such as that in Oklahoma City. Newt Gingrich was right to be outraged at this suggestion. But it was the mirror image of Mr. Gingrich's own monstrous suggestion at the end of the 1994 campaign that Democrats had created a climate that led a South Carolina woman to drown her two children. Then there was the Speaker's late 1995 assertion—made several months after the Oklahoma City bombing—that the horrible murder in Illinois of a pregnant woman for the purpose of cutting out and stealing her nearly full-term fetus was the result of failed Democratic welfare, criminal justice, and educational programs. Those comments, like Sen. Jesse Helms's statement that President Clinton should bring a bodyguard with him if he came to North Carolina, are clearly beyond the pale. Responsibility is the price of freedom, but many people in the fields of politics and entertainment seem to have forgotten this.

By themselves, words and images will not tear a society apart, but when coupled with pervasive fear and uncertainty, which seem to be plaguing large numbers of Americans who see their nation and their own prospects changing in fundamental ways, they have the capacity to inflame passions to the point where they can endanger the bonds that hold us together. And this is true whether those words and images are displayed on a movie or television screen, transmitted by a radio, or reproduced on a compact disc.

The danger is in the messages of hatred and violence, not in which medium carries them.

Yet many on both sides still refuse to accept this obvious truth. When Barney Frank wrote to Dan Quayle in 1995 to congratulate him on his attack on gangsta rapper Tupac Shakur, he asked the former vice president, "What about Liddy?" Quayle wrote back: "They're very different."[3]

Reactions to the conduct of lawmen and possible examples of abuse of governmental police authority provide another canvas on which the contradictions of both "sides" can be seen in chiaroscuro. Liberals have long been hypersensitive to such problems as police brutality against minorities and FBI and CIA abuses of authority against antiwar activists and leftist groups, from the 1969 police killing of Black Panther Fred Hampton in his bed and the infamous COINTELpro program, to the beating of Rodney King. Conservatives have traditionally been on the side of the law enforcement agencies in these cases. They have focused more on the wrongdoings of those against whom the excessive authority was used than on the authorities' abuses of legal and constitutional rights.

Suddenly the roles reversed when those against whom federal police power was used were found on the Right fringe instead of the Left. Liberals are more interested in the child rapes committed by David Koresh than they are in abuses of power by Alcohol, Tobacco, and Firearms agents at Waco in 1993. They are more concerned with the white supremacist ideology and violent revolutionary objectives of Randy Weaver than they are with the tactics used by the FBI in the 1992 raid on Ruby Ridge. For their part, conservatives generally say that whatever crimes the Branch Davidians and the Weaver group were committing in their heavily armed compounds are irrelevant. We should be concerned instead, they insist, with the outrageous actions of federal law enforcement agencies.

Apparently liberals and conservatives both decide how they should react to the use of excessive force and violation of constitutional rights by law enforcement officials on the basis of whether these abuses are committed in pursuit of left- or right-wing groups.

INDIVIDUALS OR GROUPS?

Then there is the question of whether people should be seen exclusively as individuals or as members in groups or categories is significant. There was a time in this country—and it is not that long ago—when many conservatives, especially those in the economic and social elite, favored prejudging people on the basis of such factors as race, ethnicity, religion, or sex. Those who were in the "wrong" category would be excluded from many desirable places in life. Segregation and such practices as the exclusion of

Jews, women, and various other categories from clubs had nothing to do with individuals.

The initial thrust of the Civil Rights movement was based on the idea that people should be judged as individuals, not on the basis of the categories in which they could be placed. Martin Luther King's famous call for people to be judged not "by the color of their skin, but by the content of their character" was a liberal rallying cry for assessing people as individuals.

Rather quickly in the sixties, however, positions on group and individual identity began to shift. Liberals came to argue that, since people had been discriminated against by reason of the categories to which they belonged, remedies must be applied on the same basis. This led to affirmative action policies in which members of categories that had been discriminated against in the past were to be sought out to fill positions, regardless of whether they had *personally* suffered from prejudice. Principally to combat affirmative action and other forms of group entitlement, conservatives gravitated toward the see-everyone-as-an-individual position that had recently been vacated by liberals.

But these positions were not taken consistently. While liberals tend to think of blacks as a group for correcting past injustices, they quite rightly insist that young black males not be seen as a group when it comes to fearing crime. They are prepared to use victimization by association as a foundation for corrective policies, but adamantly reject guilt by association (at least for those previously discriminated against). For their part, conservatives argue that each individual should be judged on his or her individual merits, regardless of membership in groups that have been held back *as groups* in the past. Yet conservatives are more apt than liberals to judge a young black male as a threat because of his race. Conservatives resolutely reject victimization by association, but more readily accept guilt by association.

Liberals, in short, want to act on a group basis when that appears to be in the best interests of those who have suffered from bias in the past, but on an individual basis when treating those who have been discriminated against in the past as a group would be detrimental to them.

It is interesting that the same conservatives who now insist that everyone should be judged as an individual, not as a member of a group, readily apply guilt by association to war situations. For example, most conservatives respond to suggestions that it may have been a mistake to use atomic bombs on Japanese cities with such rejoinders as: "*They* started it, didn't they?" "*They* attacked Pearl Harbor, didn't they?" and "Don't you know what kind of atrocities *they* committed in China?" "If *they* hadn't bombed Pearl Harbor, we wouldn't have dropped the big one on *them* at Hiroshima." In a similar vein, many people (often self-professed conservatives) will justify such acts as the fire-bombing of Dresden by pointing to the Holocaust or other atrocities that *they* (the Germans) committed.

One thing that these arguments demonstrate is the danger of vague antecedents. Is the antecedent to the *they* that committed the horrible acts the same as that of the *them* whose punishment is being justified? The point I am making pertains not to the argument that killing personally innocent children, women, and men was, unfortunately, a necessary evil in order to win the war and save the lives of Americans. That is another matter, one that I am not debating here. Rather, I am addressing the contention that killing individuals who were guilty of nothing themselves is *justified*, because they are members of a group that collectively did evil things. How does this differ from blaming all whites for slavery or all men for misogyny, or . . . you name it?

It seems that conservatives are saying that if a group did something wrong in the past, all individuals in it may justly be punished (although few are willing to apply this argument to white males). This is, in essence, the contention that the sins of the fathers (or the sins of the brothers, husbands, neighbors—what have you) taint the sons—the whole group. But what about sins *against* the fathers? Would it not be consistent to say that if descendants may be punished for what their ancestors did, that descendants may also be compensated for what was done *to* their ancestors? Doesn't this point to giving benefits to Native Americans and African-Americans for what was done to their forebears?

There arise all sorts of complications when we begin to punish or compensate people for what others, past or present, in their category did. Is a white woman, for example, to be considered a victim on the basis of her sex or an oppressor on the basis of her race?

Blacks are often "blamed as a group for the misbehavior of a single individual," as *Philadelphia Inquirer* columnist Claude Lewis has noted. Whenever a widely publicized crime occurs, blacks have been conditioned to the point that their first reaction is likely to be: "God, I hope the killer (rapist, assailant, etc.) wasn't black."[4] Of course the tendency toward group blame is not the exclusive property of any one group. Blacks have frequently engaged in it themselves, as the riots following the acquittal of the policemen who beat Rodney King made plain. The brutal attack on white truck driver Reginald Denny obviously had no motivation other than that he was white.

Then there was the rather different reaction of many blacks to the acquittal of O. J. Simpson. No outrage at a miscarriage of justice here. Rather, there were scenes from across the country of African-Americans celebrating. It was a case of identifying Simpson with a group that has long been victimized by the police and courts rather than identifying him as an individual whom a huge amount of evidence indicated had committed a vicious crime.

Contradictions abound on both sides on questions having to do with group and individual responsibility.

P.C. ON THE RIGHT

Conservatives have gotten a great deal of political mileage out of charging Democrats with being advocates of "political correctness." The terminology refers, of course, to the concept that only certain ideas are acceptable, and others should not be tolerated. Anything that is multicultural, feminist, minority-oriented, gay and lesbian, pro-victim, artistically outrageous, anti-Western, or socialist is supposed to be "P.C." Ideas, opinions, attitudes, and words that are not politically correct are castigated as "racist, misogynist, and homophobic."

Actually, the only new things about political correctness in the nineties are the term itself and the fact that it is considered to be on the Left. The equivalent of political correctness has always been with us. At various times in our history, those considered to have incorrect political views have been called "Tories," "Jacobins," "Doughfaces," "Copperheads," "Indian lovers," "Reds," "Communists," "peaceniks," "effete intellectual snobs," and so forth. Among the periods of the greatest dominance of P.C. before the name was invented were World War I and the McCarthy Era. People with "incorrect" views on the war were jailed while the United States was fighting to make the world safe for democracy. Careers and lives were destroyed left and right—excuse me, just Left—while Joseph McCarthy, Richard Nixon, and others were examining the political purity of the statements, actions, and thoughts of Americans. In the first half of the 1950s, accusing someone of being a "fellow traveler" who "follows the Communist line" was likely to be much more detrimental than calling him a "racist" would be today.

Just as political correctness was anything but a monopoly held by the Left in the past, today there exists a very clear P.C. of the Right. The most commonly used politically correct epithet for the last two decades has been *liberal*, a word that covers all manner of undefined "incorrect" positions and opinions. The use of the word as an adjective immediately dismisses as stupid, counterproductive, and mush-headed any noun it modifies. There is no need to discuss an idea that has been besmirched as "liberal." Newt Gingrich probably uses it as often as he says "frankly." (And it is about as meaningful.) The word is, as both an adjective and a noun, also among the most-used vocabulary of Rush Limbaugh and

Gordon Liddy. Any thought or person to which it is applied is thereby labeled with a scarlet "L" as politically incorrect from the conservative viewpoint. "Femi-Nazi," and "tree-hugger" are other right-wing terms that correspond to the Left's "racist, misogynist, homophobic." Each side has its own politically correct and incorrect terms and positions. If some on the Left demand that a person with a disability be referred to as "differently abled" or "physically challenged," many on the Right require that a fetus—or even an embryo—be called a "pre-born child."

THE RISE OF THE CHRISTIAN SOCIAL DARWINISTS

Perhaps the most fundamental contradiction in the radical Republican program is that so many of their policies are designed to accelerate the concentration of wealth and income among the few, yet the supply-side economy of which they are the champions is predicated on mass consumption, which requires a more equitable distribution of income.

If we balance the budget and if people were ever to heed the sound advice to balance their personal budgets by paying off their balances of debt, it is likely that the economy, with its growing maldistribution of income, would collapse. There simply would not be sufficient demand to balance the supply. It is, therefore, essential that we institute policies that attempt to achieve a more equitable distribution of income at the same time that we attempt to wean both the government and consumers from their overconsumption and debt habits. If we balance our national and personal budgets without paying heed to the gross imbalance in our income and wealth distributions, we will reap the results of one of the many contradictions in our political and economic thinking.

Finally, let me mention the contradiction on the Right over religion, Darwinism, and economics. Most of those who identify themselves with the "Christian Right" refuse to accept biological Darwinism. They reject the idea that humans could have evolved through natural selection; they say this leaves no room for God. But Darwinism is, in essence, "marketplace biology." It sees the same force of a competitive environment (which is to say, a natural marketplace) selecting the biological "winners" that free-market economics favors as the force that should select the economic winners. Totally unfettered free-market economics is, in short, grounded in the same "Godless" idea of natural selection that is the basis of evolutionary biology. Yet many—it is probably safe to say, most—of the people in the Christian Right are staunch advocates of social and economic Darwinism. If they condemn both "Godless Darwinism" and "Godless Communism," how can they so readily embrace what is in fact a "Godless Marketplace"? Wouldn't it make more sense for them to favor injecting some morality into the amoral marketplace, rather than treating the Market as a god that supersedes the God they worship on Sunday? Is it consistent to worship the traditional Judeo-Christian-Islamic God on one day of the week and treat the Market as God on the other six?

10
A Government That Listens to America: Positive—But Limited—Government

Is Government the Enemy?

"For some citizens, the Government has almost become like a foreign country, so strange and distant that we've often had to deal with it through trained ambassadors who have sometimes become too powerful and too influential—lawyers, accountants, and lobbyists. This cannot go on."[1]

The foregoing may sound like a recent pronouncement from a right-wing "militia," or at least the declaration of an archconservative Republican member of Congress, but it was in fact part of President Jimmy Carter's State of the Union Address in January 1978. That a moderate Democratic president could make such a statement nearly two decades ago suggests that the feelings that have led a group of unstable people to see themselves as engaged in war with the federal government have been building for a long time and are not confined to the lunatic fringe. The perception of one's own government as a foreign country is the first step toward declaring war on that government. It is, of course, only the psychopaths who can see blowing up innocent people as a justifiable action. But the deep anxiety that lies behind that action is felt by a large portion of the American populace in the late twentieth century. A Gallup Poll taken in April 1995 found that 39 percent of Americans believed that "the federal government has become so large and powerful that it poses an immediate threat to the rights and freedoms of ordinary citizens." When the word *immediate* was deleted, the number of those who said yes rose to 52 percent.[2] The bombing of the Oklahoma City federal building later that month apparently had a substantial effect in improving public attitudes toward the government, at least in the short run. A *Washington Post*/ABC News Poll about a month after that attack on the government found that well over 60 percent of the people felt that the federal government posed no threat at all to them.[3]

We Have Met the Government, and It Is Us

Republicans have been winning support by calling for power to be returned to the people, away from the government. This dichotomy between the government and the people puts the problem in the wrong terms. The great insight of twentieth-century liberalism, beginning with the Progressives (who were borrowing from the Populists of the late nineteenth century), was that, in a democracy, government need no longer be seen as the enemy of the people; rather, the people could control the government and use it as a tool—an instrument to advance the public good.

Those who roam the countryside in combat dress and cite as justification the fact that the American colonists took up arms against a government that would not give them representation fail to realize that the American Revolution took place more than two centuries ago. We no longer confront a monarch and a parliament in which we are not represented. While there may sometimes be a reason for taking up arms against an undemocratic government, there is no excuse for doing so in a democracy.

The Progressive viewpoint that the government is not the enemy of the people, but an implement for good, remains valid—but only under genuinely democratic conditions. Our government is democratic, but ours is a compromised democracy. What compromises American democracy is the influence of special interests, which often thwart the will of the people.

The problem today is less that government has gotten too big (although we must recognize that in some areas it has) than that the people have lost control over their government. "Congress has come to appear to be a coin-operated machine," Representative Patricia Schroeder points out, "—it only does something for you if you put money in."[4] The first priority for Democrats, then, is to show how the government can be brought back under the control of the people—taken away from the special interests. Republicans in the 104th Congress took an important step in curbing gift-giving by lobbyists to members of Congress. They are to be applauded for this overdue action. But much more is needed. And it does not do much good to take the position that you won't take gifts from lobbyists, but you will allow those that represent special interests that you favor to write up their own legislation. I am reminded of a comment Richard Hofstadter made about Grover Cleveland: "out of heartfelt conviction he gave to the interests what many a lesser politician might have sold them for a price."[5]

The government is—or ought to be—a synonym for "us." We need to strive for the day when we can accurately paraphrase Pogo to say: "We have met the government and it is us."

Republicans have had great success in convincing people that the Democratic Party is in the control of special interests. There has been much truth in this charge; but it is ultimately very misleading. There are special interests and, then, there are Special Interests. Democratic interest groups generally represent the not-so-special people—those who have most often been powerless in the past: workers, consumers, minorities, women, the elderly, and so forth. It is certainly true that these interest groups have sometimes exerted undue influence on the Democrats and on occasion have led the party into positions that were untenable or plainly not in the public interest. Democrats cannot let themselves become captives of labor unions, civil rights groups, the American Association of Retired Persons, the National Organization for Women, or other special interest alliances, no matter how large their constituencies. The Republicans also have close ties with some lowercase "s" special interests—aggregates of people who have little individual power, but which can exert great influence through their organizations. These include the Christian Coalition and the National Rifle Association. But the most powerful Republican interest groups are those that can be designated with capital letters, chiefly major corporations and business associations. Lobbyists from these Special Interests have, as I noted earlier, literally been invited to sit at congressional tables and devise legislation that the Republicans will then try to enact. (Democrats were also busy gathering money from these Special Interests while they were following the Coelho strategy in the eighties.)

Without a strong government to check them, these capital-letter Special Interests that are so cozy with the Grand Old Party will be able to go wild. In a conversation with me, James Carville put this prospect in his typical colorful language: "The only institution that we have that can adequately define the big things that the nation needs to do is the federal government and it is the only institution that is anywhere close to powerful enough to stand up to the big interest groups. Once you destroy that, then you've got the country by the balls." If the Republicans succeed in their assault on the federal government, Carville said, "we [will] have a fundamentally different country from the premises on which this nation was built. That is really what this whole thing is about."[6]

The most important step toward achieving the first priority of restoring confidence in government by returning government to the control of the people is one that was attempted, albeit half-heartedly, by Democrats, but blocked by Republicans, in 1994: to eliminate—or at least severely limit—the power of Special Interests through campaign finance reform and lobbying reform. Public financing of all campaigns (exactly the opposite of what the Republicans are trying to do, with the proposal they buried in their 1995 budget plan, to do away with public financing of presidential campaigns—the one effort at disinfecting the political process that has clearly worked[7]) is the only feasible solution. And—although this is very hard to get many people to see—it would be much cheaper than the private financing that results in so much wasteful spending desired by those who currently pay campaign bills.

Aside from the obvious problems associated with influence buying by Special Interests (and special interests), the private financing of campaigns for public office contributes to our present malaise in another, little-noticed but highly significant way. The alternative—or complement—to raising money from special interest political action committees is to raise it in small amounts by direct mail. The Republicans and associated conservative groups perfected this method long before the Democrats and liberal groups, but everyone is now engaged in the practice. On the surface, the idea of financing campaigns through the small contributions of millions of people who agree with a candidate, party, or organization seems eminently democratic. In fact, direct-mail fundraising is playing an important part in poisoning our democracy because it encourages division and extremism. Direct-mail experts know that the best way to raise money is by terrifying their potential supporters. This can most readily be accomplished by painting "the other side" as being in league with the devil. When parties, candidates, and groups try to raise political money from small contributors, the caricature of members of the opposition as being more extreme than they actually are becomes the standard practice. A clear demonstration of this rule is the fact that the infamous 1995 National Rifle Association fund-raising letter that characterized federal law enforcement officials as "jack-booted government thugs" garnered more responses (ca. 900,000) and brought in more donations (nearly $1 million) than any previous fund-raising solicitation in the history of this highly effective special interest group.[8]

The use of extreme appeals to raise funds leads to deeper division, making cooperation and compromise for the common good more difficult. Public financing would, therefore, lessen the divisions in our society at the same time that it would diminish the influence of special interests and give people a greater sense of control over their government.

Bill Clinton's objective of building a government that "looks like America" is a worthy one. At least as important, however, is a government that *listens to* America: *all* of America, not just the interests and Interests. Nothing would be more important in overcoming the cynicism that is eating away at American society.

The Hole in the Electorate

That cynicism is a major reason for the appearance of a "hole in the electorate" that is as threatening to our polity as the growing hole in the ozone layer is to our health. "One of the problems the Democrats especially have is there are very few people really paying attention," Senator Bumpers said in our interview. "Only 38 percent of the people are voting and the people who are not voting are our normal constituents. So we have a steep hill to climb. For example, I heard Jesse Jackson saying the other day, and it's absolutely true, if 2 percent more of the larger inner cities had voted, we wouldn't have that [1994 Republican] revolution. So that's the real dilemma of the Democrats, too." Bumpers noted that it is not just people in the inner cities who have given up on voting. "You're talking about people who have just been cut loose, just like ships at sea. People who thought they were economically secure for the rest of their lives, and suddenly there's a big merger and 7,000 people are laid off."[9]

Joe Kennedy pointed to the same problem of the hole in the electorate. "When my parents and grandparents were growing up in America, poor people were black, yes, but they were also Greeks, Irish, Jews, and Catholics and Italians. One thing they all had in common was that they voted. Today, poor people are black, they're white, they're brown, and they are yellow, and the one thing that they have in common is that they *don't* vote," said this son of one of the last politicians who inspired the poor to vote in large numbers. "So what happens is, the base of the Democratic Party has so radically shrunk compared to the base of the country, that our ability to create an agenda has been severely limited by the driving force of electoral politics: who votes. So, it seems to me that you've got to recognize that you can't just scold people into voting. They've got to think that they have a horse in the race. They've got to think that there is something in it for them. So, bemoaning the fact that people don't vote, isn't going to change anything."[10]

David Bonior maintained that this is the biggest political problem for Democrats. He said that the party talks about issues for this group and that group, but "the best and most efficient way of moving into power again is just to activate the folks who just don't participate. And that means incredible community organizing, which we have gotten away from." Like so many other leading Democrats, he pointed to the error of letting the party become dependent over the last twenty years on heavy contributions from PACs and corporate executives. "We've gotten away from grassroots community-based activity in neighborhoods to activate people. I mean, we've got to get back to that. We really have no choice now, and if we're smart we have got to give those people some hope, some reason to believe that their lives will be different if, in fact, they participate and elect Democrats. We've just got to get on it. That means hands-on and being with them in the community, not just two months before the election." He went on to offer some specifics: "Some of these communities who have not been voting—we need to be standing with these folks during the downsizing and when they have been laid off, when kids and neighborhoods are being threatened with violence—we need to be on the street walking those neighborhoods with those parents and safeguard their school and neighborhoods. We have to be visible that way. And we're not there yet, psychologically, to do that; but we're trying to get people there."[11]

In addition to this sort of direct demonstration of concern, what is needed in order to bring the nonvoters to the polls (and to get them to vote for Democrats) is "basically a message which speaks for the American worker," Bonior declared. "Whether it's income from their jobs for their families, for their kids' education. It's not that complicated of a message. It's basically the things people talk about when they are at the kitchen table. And we need to do it with more clarity, more unity, a louder voice and not get sidetracked with a lot of other issues which tend to pull us apart, diffuse our message, and cause political problems for us."[12]

People desperately want a government that listens to America. They don't believe they have that now. Rosa DeLauro told me about a woman who had come to talk with her in Connecticut. "The woman said, 'I wish for one time, the people in Washington would put their feet in our shoes and understand what our lives are about.' I think if the Democrats can identify truly with what people's lives are about and are looking for ways in which to deal with what their lives are about, then I think we will see that there will be a connection," DeLauro said. "People believed that at one point and are not so sure about that today."[13]

If there is to be any hope for the country, as well as for the Democratic Party, the people who feel that the government isn't listening to them must be shown that that will no longer be the case. They need to have, as Kennedy put it, "a horse in the race." Once they are convinced that they do, the hole in the electorate will be filled in.

TAKING ON THE GOVERNMENT

In addition to the correct perception that government is often not listening to ordinary people but is instead beholden to special interests, there are several other reasons why so many Americans have lost faith in government. One is that they do not clearly see benefits coming to them in return for their tax money. "No western industrial nation spends as much of its budget on interest and defense as we do," Paul Simon notes. "These are things that don't help the average citizen in any tangible way. And so he sees the federal government as absorbing a lot of revenue. He doesn't see a state health-care system, he doesn't see us moving on the problems of our society, and so he or she becomes skeptical about the federal government."[14] It may well be that the provision of health care, even if it increased taxes (offset by the elimination of private health insurance premiums), would make the government more popular, since it would be a case in which people could readily see a return on their taxes.

Another reason for the decline in confidence in government is the massive campaign that well-financed antigovernment activists have conducted for the past two decades. It is tough to persuade people that active government can be beneficial to them, as Dale Bumpers noted, "with 500 talk show hosts giving you anecdote after anecdote of how somebody ripped off the system and resonating so well with their audience, which for the most part are people who have either made it reasonably well or those who are struggling and think that affirmative action is the reason they are not doing better."[15] The trashing not only of politicians, but of everyone who works in government has become epidemic. This denigration of public service not only weakens community and cooperative values, but it leads to a further decline of democracy.[16]

But, in a great irony, the way for the right-wing critics of government was paved by the Left. Even in its best days in the early, "good" sixties, the so-called New Left was highly critical of the liberal state that had emerged from the New Deal and was nearing completion in the Kennedy-Johnson years. Assuming conservatism to be irrelevant, young thinkers and activists turned against what they dubbed "the liberal establishment" in an internecine conflict that severely wounded the reputation of the federal government without the Right needing to fire a shot. The arguments of the New Left against bureaucracy and in favor of small communities were reshaped by the Right into defenses of business against government interference. And, as I have already explained, the demands that arose on the Left in the sixties for complete freedom in cultural areas created a climate in which economic laissez faire seemed naturally to flourish. "All of this," as E. J. Dionne has written, "made it easier for people who supported the antiwar movement and listened to the Jefferson Airplane when they were twenty to vote for Ronald Reagan when they turned thirty—and continue to enjoy rock 'n' roll."[17] The Right's victories over liberalism since the seventies have come over an opponent already softened up by numerous body blows it had absorbed from people in its own corner.

There were, of course, many genuine misuses of power for leftist critics of government to point out. Particularly damaging were the abuses by law enforcement agencies such as the FBI. The tendency of people on the Left to distrust government law enforcement agencies was sufficiently ingrained that most people on the Left continued to see these organizations as the enemy and did not notice that the right wing had reached the same conclusion. Now, after the reaction to Ruby Ridge and Waco, we realize how deep the antipathy to the government is among right-wing groups. Although the Left's view of law enforcement agencies may be slowly improving, we are now in a period in which it seems that almost everyone is against government lawmen and -women in one context or another. This adds to the difficulty of persuading people that government powers can be used to their advantage.

WHAT WE HAVE ACCOMPLISHED THROUGH GOVERNMENT

But that case must be made. It is essential to resist the simple thinking, advocated by so many "conservatives," that sees almost all government as bad. Instead, we need to try to sort the good from the bad. Progressives must show a greater willingness than they have in the past to jettison programs that do not work. But we must also have the courage and good sense to applaud vigorously the many successes that have been achieved by government. "Courage," as Rev. Billy Graham once said, "is contagious. When a brave man takes a stand, the spines of others are stiffened."

There should be no mistake that there is a baby—or, rather, a fully developed adult—well worth saving in the federal bath water. Excesses in government regulation obviously exist. But we should be careful about acting on the basis of anecdotes. Federal programs launched by the Roosevelt and Johnson administrations (Social Security and Medicare) have transformed senior citizens from the age group with the highest percentage of poverty to that with the lowest. (The poverty rate among those over sixty-five has been cut by two-thirds.) The federally enacted GI Bill educated and trained a generation of veterans and materially assisted millions of people to raise themselves into the middle class. Federal environmental regulations put into effect since the late sixties have drastically reduced air and water pollution. There was less air pollution in the United States in the mid-1990s than there had been twenty years before, even though the nation was using twice as much energy as it had in the earlier period. This means that, as a result of federal regulation, the rate of air pollution has been slashed by more than half in two decades. Without that government intervention, it is likely that the air today would be more than twice as dirty as it is. (A striking example of the degree to which Americans fail to understand what the government has accomplished is the finding of a 1995–96 survey that 57 percent of Americans think the quality of air we breathe today is *worse* than it was twenty years ago, while only 18 percent think it is better.[18])

The Republican-controlled Congress elected in 1994 set as one of its major goals the gutting of these environmental protections. One of the riders they attached to the EPA appropriation bill in 1995 would block the EPA from implementing standards for water quality in the Great Lakes.[19] Federal regulation has succeeded in transforming the Cleveland waterfront from a literal cesspool, a place where the Cuyahoga River once caught on fire, to a vibrant place where it is safe to fish, sail, and enjoy life on the shores of Lake Erie.[20]

The Civil Rights Act of 1964 and the Voting Rights Act of 1965 have had an enormous positive impact in pushing the reality of America closer to the promises of freedom and equal rights upon which the nation was founded. School lunches; Headstart; and the Women, Infants, and Children nutrition program are among other federal initiatives that have been proven to work. Progressives need to regain their courage and their voice and speak up for their many successes.

There was a time when Democrats were not reticent about the accomplishments of positive government.[21] In the fall of 1964, when an unprecedented crowd in excess of 200,000 turned out for a campaign appearance by Lyndon B. Johnson in Providence, Rhode Island, the president clambered up on his car, seized a bullhorn, and bellowed: "I just want to tell you this—we're in favor of a lot of things and we're against mighty few."[22]

Never had a statement better captured the spirit of a time or more succinctly encapsulated the liberal outlook. That approach perfectly matched the American viewpoint in the first half of the sixties; it also meshed with the usual American optimism and "can-do" attitude. Johnson's answer to every seemingly intractable problem was the same. Is it possible to protect the civil rights of black Americans that have been trampled upon for nearly a century? *We can do it*, Johnson said in 1964. Can we fight a successful war on poverty? *We certainly can*, the Democratic president of 1964 affirmed. Can we provide health-care security for the elderly and the poor? *Yes, we can!* LBJ insisted in 1964. Johnson was a believer in affirmative action by government, which sounds better than the alternatives of "negative action" or inaction.

The most dramatic change since the sixties—or the early, "good sixties"—is that from optimism to pessimism, from a "can do" to a "can't do" attitude. The Republican position today on almost every question is the opposite of LBJ's. Can we provide security to all Americans so that they will not have to fear losing their health insurance if they suffer a serious illness or change jobs? The Republicans answer: *We can't do it*. Can we reduce the leverage of big-money interests on our government? *No, we can't do that*, the Republicans now respond.

The Republicans have reversed Lyndon Johnson and, three decades after he won a landslide victory by taking a positive view of almost everything, they are saying to voters: *We just want to tell you this—we're* against *a lot of things and we're in favor of mighty few*. That this strategy proved successful at the polls in 1994 demonstrates just how much the nation changed in thirty years. While the Republicans like to present themselves as the true Americans, their appeal to pessimism reflects a fundamental shift away from the most basic of American attitudes.

Barry Goldwater was preaching negativism in an age of great optimism. The results were disastrous for him and the Republicans. Three decades later his party is once again preaching (and practicing) negativism, but Republicans are betting that this now matches the national mood. That it apparently does is a sad commentary on the state of our nation.

What progressives need to do is to show people how government can be a positive force in their lives by helping them respond to the new problems created by technological change and the internationalization of the economy. Government should be used to assist people to advance themselves: to *enable* them to cope in the new, difficult, and rapidly changing world in which they find themselves. "I think we should have an enabling, not a punitive, approach to such things as welfare reform," Senate Democratic Leader Tom Daschle says.[23] The GI Bill is the classic example of the government playing this role through what might be termed "enabling legislation." What the Republicans are proposing today often amounts to "disabling legislation." An example that contrasts directly with the GI Bill is the Republican effort to decrease funding for student loans, which will increase the debt burden with which millions of Americans leave college. The GI Bill helped people get a start in the race toward a better standard of living. Cutting the college loan program obliges students who do not come from affluent backgrounds to start that race with heavy weights tied to their legs. Far from "getting the government off our backs," this places the government, in the form of a bill collector, *on* the back of the young person beginning a career.

Anything with sufficient power to do substantial good necessarily has the strength to be a danger. Democrats and progressives must not fall into the trap of seeing government as the solution to every problem. But neither is government the cause of all—or most—problems. We must vigorously defend the accomplishments that we, the American people, have achieved through the instrument of government. And there are plenty to defend.

Government has provided us, either directly or in partnership with private enterprise, with: a high degree of assurance that the foods and medicines we consume are safe, Social Security, the best military in the world, the elimination of Nazism, the Salk vaccine, the Interstate highway system, a system of public higher education that is the envy of the world,

Medicare, space exploration, substantially cleaner air and water, the virtual elimination of hunger and malnutrition in this country, the eradication of smallpox, victory over Communism, and the Internet, to name just a few of the great things government has accomplished.

Which of these do we want to give up? Who among us wants to repudiate these achievements of government—achievements made by *us*, working together through the instrumentality of government?

A unified nation utilizing government was able to win victories over Nazism and Communism. Should we not at least try to do the same with the problems causing the Psychic Crisis of the Nineties?

THE CRITICAL NEED FOR LONG-TERM THINKING

Democrats need to show voters (and potential voters) the sorts of things government can do to enable them to cope with the new world of technology and competition that we are facing. A few examples were offered by Paul Begala and David Bonior.

Begala believes that the major economic statistics that are determining people's lives are the unemployment rate and wage growth. The Clinton administration was very successful in job growth, but could not budge wages. "The economists tell us that it is a very long-term thing; that there is just no chance that you can move wages in just two years. It took twenty years to stall them and it will take twenty years to move them," Begala said. This points toward the need for long-term solutions, but that is very difficult in a culture and economy that are based on short-term thinking. What the Clinton administration set out to do, Begala said, is to begin with an immunization program. "We were only ahead of Bolivia and Haiti—in the whole hemisphere—in immunization. So the two-year-old is going to be immunized. Two more years and she will get Headstart. And then she will go into what ought to be a better public school because of Title One and these things that Secretary Riley and all of them are doing. Move through that. Have college as an option, a real option, even if she is a poor or middle-class kid. Then, in twenty years if we do our job, she will have a good income and a good job and will be part of a pool of people who are moving incomes up now because they have better skills."[24]

It is an impressive vision, but how do you get people who have been conditioned by our consumption-ethic economy to look for instant gratification and have had it driven into their heads that the government is incapable of helping them to accept a government plan that may take two decades to deliver good results? While wages remain stagnant, Republicans come to voters and say, "OK, we tried it that way. They had two years. Let's move on. Let's try something else. Let's try a quick tax cut to put money in your pocket; let's beat up on some people who don't look like you."[25]

So Democrats will need to offer something that will produce tangible results in the shorter term, in addition to working on the needed long-term programs. "We can do things that tell people that we care about their incomes," David Bonior said. "Minimum wage is an important message to send—it doesn't go to everybody, but it says we're for increased wages. We do a lot in terms of retraining: making sure the people understand that we are going to be there for them if they get displaced, although people don't want to hear that they are going to lose their job several times in a lifetime. They get nervous about that. But you've got to have something there for them, when, in fact, these things happen." He goes on to say that support for education is essential because people fear that their children will not be able to do as well as they have and "at least you have to give them hope as far as the resources that are out there so that the children have the opportunity to develop—to do the best that they can, given the situation." Bonior also advocated dealing with people's feeling of insecurity in their schools and communities by putting "more police officers on the streets instead of building more prisons, I think that would be a welcome addition in the communities."[26]

INTERDEPENDENCE

Republicans have identified themselves as being "the antitax party." They want this to be understood as "the antigovernment party." But it also means "the anti-'us', pro-'me' party." This can be seen in "Tax Freedom Day," the invention of self-proclaimed "conservatives" who complain about the portion of each year that they work for the benefit of someone else: the taxman.[27] In the early 1990s, the day on which these analysts said the average American had made enough to cover all taxes and started working for him- or herself, came in early May. "That is a long time to wait for emancipation," lamented William F. Buckley, Jr.[28]

Emancipation is just the word for it. The concept of Tax Freedom Day is based upon the modern belief in complete independence—the notion that we are wholly separate atoms that form no compounds. The underlying assumption is that we do nothing together. There is, of course, no doubt that some of the money collected from us as taxes and spent collectively goes to foolish, needless purposes. But, then, so does much of what we spend on our own. The fact is—and always has been throughout human existence—that we can and must do some things together. These are the things we pay for through taxes.

Tax Freedom Day is meant to indicate that it is only what someone earns after that date that goes to meet his or her needs and wants; it implies that all that the person makes up until that day goes to others. This is nonsense. What I spend on my own goes to *me*; but what I pay in taxes goes not to *them*, but to *us*. It is only because so few among us any longer think in terms of "us" that anyone pays attention to such a self-oriented idea.

There are two ways in which a person can spend his or her money to meet his or her needs or wants: separately or together with others. Taxes collected by various levels of government provide for our national defense, highways, schools, police, parks, retirement pensions, environmental protection and cleanup, medical research, technological advances, and hundreds of others things that fall into one of two categories: things that we cannot do separately or things that we have concluded *we* can do better and more efficiently together than they could be done by separate "I's." That there are things better done together is obvious. It is, for example, a rare "conservative" who seeks to purchase health insurance outside of a group.

Surely there is room for debate about which things belong in these categories. But once we have decided on what *we* need to do together, the only responsible next step is to agree that *we* must pay for these necessary things. The payment should be based on a fair, equitable system that calls on those who have the most to bear a larger portion of the burden. But we are all part of "us," and we all have an obligation to contribute to what *we* need.

The concept of complete "independence" is literally inhuman. The only creatures that truly need no other member of their own species are those that reproduce asexually. Division requires cooperation. So long as members of a species are undifferentiated in terms of function, they can be genuinely independent. Egoism is the natural philosophy of amoebas (who get along nicely without taxes) and, it seems, Republicans, but it is unnatural for complex social animals—most of all for humans.

Humans have created more complex societies than have any other species. Our divisions of function and labor define us as interdependent. The more complex our societies become—the greater the division of function and labor—the more we must cooperate. Because we have divided what is necessary for survival, we are obliged to come together.

Oddly, though, as we have created ever more complex, interdependent societies, many of us have simultaneously adopted an ideology of full independence. That ideology has become more popular as it has become more inappropriate.

Human nature is an amalgam of selfish and social motivations. This means that our basic needs can be satisfied neither in a system that ignores the individual, such as communism, nor in one that pretends that each individual is entirely independent, which is what the Tax Freedom Day "conservatives" desire. Those who see taxation as theft understand why communism cannot work, but they fail to comprehend that pure egoism is just as inhuman.

Taxes are the dues we pay as highly interdependent, social creatures. None of us wants to pay more of them than is necessary; but once we have decided what it is necessary for us to do together, we must realize that paying for these things does not constitute having our money stolen from us. We pay taxes because every day is actually an interdependence day.

ENOUGH GOVERNMENT

The critical need in assuring that we attain the optimum amount of government, beyond bringing government back under the control of the people and getting it to start genuinely listening to America, is to begin to sort out what we can best do together from what we can best do separately. Republicans keep arguing that "people spend money better than government does."[29] This is *sometimes* true, but certainly it is not in all cases. Would we be better off spending our own money to hire police protection individually? Military protection? Roads? Schools? Each objective should be examined on the basis of whether it can more efficiently be done individually or together. Then each government program should be put to the test of whether it is worth its cost to the average taxpayer. This method of judging government programs is quite simple: divide the program's cost by the total number of tax returns. This will allow people to decide whether each of the various things the government does is worth doing by seeing what it actually costs *them*.

Ronald Reagan insisted that "Government is not the solution to our problems . . . Government is the problem."[30] We should not try to deny that some things government has done have contributed to our problems. But government can also provide *part* of the solution. In fact, it is more that certain people have been *in charge of* the government than government *per se* that have been part of the problem. Especially harmful have been major figures in government from opposite ends of the spectrum: those who thought government could do almost everything and so vastly over-promised, creating expectations that could not be met, and those who maintain that government can do almost nothing positive and make this a self-fulfilling prophecy when they are in office.

Taking a knee-jerk position in favor of or in opposition to government action is ideological folly; rather, we should examine particular problems to determine what should be left entirely to individuals; what we can do better together, as a people, through the government; and in what ways the government might be able to facilitate individuals and families in helping themselves.

We must employ common sense, not extremist ideology in determining the sort of changes we need. Some of our opponents reflexively condemn any government action. This is as foolish as the opposite extreme of favoring government activity in any and all areas. Either of these ideological positions is potentially disastrous. One way that Democrats and progressives might begin to get away from the perception that they are people who never met a government program they didn't like or were not willing to consider cutting is suggested by Senator Daschle: "I think maybe we shouldn't be proposing *permanent* government programs. We should have specific programs to deal with particular problems within a set time period."[31]

Some things can be done better individually; others can best be done together. Not doing together those things that make sense to do together is foolish; it is letting ideology stand in the way of common sense.

That's just what some Republicans are doing. They are such ideologues that they want to dismantle not only those programs where the government has been doing things that individuals can do better themselves, but also those where joint action is obviously more sensible than separate actions. Ellen Goodman has put it well: "The GOP Congress isn't just trying to balance the budget. They want to end the idea of government as an agent of mutual responsibility."[32] Exactly. And that is the line that separates progressives from so-called conservatives. We believe that it is essential to employ government as an agent of mutual responsibility. No solutions for *us*, rather than *me*, are possible unless we are willing to try to use government effectively. And, in the kind of world we are living in, as Bill Clinton once said to me, "the people who work together are those who climb."[33]

We need *enough* government, but not *too much* government; and we need the right *sort* of government. Mario Cuomo says it best: "Of course, we should have *only* the government we need. But we must insist on *all* the government we need."[34]

11

A Renewed Social Contract for America

Webs Instead of Wedges

Republican campaigns during the last several elections have been based on what the late political strategist Lee Atwater termed "wedge issues." The positions that the party has collected under the banner of "family values"—opposition to abortion, homosexuality, and feminism, combined (as Patrick J. Buchanan reminded us with his 1992 convention speech and again with his campaign for the 1996 Republican nomination) with religious intolerance, racism, and xenophobia—are used as "wedge issues." The purpose of a wedge is, of course, to divide. Wedge issues are designed to split people apart. It is a new variant of the old "divide and conquer" strategy, as Secretary Reich points out: "Ignore the real problems; get anxious people scared and mad at each other—and hope that this fear puts enough points on the board to win when the buzzer sounds."[1]

Atwater explained the underlying view of politics that produces this approach when he told George Bush during the 1988 campaign that his "'kinder, gentler' theme was a nice thought, but it wouldn't win us many votes."[2] Although the wording is of more recent vintage, the practice is nothing new. Notice how similar Atwater's 1988 statement sounds to Newt Gingrich's declaration ten years earlier that Republicans need to "be nasty" and abandon "Boy Scout words" that make for "lousy politics."[3]

In fact, the Republicans' successful use of wedge issues dates back at least to the 1968 campaign of Buchanan's former employer, Richard Nixon. Recalling Attorney General John Mitchell's advice to watch what they do instead of what they say, it is notable that while Nixon was saying that he was trying to "bring us together," what he and his staff were doing was summed up later by Vice President Spiro T. Agnew as "positive polarization—to divide on authentic lines."[4] The polarization they promoted was negative for the country, but positive for the party. Buchanan stated the objective directly in a memo to President Nixon: "Cut . . . the country in half; my view is that we would have far the larger half."[5]

The driving of wedges between larger and smaller parts of the population has been the essential Republican strategy for a quarter century. With it, the party has won all but two presidential elections in those years. Wedges helped the GOP win control of Congress in 1994. Plainly the Republicans are gleefully planning more of the same today by sounding alarms on immigration and affirmative action.

The wedges that the Republicans have driven into the American populace have harmed America greatly. While pledging their allegiance to "one nation, indivisible," Republicans have cynically utilized their wedges to divide the nation. Their wedges put the lie to their pledges.

(This is not to deny that Democrats have used wedge issues, too; they have, for example, often grasped the Social Security and Medicare wedges, which they keep within easy reach on their political tool shelf. But the Democrats have not employed wedges as frequently as have the Republicans, and they have generally been much less successful at it.)

The wedge that the GOP has used most frequently and effectively is race. From Mitchell's "Southern strategy" of 1968, through Ronald Reagan's "welfare queen" of 1980, George Bush's Willie Horton of 1988, and Buchanan's "take back America" in 1992 and 1996, to the attack on affirmative action that appears likely at this writing to be a central feature of their 1996 campaign, Republicans have tried to pit the white majority against the black minority. The arithmetic is simple: whites vastly outnumber blacks in the United States, so the party that can drive a wedge between the races and identify itself with the whites will win elections.

As they did under Nixon, the Republicans continue to say one thing and do the opposite. In 1988, George Bush called for a "kinder, gentler" nation. Four years later, his party's platform was entitled "Uniting Our Family, Our Country, Our World." Both themes echoed Nixon's "bring us together." But the basis of all three campaigns was to use wedges to do the reverse.

Wedges promote neither a kinder, gentler nation nor family values. Splitting the people and turning segment against segment prevents the nation from viewing itself as a family.

Some might discount the remarks of Buchanan as the rantings of someone on the fringe. But it was Rich Bond (has there ever been a more fitting name for a Republican leader?), the chairman of the party that often talks of "uniting our country," who made the ultimate unkind, ungentle, us/them comment when he said of Democrats during the 1992 campaign: "They aren't Americans; we are." And it was Speaker Gingrich who stated that "sick Democrats" are the "enemies of normal Americans."[6]

There is an alternative political approach. At his best (which is to say, part of the time), Bill Clinton has pursued the opposite of the Buchanan-Atwater-Gingrich practice of driving wedges into the American populace. He does not appear to have ever used the phrase in public, but the President has often spoken in private of the need to develop "web issues."

Paul Begala said in our interview that, like most political consultants, he used to look for wedge issues. But, "when I started working for Bill Clinton, he had totally different views, so much more noble. He used to say this all the time: 'We don't need wedge issues; we need web issues—that stitch people together'" across racial and other lines. "It's a very wise observation," Begala contended. "There are so few ties that bind in our society anyway," Clinton notes. "We don't have a common language; there is no compulsory military service anymore. There is nothing that throws all people together and gives them a chance to come to understand one another and see what they have in common." This is why national service is such an important issue in Clinton's thinking. While the Republicans keep looking for wedges to split Americans apart, Begala insists that "Clinton tries hard to look for webs: the things that stitch us back together."[7]

The difference was evident in Clinton's 1996 State of the Union address. He kept sounding conciliatory, speaking of "common ground" and the need to "go forward as one America—one nation working together, to meet the challenges we face together."[8] But while Democrats resoundingly applauded such lines, Republican legislators (whose leaders had found it necessary to give them a stern lecture on the need to show civil behavior and not boo the president; it seems that Mr. Gingrich's efforts to recruit Republican candidates who are as nasty, uncivil, and "un-Boy Scout-ish" as he is were highly successful) sat in silence. In the official response for his party that was accurately described in the press as "unusually blistering," Senator Bob Dole indicated that the time had come to draw the line and refuse compromise. He charged that Clinton "shares a view of America held by our country's elites," favors "special interest groups," "dependence," "handouts," and "outdated values" that hold the nation back.[9] Immediately after Clinton tried to spin webs, the Republican leader hammered wedges.

On the question of wedges or webs, David Bonior believes that Democrats should employ "a little of each." "I think the overall idea of bringing people together is a theme that's more in line with what we're all about," he said to me. "Much more so. It's who we are. We can't function unless we hug this group and hug that group and bring them all under the tent, because that's what the composition of our party is supposed to be." He is, however, a political realist: "I'm not above using a wedge issue if I can, politically." He pointed out that the Republicans "have their own fractures between very traditionalist country-clubbers and religious-right folks. Sometimes they could use a good wedge, and we will be happy to supply it."[10]

Emphasizing webs would be a wise practice for all Democrats and progressives. "I think, in general, it's better not to demagogue," Senator Simon said to me. "We shouldn't separate people that way. What we have to do is tell people what we are going to do for all of us."[11] Congresswoman Marcy Kaptur has put the web ideal well: "Let us today recommit to a higher purpose than individual gain and make our cause not, 'I the person,' but 'we the people of the United States.'"[12]

Wedge politics are a major contributor to our fundamental problem of disunity. They are the principal weapon in the destructive sort of politics that E. J. Dionne has described in the following way: "We are encouraging an 'either/or' politics based on ideological preconceptions rather than a 'both/and' politics based on ideas that broadly unite us."[13]

Joe Kennedy argued that Democrats must take the opposite approach—and that traditionally they have. "I think liberal Democrats for the most part tend to be people with some hope of trying to say, 'Look, if we bind together and find a method of establishing a sense of teamwork, of accomplishing a mission, of setting a purpose and goals, that working together we can accomplish great things in the future."[14]

Although they were never called by the name, webs have been central to the Democratic vision for decades. We need social webs at least as much as we need a social safety net. Dale Bumpers suggested that this approach was a large part of the reason for Franklin Roosevelt's popularity. "We're all better off when we're all better off," the Arkansas senator said. "Or, as Hubert Humphrey said, 'it will never be a good place for any of us to live until it's a good place for all of us to live.'"[15]

A NEW SOCIAL CONTRACT

"The need that this nation has now is for a vision of community beyond the culture of greed, for political priorities that put the needs of people first."[16] With these words, Betty Friedan put her finger on one of the central themes of a new progressive vision: *community*.

We have heard a great deal lately about political "contracts," including Newt Gingrich's brainchild, the House Republicans' 1994 "Contract with America" and the Christian Coalition's 1995 "Contract with the American

Family." But while portions of these politically motivated and market-tested contracts touch on some of our major problems, it is the breach of another contract that is at the base of our national and personal troubles.

The underlying cause of our problems can be summed up in a sentence: *The social contract in the United States has been broken.*

"I think what we have lost is the concept in America of caring about each other," Patsy Mink said in our interview. "Everybody is just into themselves. Every policy is analyzed on the basis of: 'What is it going to do for *me*?' Not to the society at large." "Young people have lost it—generations of young people have lost that desire to look at the country's needs as a whole. Their well-being is all they are concerned about. Very strange," the Hawaiian Congresswoman mused.[17]

Strange; but not inexplicable. The breaking of the social contract is at the heart of the Psychic Crisis of the Nineties. Part of the cause, to be sure, is to be found in the twin perils of technological change and international competition. When the times in general look bleak, it is difficult to be optimistic for society as a whole. So if one wants to retain hope, the easiest way to do it is to plan, in Arthur Levine's marvelous phrase, to go "first class on the *Titanic*": to see a bright personal future while the community is sinking.[18] But there is more to it than this; much more. We must understand that the unnoticed engine driving the jackhammer that has broken apart the social contract is the supply-side economy that maximizes consumption by influencing people to think in terms of "me" and "more." When value$ displace values, a climate is created in which the social contract withers.

What progressive Democrats need to do is to identify themselves as being for traditional social values and against value$. "I think the time has passed when you can organize a political party around programs," White House domestic policy advisor Bruce Reed said to me. "You can only organize them around values. The Republicans have been doing that for years, and Democrats stopped doing it some time around thirty years ago, when they finally couldn't agree on their values anymore."[19] It is past time to reach such an agreement on values again.

TWO-WAY RESPONSIBILITY

One of Ronald Reagan's most effective lines in his 1980 campaign to unseat President Carter was: "Are you better off than you were four years ago?" For Americans living outside the South (and some parts of New York City), there is no distinction between the second person singular and plural. But there was little doubt that Reagan's *you* was singular. He did not mean "y'all." He was not suggesting that people examine the condition of the society as a whole, but that each individual compare his or her situation with what it had been when Carter took office. The question was not "Are *we* better off?" but "Am *I* better off?"

If Reagan's question were asked in the mid-nineties, keeping the reference point as the mid-seventies, many Americans (in the top 20 percent, the higher their ranking, the more so) could shout, *Yes!* But there would not be a psychic crisis, and three-quarters of the people would not be telling pollsters that they believe the country is headed in the wrong direction if *we as a society* were not ready to answer, *No, our condition is worse.* And a major reason that our social condition has declined is the erosion of the social contract.

We have forgotten that we are part of a community and a society and that this involves responsibilities that flow in two directions. There are both personal responsibilities and social responsibilities. Some of us seem to think that society owes us everything, but we have no obligations to society. Others think that they have seceded from society altogether, and can "go it alone," neither helping anyone else nor asking for anyone else's help.

What we need to realize is that responsibility is a two-way street. Robert Reich calls "the marriage between personal responsibility and the responsibility of society" the "first value" of civilization.[20] We are *both* individuals *and* members of communities. We must help ourselves and others. Each political party has made half of this case in recent years, but neither party has effectively made the argument for both directions of responsibility. "More than anything." Reed rightly said, "we need moral leadership that urges people to look out for one another and themselves. We're not getting that."[21]

Two-way responsibility means that individuals must try to help themselves and be held accountable for their actions. Republicans have long preached this half of responsibility—at least to the poor. They don't seem to be nearly as enthusiastic about being held accountable for their own actions in increasing the national debt. Unfortunately, too many Democrats have been silent on this aspect of responsibility.

The other side of responsibility is social responsibility—what we owe to each other as a community or society. Democrats have long emphasized this kind of responsibility, while Republicans have generally been silent.

To put the matter simply: "conservatives" call for personal responsibility, but generally ignore social responsibility; "liberals" call for social responsibility, but tend to ignore personal responsibility.

The failing on both sides lies in seeing this as an either/or choice. We are individuals who live together in communities, not just one or the other. We *are* our brothers' and sisters' keepers; but we are also our own keepers. The "conservative" attitude says every*one* should look out for him- or herself and be responsible for meeting his or her own needs while acting in a moral and responsible fashion. That's correct.

But so is the "liberal" attitude that we have a social responsibility to help others in need. These two types of responsibility go hand-in-hand; choosing only one kind yields, at best, a half-responsibility that is actually irresponsible. You are not likely to take care of yourself if you are not willing to help take care of others. You are unlikely to "feel good about yourself" unless you care about others, too.

The radical Republicans of the mid-nineties have presented many demonstrations of where one-sided responsibility leaves us. They keep talking about the need for "personal responsibility" to replace social programs. By this they mean, for example, that not only an elderly person's assets, but also those of his or her children would be susceptible to seizure to pay nursing home bills now covered by Medicare; that pension plans might vanish or be tapped by companies and we would have to assume "personal responsibility" for our retirement; that student loans would be drying up, or the interest payments increasing, and we would have to take "personal responsibility" for our children's education.[22] That's a lot of responsibility for one person—especially one who is not among the wealthy—to shoulder without help from the larger community.

"We have to challenge people to take responsibility for their own lives and use government to do what it can, but not pretend [either] that government can solve every problem, or that getting rid of government can solve every problem," Bruce Reed says.[23]

What we desperately need to turn this country around in both an economic and a moral sense is to encourage responsibility in both directions.

Bill Clinton outlined such a renewal of the social contract through two-way responsibility in a conversation I had with him six years before he was elected president. He stated that we need a family policy that stresses more spending for poor children and pregnant mothers, more work for the mothers and more responsibility for the fathers. "We've got to save people, [but] there is a limit to what the government can do." He said we need to say to people: "You've got to change your values. If you don't choose to protect yourself—and your family and community members—from destruction, there is nothing a Democrat or Republican can do." "There has got to be a heavy dose of self-help," Clinton continued. "We've got to lift up the responsible leadership in all these communities. [There are] a lot of great role models for young children—white, black, brown, otherwise. We need to do more of that and the presidency needs to become a bully pulpit for the regeneration of life and possibility for all those people who are being lost in the social problems. A Democrat can do that better because we have more credibility on that," said the

Arkansas Governor. "We've got to help them; but it's largely a choice to survive that has to be made by individuals and families and groups that we can support, but we have to insist that that is what we are emphasizing." This, Clinton rightly concluded, has to be "a big part of the new Democratic philosophy."[24]

Here was a most astute précis of much of the new vision Democrats are still seeking. There are two principal reasons why we have not gotten there, even after the man who so clearly saw what is needed has made it to the White House.

The first and lesser problem is that President Clinton has not, because of his personal history, been able to make effective use of the bully pulpit to preach the need for personal responsibility coupled with social responsibility. By far the more important difficulty in actually achieving the renaissance of the social contract that Clinton so clearly envisioned is that, even as a president and other leaders may be telling people they need to change their values, the entire supply-side, consumption-ethic economy is telling them, through advertising and popular culture, the opposite: *You are what you have, what you buy and consume; others are merely objects to be used for your individual advancement. "You only go around once who says you can't grab all the gusto because I have it all in life I'm worth it just do it because I believe in me!"* The problem, as I noted earlier, is not that the underclass has not adopted our values, but that they *have*. If we would change their values, we had better change ours—as well as the direction of our economic culture, which is the real acid searing away the social contract.

It is certainly true, as Clinton said to me, that "we all rise or fall together" and that the problems of the underclass adversely affect the larger society.[25] But we should not lose sight of the fact that the problems of the larger society, such as the consumption ethic and the consequent "Look Out for Number One" philosophy, adversely affect the underclass, too.

An example of what two-way responsibility means is that people on welfare must be helped to become self-supporting. We should neither just throw them onto the streets to fend for themselves nor continue policies that keep them in dependency. Instead, we should develop an enabling program that requires job training and provides child care and health benefits so that welfare recipients can become self-supporting. "Welfare reform without jobs," Paul Simon rightly points out, "is not really welfare reform. [If] people can't read and write, you get them into a program. If they don't have a high school degree, you get them into something. If they have marginal skills, get them into a technical school."[26]

President Clinton believes that "the fundamental points are creating a bridge from welfare to work and expecting a greater measure of personal responsibility in return for the public support needed to construct that bridge," former White House domestic policy advisor Bill Galston says.[27]

Two-way responsibility would point toward government housing programs that move away from warehousing poor people in government-owned buildings and instead seek to accomplish something similar to what Habitat for Humanity does on a smaller scale. "We need something like a Homestead program for urban residents," Marcy Kaptur said to me. "Our goal should be equity building, which means government helping people to gain a stake in society."[28] *Precisely*.

Two-way responsibility also means that we must ask the question: "What do we owe each other as members of this society?" The answer of some conservatives to this question seems to be: "Nothing; each person is responsible for him- or herself and no one else."

But that is just not so. "We are," as President Clinton said in a July 1995 speech at Georgetown University, "literally a community—an American family that is going up or down together, whether we like it or not." What happens to others does matter to us. "If we are going to have middle-class dreams and middle-class values," Clinton continued, "we have to do things as private citizens and we have to do things in partnership, through our public agencies and through our other associations."[29]

President Clinton clearly still understands reciprocal, two-way responsibility better than most leading political figures do. He stated it nicely once again in his 1996 State of the Union Address: "Citizens must share responsibility with their government. . . . Self-reliance and teamwork are not opposing virtues—we must have both."[30] *Exactly*.

Those who rode first-class on the *Titanic* wound up in the same place as those with regular accommodations. We have broken down our connections with others in the present and with the past and future, to live "now" as isolated "selves." We have to return to thinking in terms of "we" as well as (not instead of) "me."

Connections are an essential part of responsibility. Bill Clinton has made attempts to use the bully pulpit to restore Americans' sense of connection with each other and with our forebears and descendants, but so far without much success.

For their part, Republicans' policies are likely to weaken community further. "This [Republican] contract, or con- whatever you want to call it, is going to rip apart our national community," Paul Wellstone said to me. What we need, the Minnesota senator went on, "is a set of values that will tie us together. The aspiration is for a community where equality of opportunity really is there."[31]

The disconnection of the Republicans from past and future can be seen in everything from their energy and environmental policies to their massive increase in the federal debt and their encouragement of similar increases in corporate and consumer debt. The basis of the GOP appeal is to the live-for-today mentality. "The Republicans say 'we are going to do something for you today, on an individual basis,'" James Carville notes.[32]

Rights and Responsibilities

What too many among us have lost sight of in recent years is something that the Founders of our nation realized full well: that rights go hand-in-hand with responsibilities. They understood that citizenship is a two-way street. It cannot be all take and no give. *Reciprocity*—reciprocal rights and responsibilities—must be another of our central themes.

Our failure to stress responsibilities as much as we emphasize rights is at the root of many of the social ills that plague us today. Too many people think only of themselves—expecting their rights without accepting their responsibilities. The results of the failure to make the elementary connection between rights and responsibilities are all around us, from unwed teenagers having babies they cannot support and deadbeat dads failing to provide support payments for their children to an explosion of assaults and murders in which the attacker clearly sees no connection between himself and his victim.

It is a safe assumption that these pathologies are not what Jefferson had in mind when he spoke of our "unalienable rights." He and the others who helped to establish the United States understood what some of us have forgotten: The abbreviation for "United States" is "U S," not "M E."

As we seek to expand the proper rights of all Americans, we must balance those rights with a recognition of the responsibilities that are part of membership in our American community. Natural rights are linked with natural responsibilities. Freedom is not free. The Bill of Rights is one of our proudest achievements as a people. But the unraveling of our society in recent years shows that we also need a Bill of Responsibilities.

These responsibilities can serve as a guide for both our individual actions and our governmental policies:

Bill of Responsibilities

1. We have the responsibility to understand that we are members of a community and so to consider the effects of our actions on others. Our most essential responsibility is summarized in the basic teaching of most religions: Do unto others as you would have them do unto you.
2. We must recognize our connection with and responsibility to future generations. Among other things, this means conserving limited

resources, controlling pollution, and not running up debts that future generations will have to pay.

3. We have a responsibility not to create children we cannot, or do not plan to, care for.
4. We have a responsibility to nurture, educate, and teach values to the young—and to teach those values in what we *do*, as well as what we say. We have, in short, a responsibility to *live* the values we preach.
5. We have a responsibility to respect and care for the elderly.
6. As individuals and as a society, we have a responsibility to protect and assist the weak and ill. We also each have a responsibility to care for ourselves and avoid behaviors that are likely to endanger our health.
7. We have a responsibility to do all we can to care for and help ourselves—not to expect the government or the taxpayers to support us when we are capable of supporting ourselves.
8. We have a responsibility to tolerate (within the limits of accepted values) those who think, act, or worship differently from us; to guard our liberties by respecting and protecting those of others.
9. We have a responsibility to preserve the peace. This means that we should do everything we can to avoid getting involved in war, but also that we have a responsibility to maintain an adequate military that will make it clear to any irresponsible regimes that may arise anywhere in the world that we have the means and the will to resist aggression.

HARD-HEADED AND SOFT-HEARTED

In December 1994, outgoing Democratic Congressman Dave McCurdy, who had just lost his bid to be elected to the Senate from Oklahoma, complained that President Clinton has the head of a New Democrat, but retains the heart of an Old Democrat.[33] McCurdy meant this to be part of the flood of Clinton-bashing that had become so popular in the wake of the 1994 electoral debacle. But what he charged the president with being is exactly what Democrats should aspire to be: hard-headed and soft-hearted. This is certainly preferable to the opposite condition, one in which many Republicans find themselves. Their proposal to take children from their mothers and put them in orphanages is a perfect example. It would be both harsh and expensive: hard-hearted and soft-headed.

There is nothing wrong with being soft-hearted, so long as one has a hard head to go along with his or her soft heart. Franklin Roosevelt summed up what should remain a basic Democratic credo when he declared in 1936: "Governments can err; Presidents do make mistakes, . . . But better the occasional faults of a Government that lives in a spirit of charity than the constant omissions of a Government frozen in the ice of its own indifference."[34]

If "a spirit of charity" is taken to mean cooperation, compassion, and two-way responsibility, not spirit-deadening, dead-end giveaway programs, this statement is a perfect summary of one of the major differences between the parties. Should Democrats ever abandon their soft-hearted spirit, their party would cease to have a reason to exist.

Americans are yearning for a return to the principles, ideals, and cooperative values taught by our great religions. These are the values that have made America great. There is nothing new about these principles. Community, connection, interdependence, reciprocity, and responsibility are venerable American values.

Puritan leader John Winthrop summed them up as early as 1630: "Particular estates cannot subsist in the ruin of the public," he said. People in the community must "partake of each other's strength and infirmity, joy and sorrow, weale and woe," Winthrop declared. "If one member suffers, all suffer with it; if one be in honor, all rejoice with it." "We must bear one another's burdens, we must not look only on our own things, but also on the things of our brethren," this longtime Governor of the Massachusetts Bay colony concluded.[35]

What we need today is not a new deal, but a renewed deal: a revival of the ideals and values that made America great, a renewal of the social contract.

Sink or Swim—Two Visions of the American Future

The contrasting visions of Democrats and Republicans, progressives and conservatives, on how to deal with the three-fold crisis facing Americans—the rise of a two-tier, winner-take-all economy, the collapse of values (including community, responsibility, reciprocity, and future orientation), and the growth of a poisonous cynicism and lack of faith in public institutions—must be brought into sharp focus.

I have argued throughout these pages that the deep, underlying source of these intertwined problems is the supply-side economy in which we have let ourselves become dependent on maximizing consumption. If this is so, ultimate solutions must address bringing about major changes in the economy.

Short of those very difficult and necessarily slow changes (for which there appears to be zero probability that Republicans would even recognize the need), there are clear differences in approach to the more immediate problems facing the nation. As we move into the brave new economy, there are two very distinct, competing visions.

The Republican vision is already fully formed. Paul Begala outlined it correctly: "It is: 'I want you to have more and more freedom, more and more disposable income, less and less taxes, more and more independence, plus less government. That's our vision.' And I think we need to say to that same person, 'What good does it do you to hear some politician prattle along about getting government off your back? You have been laid off from U.S. Steel in Bucks County, Pennsylvania. And that job is gone. And you want to go to work for Microsoft. Bill Gates ain't going to train you. That's not his job. . . . So government is off your back. Congratulations! You know that as you sit there watching your unemployment benefits going away, watching *Oprah*.'"

"This is really big and fundamental," Begala continued. "I think that there is this race going on to try to find this new world, and the Republicans have a clear and simpler message. And it has the short-term benefits of being very in touch with their traditions."[36]

That simple GOP message emphasizes individualism and freedom, not government. The trouble is that it doesn't explain a way out. It's a hollow message. "Basically, the Republicans would leave people on their own, to sink or swim," as Tom Daschle said.[37]

We are seeing the results of that. Twenty percent are swimming (one percent like Olympic champions), many more are barely treading water, and the rest are sinking. Republicans have no problem with private floatation devices, such as large inheritances, but they don't want to provide lifeboats for those who need them.

In contrast, Democrats need to acknowledge that many of the bureaucratic solutions they've tried in the past have not worked well.

"But that doesn't mean that there is nothing that we can do to meet this new world," Begala said. "And it is—I think in a lot of ways—a more confident message, too."[38] It is a vision confident not just of a blinding bright future for a few big winners, but of a good life for all of us.

In the progressive vision of the future, the government provides assistance that enables people to advance in the new world economy, from childhood immunization through Headstart, school lunches, solid education, college loans, and lifelong job retraining.

The basic difference between these two visions of the future is that Democrats can say to people facing the highly competitive world: *You are not alone*. Republicans, on the other hand, say: *Oh, yes you are. Good luck to you (you'll need it). No one really cares if you can get yourself in a position to compete and succeed.*

INVESTING IN THE FUTURE

In 1995, Republicans suddenly rediscovered the budget deficit that they had done so much to create over the preceding decade and a half. Now, following, as we have seen, a long-term strategy some of them had devised at the beginning of the Reagan Administration, they used the deficit as an excuse to dismantle the federal social programs that had been their target from the start. Their announced desire to balance the budget and so stop borrowing from future generations gave Republicans the appearance of being concerned with the future. But it is a future centered around the winner-take-all society, with few places of importance or even decent living standards for the rest.

The future is one of the major themes for a new progressivism, but the future is not unidimensional. We have, as Education Secretary Dick Riley points out, many other deficits besides that in the annual federal budget: "an education deficit, a deficit in concern for the environment, deficits in urban development, and progress deficits and hope deficits for a lot of people."[39]

What all of this adds up to is an "investment deficit." Failure to invest in ways that will prepare our people for the challenges of the twenty-first century will do at least as much to subvert the future as leaving a large debt will. Underfunding of such programs as WIC and Headstart amounts to undermining the future. Studies indicate that $500 spent on prenatal care greatly reduces the number of low-birthweight babies. Intensive neonatal care for such infants costs a minimum of $2,500 a day and can last for months. Headstart is a program proven to reduce dropout and crime rates among those who participate in it. But the Republican attitude seems to be: *Save a little now; let someone else worry about the much greater costs later.*

Despite the guffaws that greeted Bill Clinton's attempt to make a distinction between "investment" and "spending," there is a crucial difference between spending money in ways that will save money and resources and help people in the future and simply spending for present purposes. The former is clearly wise, and investment should be an important theme for Democrats.

There is a crucial distinction between programs, such as the GI Bill, immunization, nutrition, Headstart, crime prevention, and so forth—programs that save money in the long run—and those that just represent money spent with no return. In keeping with their individualistic and short-term outlook, Republicans favor just giving money back to taxpayers (especially well-to-do ones), without any plan to encourage behaviors that will yield dividends in the future. Democratic proposals for tax reductions have centered, in contrast, on encouraging desirable activities.

President Clinton proposed to combine a tax cut with an investment strategy by, as Bonior put it, "packaging it, not as a tax cut, but as an investment. It is an education tax cut basically, but we are packaging it as an investment in resources that will provide dividends down the road. Ten thousand dollars deductible for educational expenses, reduction on the student loans, some IRA advantages to put away for education and a tax-free savings account for little ones who grow up and are ready for college."[40] "Here's how we're going to do our new investment in education," Begala said. "We will allow you to deduct tuition, job training."

He points out that corporations can deduct advertising costs. "I mean, right now corporations are using Joe Camel to sell cigarettes to children. But, you and I can't deduct our kids' tuition. That's nuts. Those two expenditures are not societally comparable. One is preferable to the other, and the one that is preferable is the one that doesn't have any tax deductions now." This is an example of how government can help people prepare for the new world without using bureaucracy. This approach was once considered a Republican idea, but President Clinton took it up, saying, "Who cares whose idea it was to begin with? We cut a lot of bureaucracy by doing it. We're the activists here. More people will be educated and trained, and that's good."[41]

Investment is a way to talk about what we need to do that may be more acceptable to late-twentieth-century American ears than sacrifice is. As Bill Clinton noted in our conversation, Ronald Reagan was good at "talking the language of sacrifice." Clinton declared that Reagan was "a brilliant student of human nature. He understands that we all want to believe that we are sacrificing, that we are tough, that we are re-generating ourselves." But, Clinton maintained, what Reagan actually did was give the country something-for-nothing by pursuing a massive buy now/pay later plan. *Real* sacrifice is a tough item to market.[42]

A TRUE BALANCED BUDGET

But while we need to be very much concerned with investment, it is also essential that we move toward a balanced budget. It has always been foolish to think that it is good for progressive Democrats to be opposed to a balanced budget. This does not, however, mean going along with the Republican priorities. Progressive Democrats need our own balanced budget.

"We shouldn't have Newt Gingrich's balanced budget," Joe Kennedy said in our interview. "But the fact that we are spending more money on Star Wars and more money on B-2s and more money on F-22s, more money on a whole range of weapons systems, that the military themselves say that they don't need and don't want, and yet we do it for them anyway, because of lobbyists and a lot of rhetoric that surrounds the notion that we want a strong national defense, is just ridiculous. The fact that we are willing to spend billions and billions of dollars on corporate welfare—I mean, come on! We are spending hundreds of millions of dollars to build roads into forests where virgin lumber is going to be cut down and sold to the Japanese as pulp so that we can buy back fiberboard from them. This is crazy. It's un-American. It's stupid. It's just a subsidy to corporations. It is not Democratic. It is not liberal. It is what the Republicans get away with. Give me a break. Stop it!"

Kennedy went on to make the strong case that "robbing our children to pay for our excesses today is also crazy." Not only is it immoral, but piling debt on our children is not helping the poor now. "Every major program affecting the poor has been cut and interest on the debt, which basically goes to rich people, and defense spending have skyrocketed. That's just plain idiotic," Kennedy concluded.[43]

What Democrats need to defend are enabling programs for the poor, along with the social safety net, not simply a balanced budget as if that were something automatically good in itself. (We must be careful, though, and not move precipitously to balance the budget, lest we cause our top-heavy economy to lose its equilibrium and suffer a catastrophic fall. It remains a serious possibility that balancing the budget while income distribution is so unbalanced might yield an economic collapse.)

The Limits of the Market

"Their vision is so narrow," Patsy Mink said to me of the right-wing Republicans. "They just want a small government. They obviously believe that the market will take care of everything—the market will take care of the sick, provide jobs, reduce the trade deficit."[44] If left free to work its magic, the market will solve all problems, they think. This is the fundamental problem with the Republican philosophy. The Market is their God. They genuflect in front of the New York Stock Exchange and trace the sign of the dollar on their chests. The market is, to be sure, a very powerful force. Were we polytheistic, we might readily accept the Market as one among the deities. But it is a fundamental mistake to confuse the market with a single, omnipotent Deity. It is a deity that lacks some of the attributes that most of us expect from our God, such as justice, compassion, and morality.

When the Market is taken as an omnipotent God, it becomes an excuse for actions that run counter to decency, morality, and traditional values: *Well, we might not* like *to "downsize" thousands of our employees out of jobs, possibly ruining their lives, but we have no choice. We must stay competitive. The Market* requires *us to do it.*

What the worship of the omnipotent Market can do to values was nicely shown by the response of a man in Richmond, California, to a National Public Radio interviewer when he was asked early in 1996 about the possibility of curbing violence and sex on television and in movies. "It's a marketplace, after all," he said reverently. "If there's a market for it, how can you tell people they can't produce it?"[45] Could the same not be said of heroin, cocaine, or atomic bombs?

The market promises—and delivers—wondrous goods and services. No economic system can come close to matching the productive forces that it can unleash. While this enormous productive capacity is an obvious blessing, it is not an unmixed one. It had, as I explained in Chapter 3, resulted by the early twentieth century in such an enormous and rapidly growing supply that it seemed necessary to begin artificially to stimulate consumption, which, in turn, required a lifting of restraints on basic acquisitive urges, and so the subversion of those traditional values that had helped to keep them in check.

The social Darwinian "conservatives" who argue that, as the classical economists (after whose scheme of brutal, unrestrained free-market competition Darwin modeled his view of "marketplace biology") insisted, that morality has no place in a market-based economy (no more than it does in Darwin's nature) are right. Their economics may have become a *less* dismal science with the amazing productivity of its supply-side phase, but that is precisely why it destroys values.

Since the market is amoral, anyone who desires *both* the benefits of the productive forces that this economic system unleashes *and* the preservation or revival of traditional values (and most Republicans, as well as most Americans, profess to want both of these objectives) *has to* accept that morality will be imposed upon this amoral system by regulation.

"As corporations have focused more and more intensely on increasing shareholders' returns and less and less on improving the standard of living of their workers," Reich says, "it should be no surprise that the stock market has soared while pink slips have proliferated and the paychecks of most employees have gone nowhere." The Secretary of Labor says that if we want corporations "to put greater emphasis on the interests of their workers and communities, society must reorganize them to do so."

One small step in this direction has been suggested by Secretary Reich and several leading Democrats in Congress. If too many corporations are insisting on giving the profits from increased productivity to shareholders and CEOs, but not to workers, these Democrats say we need incentives to change corporate behavior. Sen. Edward Kennedy proposed legislation to lower the tax rate for businesses that meet standards of "good citizenship" in such areas as "creating jobs, avoiding layoffs 'simply to maximize profits,' paying adequate wages, and providing training for their workers."[46]

THE FAIR DISTRIBUTION OF INCOME

Contrary to what the champions of a totally free market tell us, the distribution of income and wealth is a matter of public concern. Certainly our major goal should be providing equality of opportunity. Of course, we neither can nor should try to produce equality of results. But we can temper some of the worst inequalities of results. This is not an either/or question. The choice is not only between the extremes of a totally unfettered capitalism and socialism. It is possible—and necessary for our well-being as a society—to have a "slightly fettered free market."

The justification for "letting the dollars fall where they may" is that our system is a meritocracy. There is a great deal of truth in this, but the smug assumption (usually held by those at or near the top) that it is always true that whoever has a lot deserves all he or she has, regardless of how much that is, does not necessarily follow.

Which skills and talents are worth rewarding? How great a difference in reward should a small difference in a particular talent produce? These are questions that should first be sorted out by the market, but if we do not make the mistake of confusing the market with God, there is no good reason why some adjustments cannot be made when obvious injustices are propagated by the market.

Today, someone who can use a rounded piece of wood to hit a small spheroid thrown toward him on a rapid, curving trajectory may command millions of dollars in compensation. A century and a half ago this same talent would have been virtually worthless in the marketplace.

We should not think that macroeconomic, technological, and cultural changes that put much more income in the hands of a few "winners" and less in those of most others means that the winners suddenly have more merit than they did before.

Of course, we cannot have the government parceling out shares of income. The market must remain the basic way in which rewards are allocated. But, to preserve the public interest, some checks have to be placed on this process. To employ an absurd example to make a point, what if one person could accumulate *all* of a society's wealth? Or, what if 1 percent of the population received 99 percent of the income? There must be an optimum range of income distribution, although we may never be able to determine what it is, and government has no business trying to achieve anything approaching it, anyway. But we, as a people, do have an interest in seeing to it that our distribution does not get *too* far out of kilter.

A carefully crafted system of progressive taxation is a major instrument for this task.

FLATTEN THE REGRESSIVE TAX, NOT THE PROGRESSIVE ONE

Progressives and Democrats clearly need a "Big Idea" to free them from their Chapter Eleven of ideas. It must be an idea that both clearly demonstrates the different values of the parties and addresses the fundamental problem of the widening gap between the rich and the rest of America.

One way to accomplish this would be by redefining the difference between the parties on taxes. Voters currently identify Democrats as the "pro-tax party" and Republicans as the "anti-tax party." Democrats need to emphasize that Republicans have omitted a few critical letters from the name they have given us. We are not the pro-tax, but the pro-*gressive*-tax party. The Republicans are not anti-tax; they are anti-progressive tax, as they have made clearer than ever in recent years. Ronald Reagan somewhere picked up the notion that "we have received this progressive tax direct from Karl Marx, who designed it." Reagan declared the need to end "this evil day of progressive taxation." He wanted to eliminate completely taxes on inheritances, corporate profits, and capital gains. Reagan's Attorney General, Ed Meese, declared: "the progressive income tax is immoral."[47]

The preservation and restoration of a progressive tax structure must be a central feature of Democratic policy. The question is not whether to tax; it is *whom* to tax and at what rate? If progressives and Democrats do not draw a line in the sand over the defense of the principle of progressive taxation, they might as well run up the white flag and disband the party. "I'm going to resist the idea of a flat tax with my last breath," Dale Bumpers said to me. "That is nothing in the world but a Republican ploy that has been generated by all these various Rush Limbaugh flacks around the country." He went on to say that the nature of progressive taxation has never been well understood by the American people. "And the flat tax sounds so simple and you can file it on a post card. Dick Lugar is always saying that we ought to have one sales tax, and that ought to be it. You can't believe that this kind of powerful nonsense resonates as well as it does; but it does. And I can tell you the Democrats—if they cave in on the flat tax, I'm going to resign from the Democratic Party. I feel as strongly about that as any issue I can think of."[48]

More Democrats should take that pledge. Progressive taxation is the *sine qua non* of progressive social policy. It merely says that those who enjoy the greatest benefits in the society should be expected to pay the highest "dues" for membership in it. If we abandon the principle of basing taxation on ability to pay, the radical rich will have won the Super Bowl—and the rest of us need not bother to come back for the next season.

Here's a good candidate for the "Big Idea" Democrats so badly need: Remove the cap on income susceptible to Social Security taxes ($61,200 in 1995) and lower the rate of that payroll tax.[49] As it stands now, a near-minimum-wage worker making $10,000 annually pays 6.2 percent of his/her wages in FICA taxes, while a CEO who carries off $5 million pays only 1.52 percent of his income for the same purpose. (And, on his $203 million compensation from Disney in 1993, Michael Eisner owed approximately 0 percent [0.0022%, to be more precise] in FICA taxes.)

Americans pay two principal taxes to the federal government. One is mildly progressive, the other extraordinarily regressive. The Republicans propose to flatten the progressive one, thereby helping the rich, but to leave the very regressive one untouched, thus doing nothing for the middle class or the poor. Democrats have a golden opportunity to take the opposite position: keep the income tax progressive and flatten the regressive FICA tax.

Republicans have indicated a willingness to means-test Medicare benefits. The FICA tax is currently based on a *negative means test*: the less one earns, the larger the share of his or her income that is taken by this tax.

Why not apply means tests to taxes? That is all that progressive taxation is. Of course, lifting the cap on income susceptible to the FICA tax would *not* means-test it; it would merely remove the negative means test on which it is now based. It would not make this tax progressive; it would produce a *flat tax*. That's what most Republicans claim they want, so how could they argue against a flat tax to support Social Security?

Nearly half of all income now goes to the top 20 percent of income recipients, which is approximately the same as the group that earns above the current FICA cap. This suggests that a conservative estimate would be that applying the FICA tax to all income would allow the rate to be reduced at least to the 4.5 percent range. (A way to include other forms of income, in addition to wages and salaries, in FICA taxation would have to be devised.) The effects of such a change would be dramatic. The FICA tax paid by a person earning $35,000 a year would be reduced by approximately $600 annually, adding $50 to his or her monthly take-home pay. The wage earner making the 1995 cap of $61,200 now pays about $3800; at 4.5 percent, that would drop to around $2750, adding almost $90 a month to her/his take-home pay. What's more, this would not be money people had to wait to receive in tax refunds; they would see it directly added to every paycheck. And, although persons earning above the current cap would pay tax on all their income, their total FICA tax would remain below what they now pay until they passed about $100,000 in annual income.

This proposal would stimulate the economy by giving consumers more money, begin to combat—albeit only in a small way—the fundamental problem of a growing maldistribution of income, and be a great boon to small businesses (which rarely pay any employee above the current cap and so would see their share of the payroll tax substantially reduced). It would spur job creation and reduce unemployment, since the size of the payroll tax is one of the greatest obstacles to hiring new workers. It would also be something of a disincentive to the payment of the huge salaries that many Americans find so disturbing. Perhaps Jerry Jones would pay Deion Sanders a little less if he had to pay the employer's share of the FICA tax on *all* of it. If we have to live, at least for now, with a winner-take-all economy, we can at least take a little bit back from the winners.

This is, moreover, a way to assure the solvency of Social Security and Medicare, since by significantly reducing the tax rate now, there would be room for modest increases as needed in the future to cover the huge number of retirees in the Baby Boom generation. This, in turn, would restore confidence in the system. Younger people would have a strong assurance that Social Security and Medicare will be there for them when they retire, lessening one of the worries of the Psychic Crisis of the Nineties.

The only people who would pay significantly more are those making above about $150,000 a year—precisely those whose incomes have been skyrocketing in recent years while all others have been left in the dust. This could be a key to reuniting Democrats and winning back the allegiance of a unified middle and lower class.

How could the GOP argue against it? Surely they would scream "class warfare," their standard response to any proposal for fairness and equity. In fact, the regressive FICA tax that presently exists is part of the class warfare on the middle class and working poor that Republicans have waged for many years and that is being increased almost daily by the Republicans in Congress. The FICA flat tax would merely be a defensive maneuver in the class war in which Republicans and the wealthy are very much on the offensive.

There is only one argument against this: that Social Security is a retirement fund, and no one should have to pay vastly more in taxes than she or he will receive back in benefits. But this argument has already been undermined by the lifting of the cap on the Medicare tax, by the fact that almost all participants now receive far more than they put into the system, and by the fact that the system is actually run on a pay-as-you-go basis.

This idea would correct one of the basic mistakes in the original Social Security Act. The potential benefits far outweigh the solitary objection that this is a pension system and obliging the rich to pay much more than they will get out of it is unfair to them.

This proposal has everything to recommend it. Economically, it would put significantly more money in the hands of middle-class and poorer consumers, thereby providing stimulus to the economy, and it would materially assist small businesses. Morally, it would be a step to begin to counter the rapid skewing of income to the few at the expense of the many. Politically, it would bring together the middle class and the poor, allowing the Democrats to make an effective and honest case that they are looking out for the well-being of the vast majority of Americans, while the Republicans are presenting proposals designed to assist only the rich.

Removing the cap on income susceptible to the FICA tax and lowering the rate of that tax is the right thing to do in terms of economics, morality, and politics.

What are the Democrats waiting for?

DOWNSIZE THE WORK WEEK, NOT THE WORKFORCE

Let me offer one other specific proposal that would directly address a major part of the three-fold predicament in which we find ourselves. The greatest force behind the loss of jobs is the rapid expansion of computer-based technology. In the last half century, American productivity has more than doubled, yet Americans who are employed are actually working more hours today than they were in the 1940s.[50] The basic reason for that increase is that the cost of benefits has made it cheaper for employers to pay fewer workers to work at time-and-a-half than it is to pay benefits to a large number of employees. Reducing the FICA tax is one way to lessen that cost. Another way to provide work for more people would be to increase the cost of having employees work overtime from time-and-a-half to double-time. A third would be an effective national health-insurance system, which would reduce this cost of hiring additional workers.

The basic problem, though, is clearly that there has been no reduction in the work week in the United States since 1938, when the 40-hour standard was established. It is only common sense that workers should share in the enormous gains in productivity since that time by enjoying a shorter work week. One of the most frightening prospects facing us is that there is already not enough work—especially good jobs at decent pay—to go around, and computer technology threatens to make the imbalance much greater in the near future.

"There is," as the then-Secretary Treasurer of the AFL-CIO, Thomas Donahue, said in 1993, "no question that the long-term salvation of work lies in reducing working hours."[51] The choice is clear: We can continue to downsize the workforce, leaving all the gains from technology to go to the few; or we can downsize the work week, providing a broader sharing in those gains. It is obvious which side of this question progressives should be on.

The Republican position is, as usual, the same as that of big business: that gains from increased productivity stemming from new technology belong to the shareholders and the managers of the corporations, and that workers have no claim on them.[52] This leads to fewer jobs and, at least in the short run, to higher dividends, higher executive salaries and bonuses, and higher stock prices. But at what cost to the society as a whole?

If there is going to be less work—and that seems certain—the choice is whether the resulting free time will be in the agonizing form of unemployment for growing millions or the pleasant form of added leisure for people working fewer hours.

Progressives should point out that a shorter work week will not only result in economic gains (since it will reduce the amount spent in unemployment benefits and welfare and will help to maintain markets for the products and services the economy provides in such abundance), but it is also a family values issue, since it will save jobs and allow working people to spend more time with their families.

There is but one substantial objection to this course of action. Since the other side of our current economic problems is global competition, a shortened work week might increase our labor costs and put us at a competitive disadvantage. This is a serious concern, but several studies indicate that there are ways around this problem. Surely, however, we should seek international agreements on reduced working hours. Such worldwide agreements are going to be needed in many areas as we try to cope with the unprecedented problems of technological unemployment in a worldwide marketplace.

ECONOMIC CHECKS AND BALANCES

Extremist thinking, whether that of a Karl Marx or a Milton Friedman, will lead us into trouble. As hybrid plants are generally stronger than pure varieties, a hybrid socioeconomic philosophy is likely to be preferable to either pure system.

The collapse of the Soviet Union liberates the Left from associations—certainly never remotely warranted in the case of democratic socialists or liberals—with totalitarian communism. On a much less spectacular level, the partial eclipse of New Deal liberalism in the penumbra of a temporarily ascendant radical Republicanism, frees American progressives from over-reliance on bureaucratic structures and obliges us to rethink our approaches. The adoption of the extreme libertarian ideas of the "bad sixties" by the Right may allow the Left to shed that albatross, too.

It should now be possible to reconstruct a democratic (and Democratic) Left that understands both the necessity of an incentive-based economy and the need to control its excesses; a Left that recognizes both the dangers inherent in government power and the necessity of using government power in the public interest.[53] And, if we can finally escape the libertine and cultural elitist associations that are tokens of wrong turns taken in the "bad sixties," progressive Democrats may be able to bring together cultural and economic populism—a combination that seems certain to command majority support as Americans try to cope with the Psychic Crisis of the Nineties (and beyond).

In devising such a balanced system, we must recognize both the biologically evolved predispositions of humans and the values that are needed to check those among the predispositions that are not adaptive. Ideologues of both the left and the right have gone astray on this crucial point. The former have ignored the reality of selfishness as a prime motivation; the latter have abandoned the values that traditionally held greed in check. If anger and lust are among the natural predispositions of humans, but we do our best to control them, why should it be any different with this other cardinal sin, greed? But instead of trying to control greed, we have increasingly constructed our economic system upon it.

The Chinese Emperor Lin Tse-Hsu put his finger on what an unrestrained marketplace does to values when he wrote to Queen Victoria in 1839, "[I]n coveting profit to an extreme, they [the "barbarians"—the Europeans] have no regard for injuring others. Let us ask, where is your conscience?"[54] A system that extols greed has no place for conscience. Recognizing the existence—and inevitable persistence—of a particular human propensity requires us to take account of it in reconstructing our values and in devising our laws and institutions; but it does not oblige us to endorse or celebrate that tendency.

Given our innate proclivities, we must have incentives to produce. The free market, despite its shortcomings, must be the starting point for a desirable system of balance simply because production must precede distribution. Since socialism does not work as a productive system, the best it can hope to accomplish is an equitable distribution of scarcity. With the market as a basis, however, it is possible to begin with sufficient production and then make modifications in order to achieve a better distribution.

The essential truth is that, because of human nature, some form of market economics is a necessary evil. The Left errs in failing to understand its necessity; the Right goes wrong in denying its evil.

Most leftists, at least since Marx, have based their doctrine on a Lockean environmentalism that holds that such problems as greed and aggression are wholly cultural constructs resulting from what the market economy inculcates in people. A little (or, perhaps, a lot of) social engineering, and these tendencies could be eliminated, with a Walden Two, an Eden Three, or a "withering away of the state" resulting. This denial of human nature has left leftists powerless to correct the evils that have so properly appalled them.

The need is for some type of incentive-based economy for purposes of production, but some way to curb its excesses and the damage it does to cooperative values and to the environment. The way to address this problem can be found in some of our most cherished traditional values.

The consensus among the Founding Fathers of the United States was that democracy is good, but far from perfect. Accordingly, they established a political system that is basically democratic, but contains checks against the dangers of excessive democracy (for example, the passions of a moment leading to extremists gaining control of the House of Representatives, as happened in 1994, are checked by a constitutional system in which the Senate and president can apply the brakes to slow down a runaway House before it crashes).

It would be both common sense and entirely in keeping with our traditional values to follow the same course with regard to the economy. If we conclude, as I think we must, that an essentially market-based economic system is, like what Winston Churchill correctly said an essentially democratic political system is, the worst possible system except for any other one we can think of, then it follows that we need to set up a series of economic checks and balances similar to the political ones contained in the American constitutional system. In this way, we can retain the advantages of the market, as of democracy, without suffering its greatest problems.

Devising and establishing such economic checks and balances, with a priority being placed on finding some that will slowly wean our economy from its dependence on excessive consumption that has been corrupting our values and undermining the social contract, should be the foremost project of progressives.

If we can succeed to a reasonable degree in this endeavor, we will be able to answer the question, "What's Left?" by saying: A great deal, indeed, including the replacement of the two-tier, winner-take-all economy with a more just, winner-take-the-biggest-share-but-leave-something-for-others economy; the revival of values, a sense of community, and the social contract; and the slow displacement of cynicism by confidence in the potential goodness of people and institutions, leavened always with a healthy skepticism.

NOTES

Chapter One

1. Author's interview with Deputy Secretary of Education Madeline Kunin, September 26, 1995, Washington, D.C.
2. Author's interview with Sen. Paul Wellstone (D, Minnesota), March 31, 1995, Washington, D.C.
3. Author's interview with Rep. Nydia Velazquez (D, New York), September 28, 1995, Washington, D.C.
4. E.J. Dionne, Jr., "Why Not a Second Party?" *Washington Post*, September 26, 1995.
5. Robert H. Frank and Philip J. Cook, *The Winner-Take-All Society* (New York: Free Press, 1995).
6. Robert H. Frank and Philip J. Cook, "Rich Get Richer, and Poor Get . . .," *Clarion-Ledger* (Jackson, Miss.), September 17, 1995.
7. Editorial, "The Rich Get Richer Faster," *New York Times*, April 18, 1995.
8. Edward N. Wolff, "Top Heavy: A Study of Increasing Inequality of Wealth in America," Twentieth Century Fund, 1995, as cited in *New York Times*, April 17, 1995.
9. Richard Morin and Dan Balz, "Americans Losing Trust in Each Other and Institutions," *Washington Post*, January 28, 1996.
10. Associated Press story, *Atlanta Journal-Constitution*, September 24, 1995.
11. Ben Wattenberg, *Values Matter Most: How Republicans or Democrats or a Third Party Can Win and Renew the American Way of Life* (New York: Free Press, 1995), pp. 6–7.
12. Author's interview with Rep. Bernie Sanders (I, Vermont), June 28, 1995, Washington, D.C.
13. Stanley B. Greenberg, *Middle Class Dreams: The Politics and Power of the New American Majority* (New York: Times Books, 1995), p. 10.
14. Author's interview with Rev. Jesse Jackson, March 22, 1986, Little Rock, Arkansas.
15. Mario Cuomo, *Reason to Believe* (New York: Simon & Schuster, 1995), p. 19.
16. Author's interview with Bruce Reed, March 30, 1995, Washington, D.C.
17. Sen. Fred Harris (D, Oklahoma), as quoted in Peter N. Carroll, *It Seemed Like Nothing Happened: The Tragedy and Promise of America in the 1970s* (New York: Holt, Rinehart and Winston, 1982), p. 89.
18. James Carville, as quoted in Elizabeth Kolbert and Adam Clymer, "The Politics of Layoffs," *New York Times*, March 8, 1996.
19. See for example, Cal Thomas, "GOP Must Stand Firm on Abortion," *Clarion-Ledger*, December 21, 1995.
20. Author's interview with Rep. Marcy Kaptur (D, Ohio), September 28, 1995, Washington, D.C.

21. John William Ward, *Andrew Jackson: Symbol for an Age* (New York: Oxford University Press, 1955), pp. 46–78.
22. Richard Hofstadter, *Anti-Intellectualism in American Life* (New York: Knopf, 1963).
23. Author's interview with Rep. David Bonior (D, Michigan), March 30, 1995, the Capitol.
24. As quoted by Howard Fineman on *Capital Gang Sunday*, CNN, December 3, 1995.
25. *New York Times*, July 11, 1985.
26. Kevin Phillips, commentary, *Morning Edition*, National Public Radio, December 12, 1995.
27. Newt Gingrich speech, October 24, 1995, as quoted on *Washington Week in Review*, PBS, November 10, 1995.
28. Anthony Lewis, "The Big Lie," *New York Times*, December 29, 1995.
29. Background interview with a high-ranking White House official, September 1995, the White House.
30. Brian Lunde, as quoted in R. W. Apple, Jr., "Bradley's Departure a Harsh Blow for Demoralized Democrats," *New York Times*, August 17, 1995.
31. Anonymous Democratic House Member, as quoted in Robert D. Novak, "Complacency at Piney Point," *Washington Post*, May 11, 1995.
32. Yankelovich poll, December 6–7, 1995, *Time*, December 25, 1995–January 1, 1996, p. 60.
33. Bonior interview, March 30, 1995.
34. Author's interview with Paul Begala, March 30, 1995, Washington, D.C.
35. Author's interview with Bill Clinton, April 17, 1986, Little Rock, Arkansas.
36. Author's interview with Del. Eleanor Holmes Norton (D, District of Columbia), January 19, 1996, by telephone from Washington, D.C.
37. Paul Starr, in *The American Prospect*, as quoted in George F. Will, ". . . And the Two Parties," *Washington Post*, May 14, 1995.
38. Author's interview with Sen. Tom Daschle (D, South Dakota), December 14, 1995, by telephone from Washington, D.C.
39. Arthur M. Schlesinger, Jr., *The Coming of the New Deal* (Boston: Houghton Mifflin, 1958), p. 223.
40. Clinton interview, April 17, 1986.

Chapter Two

1. "Agenda for American Renewal," Bush campaign pamphlet, October 1992, as quoted in David Frum, *Dead Right* (New York: New Republic/Basic Books, 1994), p. 27.
2. Denise Woods, as quoted in Michael Shanahan and Miles Benson, "Nation's Middle Class, Beset by Deep Pessimism, Is Lowering Its Expectations," *Staten Island Advance*, May 7, 1995.
3. Shanahan and Benson, "Nation's Middle Class."
4. Robert J. Samuelson, *The Good Life and Its Discontents: The American Dream in the Age of Entitlement, 1945–1995* (New York: Times Books, 1996), excerpted in "Great Expectations," *Newsweek*, January 8, 1996, p. 26. Similar pessimistic views of the future were found in a 1996 *Washington Post*/Kaiser Family Foundation/Harvard University survey. *Washington Post*, January 28, 1996.
5. Joe Klein, "The Nervous Nineties," *Newsweek*, May 1, 1995.
6. Samuelson, "Great Expectations," p. 24.
7. Frum, *Dead Right*, p. 31.
8. Alan Brinkley, as quoted in Shanahan and Benson, "Nation's Middle Class."
9. *New York Times*, December 30, 1995.

10. Times Mirror Center for the People and the Press, opinion survey, "Voter Anxiety Dividing GOP; Energized Democrats Backing Clinton," October 25–30, 1995, released November 14, 1995, pp. 1, 3, 94.
11. Author's interview with Paul Begala (here paraphrasing Bill Clinton), March 30, 1995, Washington, D.C.
12. Carroll Quigley lecture, as quoted in David Maraniss, *First in His Class: A Biography of Bill Clinton* (New York: Simon & Schuster, 1995), p. 58.
13. As quoted in James West Davidson, *et al.*, *Nation of Nations: A Narrative History of the American Republic* (New York: McGraw-Hill, 1990, 2nd ed., 1994), p. 791.
14. Michael Barone makes a similar comparison with the late nineteenth century, but emphasizes different points, in "The New Continental Divide," *U.S. News & World Report*, November 14, 1994, pp. 44–46.
15. Frum, *Dead Right*, p. 26.
16. Wirthlin Group polls, in Ben J. Wattenberg, *Values Matter Most: How Republicans or Democrats or a Third Party Can Win and Renew American Life* (New York: Free Press, 1995), p. 117.
17. Secretary of Labor Robert B. Reich, speech on "Family Values" at the National Baptist Convention, San Diego, Calif., June 21, 1995.
18. Jeff MacNelly cartoon, in *Clarion-Ledger* (Jackson, Miss.), July 10, 1995.
19. Louis Uchitelle and N. R. Kleinfield, "A National Heartache," *New York Times*, March 3, 1996.
20. Donald L. Barlett and James B. Steele, *America: What Went Wrong?* (Kansas City: Andrews and McMeel, 1992), p. xi.
21. "Poverty in the 1990s" (editorial), *Atlanta Journal-Constitution*, March 12, 1995.
22. Author's interview with Eleanor Holmes Norton (D, District of Columbia), January 19, 1996, by telephone from Washington, D.C.
23. Rep. Marcy Kaptur, address to the United We Stand Issues Conference, August 12, 1995.
24. Patrick Buchanan, as quoted in John B. Judis, "Taking Buchananomics Seriously," *New Republic*, March 18, 1996, p. 19.
25. Uchitelle and Kleinfield, "A National Heartache."
26. *Marketplace*, National Public Radio, January 4, 1996.
27. *New York Times*, March 9, 1996.
28. Jeffrey G. Madrick, *The End of Affluence: The Causes and Consequences of America's Economic Dilemma* (New York: Random House, 1995); John Omicinski, "Americans Slicing Slower-Growing Economic Pie," *Clarion-Ledger*, September 17, 1995.
29. Bernard Wysocki, Jr., "Unstable Pay Becomes Ever More Common," *Wall Street Journal*, December 4, 1995.
30. Economic Policy Institute study by Lawrence Mishel and Jacquline Simon, cited in George F. Will, "Dukakis has Economic Weapon in Property Owners' Rise in Income," *Clarion-Ledger*, September 16, 1988.
31. Samuelson, "Great Expectations," p. 30.
32. Wattenberg, *Values Matter Most*, p. 88.
33. Robert H. Frank and Philip J. Cook, *The Winner-Take-All Society* (New York: Free Press, 1995), pp. 67–68.
34. *Ibid., passim.*
35. Average hourly earnings for private, nonagricultural industries. All dollar figures are in constant 1982 dollars. *Economic Report of the President*, February, 1995 (Washington, D.C.: Government Printing Office, 1995), as reproduced in *Just the Facts: A Citizen's Guide to Key Federal Facts* (Nashua, NH: FacTIPS, 1995), p. 60.
36. Uchitelle and Kleinfield, "A National Heartache."
37. Richard Hofstadter, "Manifest Destiny and the Philippines," in Daniel Aaron, ed., *America in Crisis* (New York: Knopf, 1952), pp. 173–200, reprinted in Theodore P. Greene, ed., *American Imperialism in 1898* (Lexington, Mass.: Heath, 1955), pp. 54–70.

38. The point about the trauma associated with the switch from "island communities" to a national economy and culture was first made by Robert H. Wiebe, *The Search for Order, 1877–1920* (New York: Hill and Wang, 1967).
39. Hofstadter, "Manifest Destiny," p. 55.
40. Samuelson, "Great Expectations," p. 26.
41. Begala interview, March 30, 1995.
42. Edward N. Wolff, "Top Heavy: A Study of Increasing Inequality of Wealth in America," Twentieth Century Fund, 1995, as cited in *New York Times*, April 17, 1995.
43. Author's interview with Rep. David Bonior (D, Michigan), March 30, 1995, the Capitol.
44. *Capital Gang Sunday*, CNN, January 7, 1996.
45. Times Mirror Center survey, "Voter Anxiety," October 25–30, 1995, p. 34.
46. Author's interview with Rep. Rosa DeLauro (D, Connecticut), September 28, 1995, Washington, D.C.
47. Richard J. Herrnstein and Charles Murray, *The Bell Curve: Intelligence and Class Structure in American Life* (New York: Free Press, 1994); Dinesh D'Souza, *The End of Racism: Principles for a Multiracial Society* (New York: Free Press, 1995).
48. Bloomberg Business News report, *Clarion-Ledger*, December 30, 1995.
49. Kurt Vonnegut, *Bluebeard* (New York: Delacorte Press, 1987), p. 75, as quoted in Frank and Cook, *Winner-Take-All Society*, pp. 1–2.
50. Frank and Cook, *Winner-Take-All Society*, p. 4.
51. Reich, "Family Values."
52. Author's interview with Rep. Jim McDermott (D, Washington), June 27, 1995, Washington, D.C.
53. Author's interview with Sen. Paul Wellstone (D, Minnesota), March 31, 1995, Washington, D.C.
54. Peter Gottschalk, as quoted in Wysocki, "Unstable Pay."
55. Thomas Geoghegan, "Why Americans Don't Save," *New Republic*, July 17 and 24, 1995, p. 30.
56. Peter Hart, as quoted in Shanahan and Benson, "Nation's Middle Class."
57. David H. Donald, as quoted in "The Downsizing of America," *New York Times*, March 3, 1996.
58. Author's interview with Rep. Barney Frank (D, Massachusetts), June 16, 1995, Washington, D.C.
59. William E. Leuchtenburg, as quoted in Shanahan and Benson, "Nation's Middle Class."
60. James Meadows, as quoted in Edmund L. Andrews, "Don't Go Away Mad, Just Go Away," *New York Times*, February 13, 1996.
61. "Poverty in the 1990s."
62. Begala interview, March 30, 1995.
63. Norton interview, January 19, 1996.
64. Jeremy Rifkin, *The End of Work: The Decline of the Global Labor Force and the Dawn of the Post-Market Era* (New York: G.P. Putnam's Sons, 1995).
65. Kaptur, United We Stand address, August 12, 1995.
66. DeLauro interview, September 28, 1995.
67. Author's interview with Secretary of Education Richard Riley, June 28, 1995, Washington, D.C.
68. John Steinbeck, *The Grapes of Wrath* (New York: Viking, 1939; New York: Penguin, 1976), p. 40.
69. Author's interview with George Stephanopoulos, June 27, 1995, the White House.
70. Author's interview with Rep. Bernie Sanders (I, Vermont), June 28, 1995, Washington, D.C.
71. Frank interview, June 16, 1995.
72. "Poverty in the 1990s."
73. *NBC Nightly News*, January 4, 1996.

74. Allan Sloan, "The Hit Men," *Newsweek*, February 26, 1996, p. 45.
75. Reich, "Family Values."
76. Ellen Goodman, "What a Sorry Message: That a 'Mensch' Is so Rare," *Boston Globe*, December 21, 1995.
77. *Ibid.*
78. Michael Janofsky, "The Browns Put N.F.L. Back in Baltimore," *New York Times*, November 7, 1995; Thomas George, "Modell Joins Newest Game in Football," *New York Times*, November 7, 1995.
79. Goodman, "What a Sorry Message."
80. Wellstone interview, March 31, 1995.
81. Rush Limbaugh Radio Show, July 14, 1995.
82. Sen. Bill Bradley (D, New Jersey), on *Meet the Press*, NBC News, July 23, 1995.
83. Ellis Cose, *A Man's World—How Real Is Male Privilege and How High Is Its Price?* (New York: HarperCollins, 1995), introduction.
84. Bonior interview, March 30, 1995.
85. *Ibid.*
86. Sara Rimer, "A Hometown Feels Less Like Home," *New York Times*, March 6, 1996.
87. Robert D. Putnam, "Bowling Alone: America's Declining Social Capital," *Current*, June 1995, pp. 3–9.
88. Richard Morin and Dan Balz, "Americans Losing Trust in Each Other and Institutions," *Washington Post*, January 28, 1996.

Chapter Three

1. William J. Bennett, *The Index of Leading Cultural Indicators* (New York: Touchstone, 1994), p. 8.
2. Ben J. Wattenberg, *Values Matter Most: How Republicans or Democrats or a Third Party Can Win and Renew the American Way of Life* (New York: Free Press, 1995), p. 9.
3. Douglas Jehl, "Quayle Deplores Eroding Values: Cites TV Show," *Los Angeles Times*, May 20, 1992.
4. William J. Bennett, on *Meet the Press*, NBC News, July 23, 1995.
5. Wattenberg, *Values Matter Most*, p. 13. Emphasis in original.
6. Sen. Bill Bradley (D, New Jersey), on *Meet the Press*, NBC News, July 23, 1995.
7. David Frum, *Dead Right* (New York: New Republic/Basic Books), p. 3.
8. Wattenberg, *Values Matter Most*, p. 10.
9. Charles Murray, "The Coming White Underclass," *Wall Street Journal*, October 29, 1993.
10. Author's interview with Rep. David Bonior (D, Michigan), March 30, 1995, the Capitol.
11. Harry L. Hopkins, *Spending to Save: The Complete Story of Relief* (New York: Norton, 1936), p. 109.
12. Wattenberg, *Values Matter Most*, p. 21 (paraphrasing George Wiley of the National Welfare Rights Organization).
13. Author's interview with Paul Begala, March 30, 1995, Washington, D.C.
14. Frum, *Dead Right*, p. 59.
15. William J. Bennett, on *Meet the Press*, NBC News, July 23, 1995.
16. I picked up this useful construction from Gary Bauer, "'Murphy Brown' Is Situation Tragedy," *St. Louis Post-Dispatch*, May 22, 1992.
17. Bonior interview, March 30, 1995.
18. Charles Krauthammer, "Cultural Crimes Against Children," *Washington Post*, July 24, 1992, as quoted in Bennett, *Index of Leading Cultural Indicators*, p. 113.

19. Irving Kristol, *The Democratic Idea in America* (New York: Harper & Row, 1972), p. 29, as quoted in Frum, *Dead Right*, p. 61.
20. Carl Rowan, "Withdrawing Federal Pittance Won't Aid in Halting Incidence of Teen Pregnancy," *Clarion-Ledger* (Jackson, Miss.), January 8, 1996.
21. Thomas Frank, "Business and the GOP: A Groovy Kind of Love," *Atlanta Journal-Constitution*, July 18, 1995.
22. Alvin Hansen, "Toward Full Employment," March 15, 1940, as quoted in Alan Brinkley, "The New Deal and the Idea of the State," in Steve Fraser and Gary Gerstle, eds., *The Rise and Fall of the New Deal Order, 1930–1980* (Princeton: Princeton University Press, 1989), p. 98.
23. Geoffrey Perrett, *America in the Twenties: A History* (New York: Simon & Schuster, 1982), p. 348.
24. Richard Hofstadter, *Social Darwinism in American Thought* (Philadelphia: University of Pennsylvania Press, 1944; rev. ed., Boston: Beacon Press, 1955), p. 150; Sidney Fine, *Laissez Faire and the General-Welfare State* (Ann Arbor: University of Michigan Press, 1956), p. 244.
25. Thorstein Veblen, *The Theory of the Leisure Class* (New York: Macmillan, 1899), pp. 241–244.
26. Perrett, *America in the Twenties*, p. 55.
27. Joan Didion, "7000 Romaine, Los Angeles 38," in Didion, *Slouching Towards Bethlehem* (1968; New York: Washington Square Press, 1981), p. 81.
28. Charley Reese, "Let Us Leave Each Other Alone," *Clarion-Ledger*, August 6, 1990.
29. Margaret Thatcher, as quoted in *Woman's Own*, October 31, 1987, p. 10.
30. Frum, *Dead Right*, p. 188.
31. Ralph Waldo Emerson, "Self-Reliance," in Lewis Mumford, ed., *Ralph Waldo Emerson: Essays and Journals* (Garden City, NY: International Collectors Library, 1968), pp. 92–93.
32. Nichols Fox, "What Are Our Real Values?" *Newsweek*, February 13, 1989, p. 8.
33. Charles F. Kettering, "Keeping the Consumer Dissatisfied," *Nation's Business*, January 1929, as quoted in Jeremy Rifkin, *The End of Work* (New York: Putnam, 1955), p. 20.
34. Anne Carson, "Putting Her in Her Place: Woman, Dirt, and Desire," in David M. Halperin, John J. Winkler, and Froma I. Zeitlin, eds., *Before Sexuality: The Construction of Erotic Experience in the Ancient Greek World* (Princeton: Princeton University Press, 1990), p. 135.
35. Bennett, *Index of Leading Cultural Indicators*, p. 9.
36. Bonior interview, March 30, 1995.
37. Bob Herbert, "Good Works? Bah!" *New York Times*, May 24, 1995.
38. Jim Wallis, "The Soul of Politics: A Practical and Prophetic Vision for Change," Summers Lecture, Millsaps College, Jackson, Miss., February 21, 1995.
39. George Gilder, *Wealth and Poverty* (New York: Basic Books, 1981), pp. 14-15.
40. Saul Bellow, *Mr. Sammler's Planet* (New York: Viking, 1970), pp. 33–34. I was directed to this remarkable statement by Daniel Bell, *The Cultural Contradictions of Capitalism* (New York: Basic Books, 1976, 1978), p. 50n.
41. Lucinda Rector, "Some Walls, Like Mine, Don't Fall," *New York Times*, December 1, 1989.
42. Author's interview with Sen. Paul Wellstone (D, Minnesota), March 31, 1995, Washington, D.C.
43. Sen. Pete Dominici (R, New Mexico), speech at the summer meeting of the National Governors' Association, July 30, 1995, Burlington, Vermont, telecast on C-SPAN.
44. John Dewey, *The Public and Its Problems* (New York: Henry Holt, 1927), pp. 153–155.
45. "Finest Worksong," lyrics by Michael Stipe, on R.E.M., *Document* (1987).
46. Sen. Phil Gramm (R, Texas), speech to National Rifle Association Convention, May 20, 1995.

47. "Smells Like Teen Spirit," lyrics by Kurt Cobain, on Nirvana, *Nevermind* (1991).
48. Frum, *Dead Right*, p. 10.
49. Solicitation letter from Household Credit Services, Inc., Salinas, California, 1990.
50. Veblen, *Theory of the Leisure Class*, p. 241.
51. Simon N. Patten, *The New Basis of Civilization* (New York: Macmillan, 1907), ch. VII, as quoted in Daniel T. Rodgers, *The Work Ethic in Industrial America, 1850–1920* (Chicago: University of Chicago Press, 1978), p. 121.
52. Bell, *Cultural Contradictions*, p. 69.
53. I have made much of the following argument in "Why Are We Accumulating 'Life Debts' Instead of 'Life Savings' Now?" *Clarion-Ledger*, January 2, 1996.
54. Thomas Geoghegan, "Why Americans Don't Save," *New Republic*, July 17 and 24, 1995, p. 32.
55. *Morning Edition*, National Public Radio, December 12, 1995.
56. Saul Hansell, "Lax Credit-Card Standards May Pose Problems," *Clarion-Ledger*, December 30, 1995.
57. Geoghegan, "Why Americans Don't Save," p. 28.
58. Rush Limbaugh radio show, July 18, 1995.
59. Bell, *Cultural Contradictions*, pp. 17, 63, 74–76.
60. Frum, *Dead Right*, p. 66.
61. George Gilder, *Wealth and Poverty* (New York: Basic Books, 1981).
62. George Gilder, *Men and Marriage* (Gretna, Louisiana: Pelican, 1989), p. 58.
63. *Ibid.*
64. *Ibid.*, p. 57.
65. Robert Wright, *The Moral Animal* (New York: Pantheon, 1994), p. 105.
66. Bradley on *Meet the Press*, July 23, 1995.
67. Sen. Bob Dole (R, Kansas), as quoted in Richard Lacayo, "Violent Reaction," *Time*, June 12, 1995, p. 28.
68. Tipper Gore, as quoted in *Clarion-Ledger*, July 10, 1995.

Chapter Four

1. Studs Terkel, speech at the Kennedy School of Government, Harvard University, Cambridge, Mass., December 6, 1995, broadcast on C-SPAN.
2. Author's interview with Paul Begala, March 30, 1995, Washington, D.C.
3. Norman Mailer, *The Armies of the Night* (New York: New American Library, 1968); Mailer, *Miami and the Siege of Chicago: An Informal History of the Republican and Democratic Conventions of 1968* (New York: World Publishing Company, 1968).
4. Allen Ginsberg, as quoted in Milton Viorst, *Fire in the Streets: America in the 1960s* (New York: Simon & Schuster, 1979), p. 76.
5. Christopher Lasch, *The Culture of Narcissism: American Life in an Age of Diminishing Expectations* (New York: Norton, 1978), p. 83.
6. David King Dunaway, *How Can I Keep from Singing: Pete Seeger* (New York: McGraw-Hill, 1981), pp. 245–48.
7. "Making Sense of the 60's", Part III, PBS, January 22, 1991.
8. *Berkeley Barb*, May 12, 1967, as quoted in Allen J. Matusow, *The Unraveling of America: A History of Liberalism in the 1960s* (New York: Harper & Row, 1984), p. 298. Emphasis added.
9. Matusow, *Unraveling of America*, p. 303.
10. William L. O'Neill, *Coming Apart: An Informal History of America in the 1960's* (New York: Quadrangle, 1971), p. 244.
11. "Port Huron Statement," in James Miller, *"Democracy Is in the Streets": From Port Huron to the Siege of Chicago* (New York: Simon & Schuster, 1987), p. 333.
12. E. J. Dionne, Jr., *Why Americans Hate Politics* (New York: Simon & Schuster, 1991), pp. 24, 31–54.

13. Viorst, *Fire in the Streets*, p. 40; O'Neill, *Coming Apart*, p. 177.
14. Author's interview with Richard Goodwin, July 8, 1985, Bourne, Massachusetts.
15. Lyndon B. Johnson, Inaugural Address, January 20, 1965, as quoted in Matusow, *Unraveling of America*, p. 153.
16. Goodwin interview, July 8, 1985.
17. Matusow, *Unraveling of America*, p. 160.
18. Sen. Robert Dole, October 24, 1995, in videotaped remarks shown on *Washington Week in Review*, PBS, November 10, 1995.
19. Peter N. Carroll, *It Seemed Like Nothing Happened: The Tragedy and Promise of America in the 1970s* (New York: Holt, Rinehart and Winston, 1982), p. 59.
20. *Ibid.*
21. *New York Times*, July 17, 1964.
22. Matusow, *Unraveling of America*, pp. 137–38.
23. Richard Morin and Dan Balz, "Americans Losing Trust in Each Other and Institutions," *Washington Post*, January 28, 1996.
24. Matusow, *Unraveling of America*, p. 154.
25. Ben J. Wattenberg, *Values Matter Most: How Republicans or Democrats or a Third Party Can Win and Renew the American Way of Life* (New York: Free Press, 1995), p. 22.
26. Author's interview with Rep. Barney Frank (D, Massachusetts), Washington, D.C., June 16, 1995.

Chapter Five

1. I am indebted to my former student, Ronald V. Jackson, for this formulation.
2. Peter N. Carroll, *It Seemed Like Nothing Happened: The Tragedy and Promise of America in the 1970s* (New York: Holt, Rinehart and Winston, 1982), p. 312.
3. *New York Times*, June 20, 1989.
4. Carroll, *It Seemed Like Nothing Happened*, p. 127.
5. *Ibid.*
6. *Ibid.*, p. 129.
7. As quoted in Carroll, *It Seemed Like Nothing Happened*, p. 128.
8. Allen J. Matusow, *The Unraveling of America* (New York: Harper & Row, 1984), pp. 137, 147–148.
9. Theodore H. White, *The Making of the President, 1964* (New York: Atheneum, 1965), pp. 200–201; *New York Times*, July 15, 1964; Matusow, *The Unraveling of America*, p. 137.
10. Carroll, *It Seemed Like Nothing Happened*, pp. 85–86.
11. Ben J. Wattenberg, *Values Matter Most: How Republicans or Democrats or a Third Party Can Win and Renew the American Way of Life* (New York: Free Press, 1995), p. 27.
12. Matusow, *The Unraveling of America*, pp. 133–138, 143–148.
13. Sen. Barry Goldwater, as quoted in *Ibid.*, p. 135.
14. Sen. Barry Goldwater, March 11, 1964, as quoted in *Ibid.*, p. 135.
15. John A. Garraty, *The New Commonwealth, 1877–1890* (New York: Harper & Row, 1968), pp. 240–241.
16. *Ibid.*, 241n.
17. These expenditures are measured in current dollars, so inflation accounts for part—but a relatively small part—of the increase. Executive Office of the President, Office of Management and Budget, *Budget of the United States Government, Historical Tables, Fiscal Year 1996* (Washington: Government Printing Office, 1995), as reproduced in *Just the Facts: A Citizen's Guide to Key Federal Facts* (Nashua, NH: FacTIPS, 1995), p. 57.
18. John Mitchell, as quoted in Jonathan Schell, *The Time of Illusion: An Historical and Reflective Account of the Nixon Era* (New York: Knopf, 1975), p. 43.

19. This point is made in greater detail in Robert S. McElvaine, "Why the Debacle Shouldn't Hearten Liberals," *New York Times*, December 9, 1986.
20. Author's interview with Sen. Tom Daschle (D, South Dakota), December 14, 1995, by telephone from Washington D.C.
21. E. J. Dionne, Jr., *Why Americans Hate Politics* (New York: Simon & Schuster, 1991), pp. 124–126.
22. Carroll, *It Seemed Like Nothing Happened*, p. 204.
23. Wattenberg, *Values Matter Most*, pp. 36–39.
24. Michael Dukakis, as quoted in David Kusnet, *Speaking American: How Democrats Can Win in the Nineties* (New York: Thunder Mouth Press, 1992), p. 31.
25. Ronald Reagan, as quoted in Carroll, *It Seemed Like Nothing Happened*, p. 344.
26. Wattenberg, *Values Matter Most*, pp. 34–35.
27. Ronald Reagan, as quoted in Carroll, *It Seemed Like Nothing Happened*, p. 345.
28. Al Gore had made the argument to Bill Clinton in 1987 that the only candidates capable of uniting the Democratic coalition in the late twentieth century were southern moderates. Bob Woodward, *The Agenda: Inside the Clinton White House* (New York: Simon & Schuster, 1994), p. 53.
29. Carroll, *It Seemed Like Nothing Happened*, p. 189.
30. Dionne, *Why Americans Hate Politics*, p. 133.
31. *Ibid.*, p. 134.
32. *Ibid.*, p. 132.
33. *Ibid.*, p. 24.
34. David Frum, *Dead Right* (New York: New Republic/Basic Books, 1994), p. 34.
35. Haynes Johnson, *Sleepwalking Through History: America in the Reagan Years* (New York: Norton, 1991), p. 153.
36. George Gilder, *Wealth and Poverty* (New York: Bantam Books, 1981), p. 41.
37. David A. Stockman, *The Triumph of Politics: Why the Reagan Revolution Failed* (New York: Harper & Row, 1986), pp. 65–68.
38. Frum, *Dead Right*, p. 29.
39. Stockman, *The Triumph of Politics*, pp. 65–68.
40. For a fuller discussion of the goals and effects of Reagan's economic programs, see Robert S. McElvaine, *The End of the Conservative Era: Liberalism After Reagan* (New York: Arbor House, 1987), pp. 71–103.
41. James Tobin, as quoted in Johnson, *Sleepwalking Through History*, p. 111.
42. Author's interview with Bill Clinton, April 17, 1986, Little Rock, Arkansas.
43. Ruth Shalit, "The Undertaker: Tony Coelho and the Death of the Democrats," *The New Republic*, January 2, 1995, pp. 17–25.
44. Author's interview with Sen. Paul Wellstone (D, Minnesota), March 31, 1995, Washington, D.C.
45. Author's interview with Rep. Tony Coelho (D, California), July 17, 1985, the Capitol.
46. Shalit, "The Undertaker," p. 20.
47. *Ibid.*, p. 22.
48. Author's interview with Sen. Paul Simon (D, Illinois), March 30, 1995, Washington, D.C.
49. Wellstone interview, March 31, 1995.
50. Shalit, "The Undertaker," p. 18.

Chapter Six

1. Maya Angelou, as quoted in *Clarion-Ledger* (Jackson, Miss.), May 17, 1995.
2. Thorstein Veblen, as quoted in Thomas Sowell, "Will Humanizing Hillary Aid Re-election?" *Clarion-Ledger*, July 21, 1995.
3. John Gunther, *Roosevelt in Retrospect: A Profile in History* (New York: Harper & Brothers, 1950), p. 5.

4. David Frum, *Dead Right* (New York: New Republic/Basic Books, 1994), p. 50.
5. Connie Bruck, "Hillary the Pol," *New Yorker*, May 30, 1994, p. 66.
6. David Maraniss, *First in His Class: A Biography of Bill Clinton* (New York: Simon & Schuster, 1995), pp. 38–41.
7. Bruck, "Hillary the Pol," p. 66.
8. Author's interview with Sen. Dale Bumpers (D, Arkansas), September 27, 1995, Washington, D.C.
9. Robert J. Samuelson, *The Good Life and Its Discontents: The American Dream in the Age of Entitlement, 1945–1995* (New York: Times Books, 1996), excerpted in "Great Expectations," *Newsweek*, January 8, 1996, p. 32.
10. Maraniss, *First in His Class*, p. 442.
11. E.J. Dionne, Jr., *Why Americans Hate Politics* (New York: Simon & Schuster, 1991), p. 14.
12. Arthur M. Schlesinger, Jr., *The Crisis of the Old Order, 1919–1933* (Boston: Houghton Mifflin, 1957), p. 427.
13. Frank Freidel, *Franklin D. Roosevelt: Launching the New Deal* (Boston: Little, Brown, 1973), p. 91.
14. Tom Teepen, "Clinton's Moves Correct, But Certainly Costly to Him," *Clarion-Ledger*, July 16, 1995.
15. Associated Press story, *Atlanta Journal-Constitution*, September 24, 1995.
16. William Safire, "His Third Left Turn," *New York Times*, November 16, 1995.
17. Todd S. Purdum, "Clinton Analyzes His Term, and Finds Himself Wanting," *New York Times*, November 2, 1995; Ben Wattenberg, "Clinton Agrees with GOP: Values Need Restoring," *USA Today*, December 6, 1995.
18. Maraniss, *First in His Class*, pp. 397–399.
19. *Ibid.*, p. 446.
20. Author's interview with Sen. Paul Wellstone (D, Minnesota), March 31, 1995, Washington, D.C.
21. Author's interview with Sen. Paul Simon (D, Illinois), March 30, 1995, Washington, D.C.
22. Author's interview with George Stephanopoulos, June 27, 1995, the White House.
23. Charles Krauthammer, "The Pushover Presidency," *Washington Post*, May 12, 1995.
24. Frum, *Dead Right*, pp. 17, 80.
25. Author's interview with David Kusnet, June 16, 1995, Washington, D.C.; author's interview with Carter Willkie, June 27, 1995.
26. Ben Wattenberg, *Values Matter Most: How Republicans or Democrats or a Third Party Can Win and Renew the American Way of Life* (New York: Free Press, 1995), p. 206; Bob Woodward, *The Agenda: Inside the Clinton White House* (New York: Simon & Schuster, 1994), pp. 40–41.
27. Woodward, *The Agenda*, pp. 52–53.
28. Franklin D. Roosevelt, 1932 Acceptance Speech, July 2, 1932, as quoted in Schlesinger, *Crisis of the Old Order*, p. 313.
29. Gwen Ifill, "Clinton: Forging Discipline, Vision and Luck Into Victory," *New York Times*, November 5, 1992.
30. *Ibid.*
31. Author's interview with Bill Clinton, April 17, 1986, Little Rock, Arkansas.
32. Elizabeth Drew, *On the Edge: The Clinton Presidency* (New York: Simon & Schuster, 1994), p. 189.
33. Safire, "His Third Left Turn."
34. Author's interview with Paul Begala, March 30, 1995, Washington, D.C.
35. Maraniss, *First in His Class*, p. 388.
36. Dick Morris, as quoted in *ibid.*, pp. 392–393.
37. Maraniss, *First in His Class*, pp. 444–447.
38. *Ibid.*, pp. 439–443.

39. Woodward, *The Agenda*, p. 23.
40. As quoted in Woodward, *The Agenda*, p. 33.
41. Woodward, *The Agenda*, p. 37.
42. The letter is quoted in Maraniss, *First in His Class*, pp. 199–204.
43. Drew, *On the Edge*, p. 387.
44. *Ibid.*, p. 70.
45. *Ibid.*, p. 71.
46. Dick Morris, as quoted in Maraniss, *First in His Class*, p. 398.
47. Maraniss, *First in His Class*, p. 384.
48. Drew, *On the Edge*, p. 15.
49. *Ibid.*, p. 18.
50. Clinton interview, April 17, 1986.
51. Peter N. Carroll, *It Seemed Like Nothing Happened: The Tragedy and Promise of America in the 1970s* (New York: Holt, Rinehart and Winston, 1982), p. 209.
52. Drew, *On the Edge*, p. 110.
53. Woodward, *The Agenda*, pp. 280–281.
54. Wellstone interview, March 31, 1995.
55. Warren Buffet, as quoted in Woodward, *The Agenda*, p. 306.
56. Clinton interview, April 17, 1986.
57. Author's interview with Rep. Rosa DeLauro (D, Connecticut), September 28, 1995, Washington, D.C.
58. Wellstone interview, March 31, 1995.
59. Author's interview with Rep. Nydia Velazquez (D, New York), September 28, 1995, Washington D.C.
60. Author's interview with Rep. David Bonior (D, Michigan), March 30, 1995, the Capitol.
61. Drew, *On the Edge*, p. 191.
62. Charles Murray, "The Coming White Underclass," *Wall Street Journal*, October 29, 1993.
63. Newt Gingrich, December 1993, as quoted in Frum, *Dead Right*, p. 13.
64. Bonior interview, March 30, 1995.
65. Adam Clymer, "Democrats Promise Quick Action on a Clinton Plan," *New York Times*, November 5, 1992. Emphasis added.
66. Woodward, *The Agenda*, pp. 43–44.
67. Drew, *On the Edge*, p. 192.
68. Bonior interview, March 30, 1995.
69. Velazquez interview, September 28, 1995.
70. Author's interview with Sen. Tom Daschle (D, South Dakota), December 14, 1995, by telephone from Washington, D.C.
71. Bumpers interview, September 27, 1995.
72. Simon interview, March 30, 1995.
73. Author's interview with Rep. Bernie Sanders (I, Vermont), June 28, 1995, Washington, D.C.
74. Drew, *On the Edge*, p. 191.
75. Simon interview, March 30, 1995.
76. Bonior interview, March 30, 1995.
77. Author's interview with Bill Galston, March 29, 1995, the White House.
78. Wellstone interview, March 31, 1995.
79. Begala interview, March 30, 1995.
80. Walter Shapiro, "Rushmore or Less," *Esquire*, July 1995, p. 33.
81. Doug Wallace, as quoted in Maraniss, *First in His Class*, p. 333.
82. Bumpers interview, September 27, 1995.
83. Drew, *On the Edge*, pp. 92–93, 176.
84. Begala interview, March 30, 1995.

85. Drew, *On the Edge*, p. 387.
86. *Washington Week in Review*, PBS, January 5, 1996.
87. Drew, *On the Edge*, p. 387.
88. Bill Clinton, Address to Democratic Leadership Council, May 6, 1991, Cleveland, Ohio, as quoted in Maraniss, *First in His Class*, p. 459.
89. Maraniss, *First in His Class*, pp. 265–286.
90. Bill Clinton, November 3, 1992, as quoted in *New York Times*, November 5, 1992.
91. Frum, *Dead Right*, p. 104.
92. Begala interview, March 30, 1995.
93. Shapiro, "Rushmore or Less," p. 33.

Chapter Seven

1. Hendrik Hertzberg, "Marxism: The Sequel," *New Yorker*, February 13, 1995, pp. 6–7.
2. *Ibid.*, p. 6.
3. Newt Gingrich, as quoted in Richard Reeves, "Democrats Need a Leader," *Clarion-Ledger* (Jackson, Miss.), April 3, 1986.
4. Edmund Burke, *Reflections on the Revolution in France* (1790) in Burke, *Reflections on the French Revolution* (London: J.M. Dent, 1910), p. 93.
5. *Ibid.*, pp. 241, 58, 32.
6. *Ibid.*, p. 242.
7. Ronald Reagan, January 28, 1982, in Reagan, *An American Life* (New York: Simon & Schuster, 1990), p. 316, as quoted in David Frum, *Dead Right* (New York: New Republic/Basic Books, 1994), p. 47.
8. Garry Wills, *Lincoln at Gettysburg: The Words That Remade America* (New York: Simon & Schuster, 1992), p. 145.
9. *New York Times*, May 24, 1995.
10. George Templeton Strong, *The Diary of George Templeton Strong*, Allan Nevins and Milton H. Thomas, eds. (Seattle: University of Washington Press, 1952), p. 233.
11. The coat is in an exhibit at Ford's Theater in Washington.
12. Ron Long, as quoted in *Clarion-Ledger*, June 5, 1995.
13. Author's interview with Sen. Paul Wellstone (D, Minnesota), March 31, 1995, Washington, D.C.
14. Tim Chavez, "States Righters Wrong in King's Era, Wrong Now," *Clarion-Ledger*, February 12, 1995.
15. Author's interview with Bill Clinton, April 17, 1986, Little Rock, Arkansas.
16. Author's interview with Sen. Paul Simon (D, Illinois), March 30, 1995, Washington, D.C.
17. Author's interview with Rep. Barney Frank (D, Massachusetts), June 16, 1995, Washington, D.C.
18. Author's interview with Paul Begala, March 30, 1995, Washington, D.C.
19. Author's interview with Bill Galston, March 29, 1995, the White House.
20. Tom Teepen, "States' Rights and Wrongs," *Atlanta Journal-Constitution*, October 31, 1995.
21. Author's interview with Rep. Chaka Fattah (D, Pennsylvania), September 28, 1995, Washington, D.C.
22. George F. Will, "Save Your Confederate Money, Boys . . . ," *Washington Post*, December 28, 1995. Emphasis added.
23. Author's interview with Deputy Secretary of Education Madeline Kunin, September 26, 1995, Washington, D.C.
24. Author's interview with Secretary of Education Richard Riley, June 28, 1995, Washington, D.C.
25. Simon interview, March 30, 1995.

26. Wellstone interview, March 31, 1995.
27. Author's interview with Rep. David Bonior (D, Michigan), March 30, 1995, the Capitol.
28. Begala interview, March 30, 1995.
29. Bonior interview, March 30, 1995.
30. Begala interview, March 30, 1995.
31. *Ibid.*
32. Chavez, "States Righters Wrong."
33. Bonior interview, March 30, 1995.
34. Author's interview with Rep. Rosa DeLauro (D, Connecticut), September 28, 1995, Washington, D.C.
35. Begala interview, March 30, 1995.
36. Author's interview with Rep. Marcy Kaptur (D, Ohio), September 28, 1995, Washington, D.C.
37. Begala interview, March 30, 1995.
38. Wellstone interview, March 31, 1995.
39. Bonior interview, March 30, 1995.
40. Author's interview with Rep. Joe Kennedy (D, Massachusetts), September 27, 1995, Washington, D.C.
41. NBC/*Wall Street Journal* poll, taken by Peter Hart and Robert Teeter, September 24–27, 1994, in Ben J. Wattenberg, *Values Matter Most: How Republicans or Democrats or a Third Party Can Win and Renew the American Way of Life* (New York: Free Press, 1995), pp. 111–112.
42. Joe Kennedy interview, September 27, 1995.
43. Harold Ickes, as quoted in Ruth Shalit, "The Undertaker," *The New Republic*, January 2, 1995, p. 18.
44. Mark Mellman, as quoted in Shalit, "The Undertaker," p. 18.
45. Wattenberg, *Values Matter Most*, p. 400.
46. Begala interview, March 30, 1995.
47. Frum, *Dead Right*, p. 23.
48. Begala interview, March 30, 1995.
49. Times Mirror Center for the People and the Press, opinion survey, "Voter Anxiety Dividing GOP; Energized Democrats Backing Clinton," October 25–30, 1995, released Nov. 14, 1995, p. 9.
50. Bonior interview, March 30, 1995.

Chapter Eight

1. Kevin Phillips commentary, *Morning Edition*, National Public Radio, May 17, 1995.
2. Bob Downs, "Business is Big Beneficiary as 'Contract' is Completed," *Wall Street Journal*, April 7, 1995.
3. William Greider, "The Education of David Stockman," *Atlantic Monthly*, December 1981, pp. 46–47.
4. Phillips commentary, May 17, 1995.
5. Mario Cuomo, telephone conversation with the author, December 15, 1994; Cuomo, speech to the National Press Club, December 16, 1994.
6. Daniel Bell, as quoted in "Good Newt, Bad Newt," *Time*, December 25, 1995–January 1, 1996, p. 95.
7. William Jennings Bryan, address before the Democratic National Convention, July 8, 1896, Chicago.
8. Author's interview with Rep. Marcy Kaptur (D, Ohio), September 28, 1995, Washington, D.C.

9. I have previously made many of the points contained in this and the next few paragraphs in "200-Year-Old 'Voodoo Economics' Alive and Kicking," *Clarion-Ledger* (Jackson, Miss.), December 22, 1991.
10. Sylvia Nasar, "The 1980's: A Very Good Time for the Very Rich," *New York Times*, March 5, 1992; editorial, "The Rich Get Richer Faster," *New York Times*, April 18, 1995.
11. Author's interview with Sen. Paul Simon (D, Illinois), March 30, 1995, Washington, D.C.
12. Author's interview with Sen. Dale Bumpers (D, Arkansas), September 27, 1995, Washington, D.C.
13. Author's interview with Sen. Paul Wellstone (D, Minnesota), March 31, 1995.
14. Author's interview with Rep. Joe Kennedy, September 27, 1995, Washington, D.C.
15. Bumpers interview, September 27, 1995.
16. Stacks, "Good Newt, Bad Newt," p. 93.
17. Bumpers interview, September 27, 1995.
18. Author's interview with Paul Begala, March 30, 1995, Washington, D.C.
19. Wellstone interview, March 31, 1995.
20. Kevin Phillips, on *Inside Politics*, CNN, January 3, 1996.
21. Lars-Erik Nelson, "B2 Vote Shows Deficit Reduction Is Not to Be" and editorial, "Star Wars Forever," both in *Star-Ledger* (Newark, N.J.), June 19, 1995.
22. Author's interview with Rep. Patsy Mink (D, Hawaii), September 26, 1995.
23. David Frum, *Dead Right* (New York: New Republic/Basic Books, 1994), p. 45.
24. Simon interview, March 30, 1995.
25. Author's interview with Bill Clinton, April 17, 1986, Little Rock, Arkansas.
26. Stacks, "Good Newt, Bad Newt," p.93.
27. Nancy Gibbs and Karen Tumulty, "Master of the House," *Time*, December 25, 1995–January 1, 1996, p. 66.
28. *United States* v. *E. C. Knight Co.* (156 U.S. 1); *In Re Debs* (158 U.S. 564); *Pollock* v. *Farmers' Loan and Trust* (158 U.S. 601); *Plessy* v. *Ferguson* (163 U.S. 537).
29. Stacks, "Good Newt, Bad Newt," p. 93.
30. David E. Rosenbaum, "Panel Calls for Flat Tax but Fails to Specify the Rate," *New York Times*, January 18, 1996.
31. George Norris, as quoted in Arthur M. Schlesinger, Jr., *The Crisis of the Old Order, 1919–1933* (Boston: Houghton Mifflin, 1957), p. 62.
32. George Will, "Dukakis Has Economic Weapon in Property Owners' Rise in Income," *Clarion-Ledger*, September 16, 1988.
33. Author's interview with George Stephanopoulos, June 27, 1995, the White House.
34. *Ibid.*
35. Author's interview with Rep. Barney Frank (D, Massachusetts), June 16, 1995, Washington, D.C.
36. Begala interview, March 30, 1995.
37. Frank interview, June 16, 1995.
38. Author's interview with Senator Tom Daschle (D, South Dakota), December 12, 1995, by telephone from Washington, D.C.
39. Author's interview with Rep. David Bonior (D, Michigan), March 30, 1995, the Capitol.
40. Author's interview with Rep. Bernie Sanders (I, Vermont), June 28, 1995, Washington, D.C.
41. Bonior interview, March 30, 1995.
42. Author's interview with James Carville, Washington, D.C., March 30, 1995.
43. Begala interview, March 30, 1995.
44. Gibbs and Tumulty, "Master of the House," pp. 65–66.
45. Frum, *Dead Right*, p. 16.
46. *Ibid.*, pp. 18, 19, 43, 62.
47. *Ibid.*, p. 33.

48. Yankelovich poll, December 6–7, 1995, *Time*, December 25, 1995–January 1, 1996, p. 60.
49. Senator Richard Lugar (R, Indiana), at the South Carolina Republican Presidential Forum, January 6, 1996.
50. Frum, *Dead Right*, p. 5.
51. Secretary of the Interior Bruce Babbitt, speech to the National Press Club, December 13, 1995.
52. Gibbs and Tumulty, "Master of the House," pp. 66–68.
53. Wellstone interview, March 31, 1995.
54. Anthony Lewis, "Is Reality Dawning?" *New York Times*, July 31, 1995; editorial, "Vicious Assault on EPA," *Atlanta Journal-Constitution*, August 6, 1995; Jane Fritsch, "Threat to Cut E.P.A. Budget Reflects a New Political Shift," *New York Times*, August 24, 1995; editorial, "Riders from Hell," *Washington Post*, October 25, 1995; Babbitt speech, December 13, 1995.
55. Babbitt speech, December 13, 1995.
56. *Ibid.*
57. Mink interview, September 26, 1995.
58. Bonior interview, March 30, 1995.
59. Begala interview, March 30, 1995.
60. Author's interview with Rep. Rosa DeLauro (D, Connecticut), September 28, 1995, Washington, D.C.
61. Gibbs and Tumulty, "Master of the House," pp. 56, 60.
62. Begala interview, March 30, 1995.
63. Gibbs and Tumulty, "Master of the House," p. 68.
64. Daschle interview, December 12, 1995.
65. Newt Gingrich, June 24, 1978, as quoted in *Time*, December 25, 1995–January 1, 1996, p. 78.
66. Gibbs and Tumulty, "Master of the House," p. 80.
67. Newt Gingrich, interview, December 13, 1995, in *Time*, December 25, 1995–January 1, 1996, p. 84.
68. Frank interview, June 16, 1995.
69. *Ibid.*, p. 78.
70. Michael Beschloss, in "Taking His Measure," *Time*, December 25, 1995–January 1, 1996, p. 98.
71. *The Capital Gang*, CNN, December 30, 1995,
72. Newt Gingrich, 1987, as quoted in Robert Wright, "Speaker's Corner," *The New Republic*, January 1, 1996, p. 6.
73. Gibbs and Tumulty, "Master of the House," p. 80.
74. Newt Gingrich, as quoted in Wright, "Speaker's Corner," p. 6.
75. Hendrik Hertzberg, "Marxism: The Sequel," *New Yorker*, February 13, 1995, p. 6.
76. Newt Gingrich, *To Renew America* (New York: HarperCollins, 1995).
77. Gibbs and Tumulty, "Master of the House," p. 78.

Chapter Nine

1. Ellen Goodman, "Wouldn't It Be Wise to Instigate Reform with Part-Time Orphanages (Day Care)?" *Clarion-Ledger* (Jackson, Miss.), February 14, 1995.
2. I made these points in "It's the Message, Not the Medium," *Los Angeles Times*, April 28, 1995.
3. Correspondence in the possession of Rep. Barney Frank.
4. Claude Lewis, "'Group Responsibility' Won't Wash," *Clarion-Ledger*, December 6, 1995.

Chapter Ten

1. Jimmy Carter, State of the Union Address, January 19, 1978, in *Public Papers of the Presidents of the United States—Jimmy Carter, 1978* (Washington: Government Printing Office, 1979), Book I, p. 94.
2. Gallup CNN/*USA Today* Poll, conducted April 23–24, 1995; reported in *USA Today*, May 16, 1995.
3. *Washington Post*/ABC News Poll, reported in Richard Morin, "Anger at Washington Cools in Aftermath of Bombing," *Washington Post*, May 18, 1995.
4. Rep. Patricia Schroeder (D, Colorado), on *This Week with David Brinkley*, ABC News, December 12, 1995.
5. Richard Hofstadter, *The American Political Tradition—And the Men Who Made It* (New York: Knopf, 1948, 2nd ed., Vintage, 1973), p. 239.
6. Author's interview with James Carville, March 30, 1995, Washington, D.C.
7. Gerald F. Seib, "How to Lure More Bad Money into Campaigns, *Wall Street Journal*, May 17, 1995.
8. *Morning Edition*, National Public Radio, May 19, 1995.
9. Author's interview with Sen. Dale Bumpers (D, Arkansas), September 27, 1995, Washington, D.C.
10. Author's interview with Rep. Joe Kennedy (D, Massachusetts), September 27, 1995, Washington, D.C.
11. Author's interview with Rep. David Bonior (D, Michigan), March 30, 1995, the Capitol.
12. *Ibid.*
13. Author's interview with Rep. Rosa DeLauro (D, Connecticut), September 28, 1995, Washington, D.C.
14. Author's interview with Sen. Paul Simon (D, Illinois), March 30, 1995, Washington, D.C.
15. Bumpers interview, September 27, 1995.
16. Author's interview with Sen. Paul Wellstone (D, Minnesota), March 31, 1995, Washington, D.C.
17. E. J. Dionne, Jr., *Why Americans Hate Politics* (New York: Simon & Schuster, 1991), pp. 52–53.
18. "Why Don't Americans Trust the Government?" *Washington Post*/Kaiser Family Foundation/Harvard University Survey Project, 1996, p. 4.
19. Anthony Lewis, "Is Reality Dawning?" *New York Times*, July 31, 1995.
20. Secretary of the Interior Bruce Babbitt, speech to the National Press Club, December 14, 1995, Washington, D.C.
21. I made the points that follow in "Nattering Nabobs are Back—This Time as Republicans," *Los Angeles Times*, October 17, 1994.
22. Lyndon B. Johnson, as quoted in William L. O'Neill, *Coming Apart: An Informal History of America in the 1960s* (New York: Quadrangle, 1971), p. 119.
23. Author's interview with Sen. Tom Daschle (D, South Dakota), December 14, 1995, by telephone from Washington, D.C.
24. Author's interview with Paul Begala, March 30, 1995, Washington, D.C.
25. *Ibid.*
26. Bonior interview, March 30, 1995.
27. I discussed this topic in "Yours, Mine, Ours—Taxes Cover All," *Los Angeles Times*, May 2, 1993.
28. William F. Buckley, Jr., "Gore, Democrats Entangling Themselves in the 'Tax-the-Rich' Rhetoric," *Clarion-Ledger* (Jackson, Miss.), May 13, 1991.
29. Rep. John Kasich (R, Ohio), on *Meet the Press*, NBC News, December 12, 1995.
30. Ronald Reagan, First Inaugural Address, January 20, 1981, *New York Times*, January 21, 1981.

31. Daschle interview, December 14, 1995.
32. Ellen Goodman, "When Politicians Push Personal Responsibility, They Mean Ours, Not Theirs," *Boston Globe*, December 31, 1995.
33. Author's interview with Bill Clinton, April 17, 1995, Little Rock, Arkansas.
34. Mario M. Cuomo, *Diaries of Mario M. Cuomo: The Campaign for Governor* (New York: Random House, 1984), p. 457.

Chapter Eleven

1. Robert B. Reich, "Family Values," remarks to the National Baptist Convention, San Diego, California, June 21, 1995.
2. Lee Atwater, as quoted in Susan Trausch, "Words Spoken by Dying Man Probably as Close as We Get to Truth," *Clarion-Ledger* (Jackson, Miss.), February 3, 1991.
3. Newt Gingrich, June 24, 1978, as quoted in *Time*, December 25, 1995-January 1, 1996, p. 78.
4. As quoted in Jonathan Shell, *The Time of Illusion* (New York: Knopf, 1976), p. 62.
5. As quoted in *ibid.*, p. 185.
6. Nancy Gibbs and Karen Tumulty, "Master of the House," *Time*, December 25, 1995–January 1, 1996, p. 56.
7. Author's interview with Paul Begala, March 30, 1995, Washington, D.C.
8. Alison Mitchell, "Clinton Offers Challenge to Nation, Declaring 'Era of Big Government' Is Over," *New York Times*, January 24, 1996.
9. Katharine Q. Seelye, "Dole Says President Defends Old Elites Seeking Largesse," *New York Times*, January 24, 1996.
10. Author's interview with Rep. David Bonior (D, Michigan), March 30, 1995, the Capitol.
11. Author's interview with Sen. Paul Simon (D, Illinois), March 30, 1995, Washington, D.C.
12. Rep. Marcy Kaptur (D, Ohio), speech at United We Stand America Conference, August 12, 1995, Dallas, Texas.
13. E.J. Dionne, *Why Americans Hate Politics* (New York: Simon & Schuster, 1991), p. 14.
14. Author's interview with Rep. Joe Kennedy (D, Massachusetts), September 27, 1995, Washington, D.C.
15. Author's interview with Sen. Dale Bumpers (D, Arkansas), September 27, 1995, Washington, D.C.
16. Betty Friedan, speech at George Mason University, March, 1995, telecast on C-SPAN.
17. Author's interview with Rep. Patsy Mink (D, Hawaii), September 26, 1995, Washington, D.C.
18. Arthur Levine, *When Dreams and Heroes Died: A Portrait of Today's College Student* (San Francisco: Jossey-Bass, 1983), pp. 103–115.
19. Author's interview with Bruce Reed, March 30, 1995, Washington, D.C.
20. Reich, "Family Values."
21. Reed interview, March 30, 1995.
22. Ellen Goodman, "When Politicians Push Personal Responsibility, They Mean Ours, Not Theirs," *Boston Globe*, December 31, 1995.
23. Reed interview, March 30, 1995.
24. Author's interview with Bill Clinton, April 17, 1986, Little Rock, Arkansas.
25. *Ibid.*
26. Simon interview, March 30, 1995.
27. Author's interview with Bill Galston, March 29, 1995, the White House.
28. Author's interview with Rep. Marcy Kaptur (D, Ohio), September 28, 1995, Washington, D.C.

29. President Bill Clinton, speech at Georgetown University, July 6, 1995, *New York Times*, July 7, 1995; Frank Rich, "The Middle Ground," *New York Times*, July 8, 1995.
30. Mitchell, "Clinton Offers Challenge."
31. Author's interview with Sen. Paul Wellstone (D, Minnesota), March 31, 1995, Washington, D.C.
32. Author's interview with James Carville, March 30, 1995, Washington, D.C.
33. Jeffrey H. Birnbaum, "Democrats Air Their Disputes with Clinton," *Wall Street Journal*, December 7, 1994; Robert Shogan, "Centrist Ally Calls Clinton 'Old Democrat,'" *Los Angeles Times*, December 7, 1994.
34. Samuel I. Rosenman, ed., *The Public Papers and Addresses of Franklin D. Roosevelt* (New York: Russell & Russell, 1938–50), vol. V, p. 235.
35. John Winthrop, "A Modell of Christian Charity" (1630), reprinted in David A. Hollinger and Charles Capper, eds., *The American Intellectual Tradition* (New York: Oxford University Press, 1989), vol. I, p. 14.
36. Begala interview, March 30, 1995.
37. Author's interview with Sen. Tom Daschle (D, South Dakota), December 14, 1995, by telephone from Washington, D.C.
38. Begala interview, March 30, 1995.
39. Author's interview with Secretary of Education Richard Riley, June 28, 1995, Washington, D.C.
40. Bonior interview, March 30, 1995.
41. Begala interview, March 30, 1995.
42. Clinton interview, April 17, 1986.
43. Kennedy interview, September 27, 1995.
44. Mink interview, September 26, 1995.
45. *Morning Edition*, National Public Radio, January 24, 1996.
46. Elizabeth Kolbert and Adam Clymer, "The Politics of Layoffs," *New York Times*, March 8, 1996.
47. Ronnie Dugger, *On Reagan: The Man and His Presidency* (New York: McGraw-Hill, 1983), pp. 101–105, 113.
48. Bumpers interview, September 27, 1995.
49. I would like to thank Martin Colucci of Atlantic City, New Jersey, and Millard Grimes of Athens, Georgia, for their contributions to my thinking on this topic, and Professor Bill Brister of Millsaps College for assistance with some of the statistics on what this change might mean.
50. Jeremy Rifkin, *The End of Work* (New York: Putnam, 1995), pp. 222–223.
51. Thomas Donahue, as quoted in *ibid.*, p. 230.
52. Rifkin, *End of Work*, p. 227.
53. Dionne, *Why Americans Hate Politics*, p. 360.
54. Lin Tse-Hsu, as quoted in Flora Lewis, "The Opium War," *New York Times*, October 29, 1989.

INDEX

INDEX